NORTHERN AFRICA:
ISLAM AND MODERNIZATION

NORTHERN AFRICA: ISLAM AND MODERNIZATION

Papers on the theme of Islamization, Modernization, Nationalism and Independence presented and discussed at a Symposium arranged by the African Studies Association of the United Kingdom on the occasion of its annual general meeting, 14 September 1971.

Edited with an Introduction by

MICHAEL BRETT

Lecturer in the History of North Africa,
School of Oriental and African Studies
University of London

FRANK CASS : LONDON

First published 1973 in Great Britain by

FRANK CASS AND COMPANY LIMITED
67 Great Russell Street, London WC1B 3BT, England

and in United States of America by

FRANK CASS AND COMPANY LIMITED
c/o International Scholarly Book Services, Inc.
P.O. Box 4347, Portland, Oregon 97208

ISBN: 0 7146 2972 3

Library of Congress Catalog Card No. 72–92960

Printed in Great Britain by
Cox & Wyman Ltd,
London, Fakenham and Reading

CONTENTS

THE AFRICAN STUDIES ASSOCIATION OF THE UNITED KINGDOM

The African Studies Association of the United Kingdom was founded in 1963, with the principal aims of advancing African studies in the United Kingdom, and the developing of facilities for the interchange of information between scholars and scientists, individuals and institutions, concerned with the study of Africa. The inter-disciplinary character of the Association has been maintained and developed, and it remains the only full inter-disciplinary organization concerned with Africa in the United Kingdom. Amongst its 500 present members are included historians, political scientists, anthropologists, economists, sociologists, linguists and educationists, and a considerable number of natural scientists, such as agriculturists, biologists, geologists and soil scientists, medicals and geographers. Epitomizing this breadth of interest is the fact that its past Presidents are Dame Margery Perham, F.B.A., Dr. Audrey Richards, C.B.E., Professor Roland Oliver, Sir Joseph Hutchinson, F.R.S., Professor John Fage, Professor Anthony Allott, Professor Robert Steel, and Dr. Ronald Keay, O.B.E. The President for 1973–4 is Dr. John Hargreaves.

Membership is open to anyone professionally concerned with African studies, upon completion of the application form, and admission by the Council.

Further details may be obtained from:

The Hon. Secretary,
African Studies Association of the United Kingdom,
c/o Centre of West African Studies,
University of Birmingham,
P.O. Box 363, B15 2SD U.K.

PREFACE

The meeting of the Symposium to discuss the topics of Islamization, modernization, nationalism and independence in Islamic Northern Africa took place on 14 September 1971 in the Macmillan Hall of the Senate House, University of London. It was opened on behalf of Professor C. H. Philips, Director of the School of Oriental and African Studies, University of London, by Dr. David Dalby, who drew attention in his introduction to the importance of the region as providing a link between the African and Oriental interests of the School. Regional studies of this kind, which the Association had already adopted for its symposium on Southern African Studies in 1969, were moreover essential for the inter-disciplinary study of Africa to which the Association was committed. Serious attention was required lest they present a fragmentary and unconnected view of several more traditional disciplines; if successful, however, they might serve to break down the barriers between such disciplines in the interests of a fuller understanding of the continent as a whole. It was meetings of this kind which could at least prepare the way for systematic research along these lines.

The meeting was divided into two sessions, the first on the subject of Islamization under the chairmanship of Professor W. Montgomery Watt, the second on the subject of modernization, nationalism and independence under the chairmanship of Professor Roland Oliver. A brief summary of the discussions has been included in the present volume, together with written observations later submitted by participants.

INTRODUCTION

The problem underlying the theme of the Symposium is one which has vexed the intelligence ever since Bonaparte set foot in Egypt in 1798, namely the relationship of Islam to the modern world created by the expansion of Europe in the course of the last five hundred years. While the discussion was broadly informative, the papers were for the most part historical in their treatment of a subject of philosophical and political controversy, which was dealt with from a sociological point of view in a volume which springs to mind in this context, *Islam in Tropical Africa*, the outcome of a discussion of a related theme, the influence of Islam in the continent south of the Sahara.[1] In making such an approach in an area defined to include the lands to the north of the desert, the advantage may stem from the disadvantage. On the one hand Islam has been seen as a fundamental and enduring structure, for good or evil,[2] on the other as a form whose value has changed with the circumstances of each time and place.[3] Between such extremes of interpretation the historian at least is cramped, not least because in Africa in particular his studies are still in their infancy. If any historical statement is a more or less sweeping generalization with regard to what was happening, outside the heavily researched past of Europe the attempt at plausibility must often be a *reductio ad absurdum*. In the circumstances it is at least as important to establish what cannot be said as that which can. The rigour may be regrettable, but clears the ground. For the problem in question it makes the point that, in spite of the very considerable homogeneity of Islam as a religion and a community, it is difficult to infer from the faith itself the reasons for its spread, or conversely from the societies with which it has been associated. While the historical fact may be noted, the relationship remains obscure. For that reason there is no very firm theoretical foundation from which to go on to consider the relationship of Islam to the modern world.

The point is the more forcible when it is recalled that Islam as it came to be formulated was predicated to a large extent upon the divorce between the ideal and the reality. The frequent statement that 'Islam knows no distinction between a spiritual and a temporal realm, between religious and secular activities',[4] consisting as it does in a 'system of rules comprising every part of a Muslim's life, from the humblest details up to the principles of his moral and social existence',[5] namely the Sharī'a, the 'way' binding upon all believers, is not a straightforward proposition. Observing with Becker that 'in accordance with the model of the Sharī'a, for a Muslim a legal prescription is not a binding rule to be followed under any circumstance, but an unattainable ideal which even the best of men can never fulfil',[6] (my translation), we may note with Professor Anderson[7] the wide discretion accorded to the state to act as it thinks fit in accordance with its power of siyāsa, policy making, and take account of the character of Islamic jurisprudence in areas where the application of the Sharī'a has traditionally been most systematic, for example in the field of family law. Jurisprudence is the operative word, emphasizing the fact that the Sharī'a is a law of scholars who at various times and in various places have recognized the validity of a great deal of non-Islamic custom and practice.[8] There is no simple rule. What is important here, however, is the dichotomy entailed within the body politic between dīn, religion, and dawla, state. Theoretically again, the two are merely aspects of the same Sharī'a, the same comprehensive way of life,[9] but the division which appeared in practice as the law itself took shape between the men of religion and the men of power, sulṭān, government, led from the ninth century onwards to a situation resembling that of church and state in Christian Europe,[10] a situation which was only modified under the Ottoman empire when the 'ulamā', 'the wise', were incorporated into a whole official hierarchy for the administration of justice.[11]

By the fourteenth and fifteenth centuries the situation was generally recognized. Islam as represented by its clerics looked to the state to provide the conditions under which a Muslim might live by his religion; the state on the other hand looked to Islam and to the clerics in particular to provide the justification for the ruler's hold on power, whether as descendant of the Prophet or as defender of the faith, whatever the circumstances rendered appropriate.[12] The practice of government was little affected, with the result that the scepticism of the clerics and of the population at large was translated into practical terms in the institution known as waqf, mortmain, in the Maghrib as ḥubus, 'habous', whereby extensive properties were placed under clerical administration, often as a kind of insurance against the fortunes of the world. Both the distinction and the attitude extended into the countryside, so that in the tribal societies of North Africa the murābiṭūn, the marabouts, were on the one hand outside the tribal system of government, and on the other intermediate between the peoples themselves as well as between the peoples and the state.[13] To the south of the Sahara many rulers looked to Islam, its doctrines and its adherents, for support; but equally the Muslim required a guarantee. An instance in which the reciprocity is almost feudal in character is provided here by R. O'Fahey.[14] In that case the sulṭān was Muslim, but in the last resort his religion was a matter of indifference, provided that the requirement of protection was met.[15] Instances spring to mind in the Sudan from the time of al Bakrī's Ghana onwards, but north of the desert they multiplied from the eleventh century with the beginning of the Reconquista in Spain and the Norman conquest of Sicily, followed in the twelfth by the Norman occupation of the coastal cities from Tripoli to Mahdiya, coming eventually to a head in the Maghrib with the colonization of Algeria. The jurists had the answer, to the effect that any government was better than none.

The situation was disguised but never substantially altered when men of religion took it upon themselves to become the sulṭān. The Safavid dynasty in Persia, the Ottoman Turks, and the dynasties of Morocco from the sixteenth century, all originated with holy men, murābiṭūn as they were known in the Maghrib, who made the transition from dīn to dawla, from one side of the medal to the other. In each case, however, it was a long process, in the course of which the man of religion was transformed into the ruler of a dominion. What is in question is a particular path to power, sufficiently unusual for each case to be studied in its own right, of which the outcome was the affirmation of the old dichotomy. Over the whole of the region from western Algeria to Egypt the path was effectively closed from the sixteenth century by the Ottoman conquest, which left the choice of ruler firmly in the hands of aristocratic and military oligarchies as the control of Constantinople weakened. This may put into some perspective the occasions when the expectation upon which successive dynasties traded, that a Muslim ruler should not only defend but be seen to defend the faith, gave rise to the demand that he should put it into practice as far as humanly possible.

We cannot know the extent to which the Rustamid imāms of Tāhart in the ninth century in what is now Algeria attempted to realize the requirements of Ibāḍī doctrine; it may be that it was only after the people of Tāhart eventually settled in the Mzab in the northern Sahara that the clerical theocracy which survives to the present day was established.[16] The Almoravids and the Almohads after them both began in this way as communities under a strict religious discipline which governed them in practice as well as in theory, but both gave rise to states in which the sulṭān was characteristically distinguished from the 'ulamā'. Such events are now remote. The aim of bringing about a Muslim state in which the siyāsa shar'īya, the power of the sulṭān to act on behalf of the law, should be exercised more nearly in accordance with the prescriptions of the law, nevertheless lived on, so that the appeal of the Ḥanbalī theologian and jurist ibn Taymīya, who flourished at Damascus early in the fourteenth century, for an umma wasaṭ, 'a nation of the middle way' which should live by the law,[17] although it brought about his imprisonment and death at the hands of authority, survived to become the inspiration of the reformer ibn 'Abd al Wahhāb in Arabia in the eighteenth century, whose preaching provoked the Wahhābī movement and led to the foundation of the Wahhābī state by the Arab chief ibn Su'ūd and his successors.[18] While the links between Wahhābism and the Sudan are far from clear, there seems to be a strong contemporary parallel in the activities of 'Uthmān dan Fodio and the subsequent revivalists of the nineteenth century, who likewise attempted to bring about a state in which the laws of Islam should be systematically applied. Yet the success was no more than partial. While Dr. Hiskett can qualify the Fulani empire from this point of view as a considerable achievement,[19] Professor Anderson can note the persistence of an accommodation with customary law which points back to the situation in lands where revivalism was not so significant a force.[20]

Such a survey evidently emphasizes the common features at the expense of the many variables; the context is lacking. What is left is a typology from which to go on to consider the changes that came about as Europe in the nineteenth century impinged upon the Islamic world. In certain cases the traditional was artificially preserved. In Algeria the emasculation of the nobility, the 'ulamā' and the murābiṭūn was accompanied by their maintenance in a system designed to prevent the advancement of the Muslim population to a position of equality.[21] Dependence upon the French sulṭān was considered due protection all the more because it was so complete; thus when after 1904 it was proposed to disestablish the Islamic cult together with the Catholic Church, the proclamation of de Bourmont in Algiers in 1830 was once again invoked as the convention whereby France had formally undertaken to ensure the proper practice of the faith.[22] At the other extreme, of colonial indulgence, Indirect Rule in Northern Nigeria served the old institutions as a guarantee. In that case it was a question also of political power in the name of Islam. Rulers elsewhere continued to appeal to religion, 'Abd al Qādir unsuccessfully in Algeria, the 'Alawī dynasty in Morocco, where the appeal failed to prevent the establishment of the Protectorate in 1912, but gave the monarchy a value which the French, the Moroccan nationalists, and ultimately the king himself were able to exploit with the results described by M. Palazzoli.[23] The growing element of archaism was nowhere more apparent than in the pan-Islamic propaganda of the Ottoman empire, which claimed for the Ottoman sulṭān spiritual and secular authority over all Muslims everywhere in an attempt to counteract the claims of Europe on the one hand and of nationalism among the subject peoples on the other.[24] It was inappropriate, and it failed. The traditional was in process of revision.

Modernization is a term which may be used not only to describe many of the material changes which have come about over the last hundred and fifty years in Northern Africa as elsewhere, but also to embrace many of the aspirations. If the changes were not always for the better, the aspirations were frequently in conflict. The state's requirement of efficiency might be directed against those who desired constitutional government or those who demanded independence. The one common denominator was the model of western Europe, in accordance with which such aspirations were formulated. It offered the example of a successful society whose ideas and practices, if systematically adopted, offered the possibility of similar all-round success. The emphasis might differ; at one extreme Muḥammad 'Alī in Egypt employed the expertise of Europe to create for himself a despotism in which 'he may have identified Egypt with himself; he never identified himself with Egypt',[25] while at the other Charles Henry Churchill, deeply involved in the local politics of Syria and Mount Lebanon, wrote a biography of 'Abd al Qādir in which the amīr is the national hero of the Romantic tradition;[26] the prescription was the same. In the nineteenth century, therefore, from the Middle East at least as far as Tunisia, the model of Islamic belief and practice came to be compared against something other than itself.

For a Muḥammad 'Alī, eliminating the economic power and the political influence of the 'ulamā' in Egypt before the French did so in Algeria, the old relationship to the sulṭān appeared as an obstacle. By the middle of the century, for a patriot like Ṭahṭāwī, Islam was a loyalty which should not interfere with that to one's fellow countrymen, for whom it was only one, if the most important, among many religions.[27] Against this twofold challenge to the central position of the Muslim community, the umma as it was traditionally known, there were on the other hand those, equally radical, who placed it with ibn Taymīya firmly in the middle, demanding not that it should retire, but that it should be transformed in accordance with its principles, which would, if properly applied, prove the indispensable key to modernization. For Khayr al Dīn, minister first to the bey of Tunis, then to the Ottoman sulṭān, its international character was an advantage.[28] Khayr al Dīn was a lonely figure; his only home was in government, where the Ottoman empire was his only hope. To the extent that his philosophy was reduced to serving the political interests of the sulṭān as pan-Islamic propaganda, it failed. By the end of the century, however, it was identified with interests at once more essential and more vital, on the one hand the 'ulamā', on the other the nation as it was known to Ṭahṭāwī.

Discrimination against a Muslim people specifically on the grounds of religion was employed by the French in Algeria from 1865 onwards. The Senatus Consulte of that year declared the indigenous non-European population of the country French subjects but not French citizens, a status which might only be granted if, along with European habits, they also chose to live by the French civil code in preference to their religious law. This applied as much to the large Jewish minority as to the Muslims, but in 1870 the Algerian Jews were naturalized by the Décret Crémieux, so that it was almost entirely the Muslim community which was left to take the consequences. The original intention of Napoleon III had been to create 'un royaume arabe' alongside the 'colonie européenne'; in the event the bulk of the country fell under French civilian control, and subject status came to mean subjection to a harshly repressive regime.[29] In Egypt as in Tunisia and later in Morocco, where the European power was acting in theory on behalf of the sovereign, the distinction was not so nice, but equally invidious. By the end of the nineteenth century the European presence to the south of the Mediterranean had grown by *force majeure* to dominate those societies which it had once encouraged, whatever the motive, to follow the European example. Now, Cromer in Egypt envisaged only the most gradual progress towards self-government. The constitution, the dastūr (destour), promulgated by the bey of Tunis in 1861, the Egyptian Assembly of Delegates, were things of the past, abolished by administrations which in political matters favoured the old at the expense of the new in the interests of stability. The European model, on the other hand, became all the more urgent. In Morocco the Japanese defeat of Russia in 1904 was greeted as a victory for modernization in the face of the kind of threat building up towards the establishment of the Protectorate at Fes in 1912.[30] The condition was clear, in effect dictated by imperial concern for territorial division north as well as south of the Sahara, the achievement of a nation state of the European type.

Against this background, modernist thinking about Islam as a means to the rejuvenation of the Muslim world found a place in the traditional categories of Muslim scholarship, notably the fiqh, the science of the law. This was in many ways the achievement of the Egyptian Muḥammad 'Abduh, who after a varied career as student, teacher, editor and judge in 1899 became Muftī of Egypt, head of the system of religious law.[31] In that capacity he endeavoured to show from inside the traditional system how reform might be accomplished in accordance with the Sharī'a as it stood. As Professor Anderson observes, the attempt involved a degree of ecleticism in the matter of authorities which went against the traditional division of jurisprudence into schools with separate if similar interpretations. For this reason it was and continued to be highly controversial, but served nevertheless to give the principle of modernization a much more firmly Islamic foundation. At the same time with 'Abduh Islamic reform acquired a nationalist character on behalf of an Egypt independent of British control. Both these elements of reform and nationalism were developed after 'Abduh's death in 1905 in the Salafīya, a movement which continued his thinking with the purpose of bringing about a return to the faith of the ancestors, disposing of the laxity which had affected the practice of Islam over the intervening centuries, while at the same time it worked for the political independence of Muslim populations in Muslim states. In connection with the Arab nationalist Shakīb Arslān in Geneva in the years after the First World War[32] it spread into the Maghrib, where the Association des Oulémas d'Algérie founded in 1931 under the leadership of ibn Bādīs attacked the so-called maraboutic Islam of the countryside, demanding a more rigorous faith as the basis of a national creed expressed in the formula: Islam is my religion, Arabic is my language, Algeria is my country.[33]

The philosophy of the Salafīya was an inversion of the proposition that Islam was the cause of the backwardness of the Muslim peoples. Tracing its descent from ibn Taymīya through ibn 'Abd al Wahhāb, it made of Islam the cardinal principle of a just and successful society, organized initially into nation states but ideally rising through regional federations such as the Maghrib to the unity of the Arab peoples and ultimately of Muslims everywhere. For many nationalists however, it was perhaps more important that Islam was more simply a means of identity. That this was so appears at a very basic level in the special case of Algeria, where the number of those who over the years applied for citizenship in accordance with the provisions of the Senatus Consulte of 1865 was minimal, a mere 2,500 by 1934. In Morocco it was apparent in the opposition to the so-called dahir Berbère in 1930, whereby the Berber population discussed in Nevill Barbour's paper[34] was rendered subject to a code of customary law in preference to the Sharī'a, an act which used the principle of 1865 to divide rather than unite the Muslim population.[35] Equally it appears, as M. Palazzoli points out below, in the use made of the monarch as a national figurehead by the Istiqlāl, the nationalist party. In Egypt it is more to be inferred from the attitude of successive governments and political parties. These have frequently employed the language of 'Abduh, and have indeed been led by men who were his colleagues, disciples and successors, such as Sa'd Zaghlūl, who as leader of the Wafd, the nationalist movement and parliamentary party which grew up immediately after the First World War, successfully conducted the campaign for Egyptian independence in 1923. Nevertheless their policies have been secularist, even in the apparently exceptional case of the Muslim Brotherhood, the party whose programme was most representative of Islamic reform.[36] The emphasis has fallen upon the power and discretion of the state as the instrument of the people for the accomplishment of the basic task. In this political situation, familiar in Europe since the French Revolution, now firmly rooted not only in Egypt as a result of European control, Islam as the religion of the majority has been more of a justification than a command.

As the title of Hourani's book, *Arabic Thought in the Liberal Age*, implies, all this is nevertheless very 'bourgeois', not only in the sense that it was largely the work of the 'middle classes' of Egyptian and North African society, those with the education for the purpose, but also in the sense that it was largely in reaction to the values and judgements of the increasingly middle-class society of Western Europe with its typical institutions. It might well be asked to what extent it corresponded to the realities of the countries in question. To the extent that the response was forthcoming, and that it amounted to a growing and increasingly effective demand for modernization on European terms, it might be said that the correspondence was exact, that the avowed aims determined the course of the history to such an extent that no more should be asked, that the study is simply one of a progressive transformation. On the other hand events have given rise to two different propositions which in a curious way are not unrelated, and may serve to place the other in perspective. In the first place, by way of illustration, there is that generated by the Algerian war of independence in the work of Frantz Fanon. This is a neo-Marxist theory of popular revolution based largely on the peasantry, laying stress in consequence upon the lower rather than the middle and upper classes, whose opinions are evaluated according to their relationship to the situation and interests of the people at large. Its importance for the present purpose lies in the attention drawn to traditional values in the process of change.

Popular opposition to imperial government became apparent in Egypt over the Dinshawāy affair in 1906, in which a number of villagers were hanged or flogged for an attack upon a party of British officers,[37] and took the form of popular support for nationalist movements and leaders from Muṣṭafā Kamīl (d. 1908) onwards. In the Maghrib, the pacification of Morocco was hardly complete when it showed itself throughout French North Africa in the riots and demonstrations which were a feature of the 1930s up till 1938, when the more militant leaders found themselves in prison or exile. It reappeared after the Second World War. Fierce reprisals for the killing of Europeans at Sétif in 1945 kept Algeria quiet for some ten years, but in Morocco and Tunisia opposition had grown to the point of insurrection by the early 1950s. According to Berque, the significant feature was the growth of an urban proletariat, which provided the necessary support for demands previously restricted to an educated minority. The turning point occurred in 1934 when the contradictions of the colonial system became apparent: prosperity began to revive after the Depression, but could no longer satisfy those driven into the cities by the development of a modern economy. The regime was obliged to resort to a sterile repression.[38] According to Fanon, writing of course about the 1950s, it was the people at large who responded naturally to the initiative of the FLN, for which they had waited over the years. The emphasis is less upon the ways in which the opportunity arose out of the colonial situation, important as these may have been, as upon the continuity of feeling which qualified the course of events and ultimately determined its outcome. That there is a difference from the theme of *Arabic Thought in the Liberal Age* can be seen in Fanon's evaluation of the relationship between tradition and modernity. Whereas the subjects of Hourani's book were concerned from the outset with the reform of traditional ways, Fanon laid stress upon the value of conservatism as the natural and proper response to colonial rule. The time for modernization was the moment of insurrection, when it might serve the purpose of progressive popular revolution.[39]

The corollary of this thesis is Fanon's famous denunciation in *The Wretched of the Earth* of the educated *élites* of independent Africa as a 'false bourgeoisie', lacking the essential feature of the European class, the ownership of the means of production. Their modernity is in fact a capitulation to the colonizer, a servile imitation. Only to the extent that it prepares and assists the revolution is it justifiable. Traditional culture on the other hand is equally qualified as a means to the end, a defence against aggression which must change in value or disappear when the real victory over colonialism is at hand. What is important here is not the relevance to current Marxist thought about the role of culture and cultural alienation in the class conflict in the age of mass communication. Nor is it the argument for some form of pre-colonial nationhood represented by popular culture. It would be a mistake to follow it into the cul-de-sac of national myth, of the kind which would make of 'Abd al Qādir in Algeria the leader of the people against the invader despite the treason of the ruling class.[40] More to the point is the relativity which places the question of tradition in a new light. Here, however, Fanon's position is a logical extreme. Starting from the basic assumption that values change with circumstance, it is possible to argue the opposite, and to conclude that adherence to tradition has equally and perhaps more effectively served the purpose of reaction rather than revolution.

A proposition of this kind emerges somewhat piecemeal from the work of African historians. Their studies of the response to colonial government in various parts of the continent have tended to break down a simplistic division of the African population into those who resisted and those who collaborated, showing that those who resisted in some ways collaborated in others, and vice versa.[41] The result may be expressed in an examination question about the extent to which traditional authority survived under European rule. Muslim Africa provides a number of examples, of which one of the most interesting to the south of the Sahara, leaving aside the case of Northern Nigeria, is that of the religious orders in Senegal, notably the Murīdīya.[42] In Algeria, by the side of the old nobility, the marabouts maintained themselves in one of their original positions, intermediary between government and people, to encounter the anger of the Salafīya at their neglect of their people and their faith.[43] In Morocco there was nothing to equal the spectacular alliance of the Glawi family with the French, but Gellner can note in the High Atlas that the 'saints' have survived the imposition of bureaucracy to do well at local elections.[44] Few such examples, however, are as outstanding as the two presented to the symposium, M. Palazzoli's discussion of the monarchy in Morocco, and Professor Sanderson's case for the origins of Sudanese independence.[45] No easy generalization is at hand for these instances; John Waterbury has seen the royal hegemony in Morocco sociologically, in terms of a system of checks and balances such as that described by Gellner,[46] which would be typical of North African and Middle Eastern societies.[47] By the constraints imposed upon initiative, the result would be stalemate not only for the individual but for the group as a whole, a fact which would explain a general failure to develop as well as the particular success of a traditional authority. M. Palazzoli likewise touches upon the problem of 'under-development' when considering the question of political strategy. In this respect, however, it may be wondered to what extent Moroccan society, and by implication that of the area in general, is the cause as much as the victim of its predicament.

Waterbury's thesis might be regarded as a more fashionable version of Renan's contention that so far as progress was concerned, Islam was like an iron band around the head of the believer,[48] with religion now subordinate to local culture on the principle summarized by Bourdieu, that in matters of faith a society will select those features it requires and ignore the rest.[49] Bourdieu on the other hand would not deny the implication of M. Rodinson's demonstration of the concordance of Islam and economic enterprise,[50] that it is the circumstance which counts. He offers indeed a description of the way in which economic transactions have been habitually translated into moral terms (along the lines of 'an Englishman's word is his bond'), which might serve as a model of the way in which economic innovations may be accepted.[51] It is true that the modernization of the economy of the area, north and south of the Sahara, has had a peculiar history. Where the British in Egypt were politically reactionary, economically they were most assiduous, not merely in fulfilling their obligations to the European community by managing the finances of the state, or in pursuing their imperial strategy in the matter of the Suez canal. They continued and greatly improved upon the initiative of Muḥammad 'Alī in providing not only for the cash crop, cotton, but for agriculture in general, with the systematic control of the Nile. The effort extended to the Sudan with the Sennar dam, the Gezira scheme, and the railways. The fiscal aspect of such operations was more prominent to the west, where for both the British and the French groundnuts became the staple of the savannah belt. In the Maghrib the situation was complicated by colonization, which represented an immense direct and indirect investment. Whatever the details, the story may seem dictated with little reference to native wishes.

This, however, would be to ignore the fact that as in the political field, from which indeed it is only to be distinguished for the sake of convenience, from the cotton farmers of the Gezira to the migrant Algerian labourers in France, the result depended to a considerable extent upon a chosen response. Opportunities have doubtless been severely limited, just as they have been evaluated with reference to traditional ways of life; the Murīd settlements in Senegal, growing groundnuts on hitherto uncultivated land, offer a specifically Islamic instance. Inevitably they have been taken also in the interests of old as well as new sectors of the community, the landlords of Egypt before Nasser, the traders from the Mzab in the Algerian Sahara,[52] alongside the impoverished immigrants into the bidonvilles and the westernized middle classes. The adaptation is still apparent, and may be expected to continue. Whether it will further the end of a society in which adequate wealth is adequately distributed is another question. Dealing with the Maghrib, Amin can show the crippling effect of a flight of capital in the years after independence.[53] What is required, however, seems to be not merely a return to previous levels of investment, but a very different outlay. The fact is that these various countries, including Egypt, have inherited what may be called the syndrome of under-development, on the one hand dependence upon the export of primary products for the world market, insufficient even with the addition of foreign aid to provide for more than a fraction of the growing population, and on the other the immense difficulty of diversification in the face of the economic growth of the developed countries. It is particularly apposite that this collection includes the paper by Dr. Allen on the agriculture of Tripolitania, which illustrates some aspects of the situation with a particularly clear-cut subject.[54]

Libya has frequently been regarded as a creation *ex nihilo,* a huge expanse of desert turned into a state because the great powers could not agree upon its allocation, which belatedly acquired substance with the discovery of oil. In fact, to some extent because of the small scale of its population, it offers a good case history of the considerations outlined in this introduction. In a classic work,[55] Evans-Pritchard provided an historical account of the Sanūsī order in Cyrenaica which might be taken as a model of the way in which a traditional authority, here specifically Muslim, can undergo a progressive transformation. The founder of the order was a contemporary, to all intents and purposes a fellow-countryman, of 'Abd al Qādir in Algeria, whose time in Arabia, if it did not make him a follower of ibn 'Abd al Wahhāb, placed him among the earlier advocates of a return to a more conscientious Islam, with a missionary intention. He settled in Cyrenaica as a murābiṭ, a holy man after the fashion of the Ihansalen described by Gellner in the High Atlas.[56] He and his followers, in the stateless society of the Arab beduin, acted in the same way as mediators. The difference was that they were more centralized, and as missionaries looked beyond the local society to Tripolitania, the Fezzan and the Central Sudan. There in particular they acquired a notable position, but were driven out by the French at the beginning of the present century. Against the French attack their leader Aḥmad took up arms, which were then employed in the north on the outbreak of the Italo–Turkish war in 1911. According to Evans-Pritchard, the Cyrenaican tribes who normally lived in a state of mutual opposition, but naturally united at every stage from the family group up to the tribal confederation in the face of external attack, considered themselves as a whole in opposition to the Ottoman administration of the area. In the face of the Italian attack, however, the principle of alliance was extended to include the Turks as fellow Muslims, so that the beduin made common cause with the Ottoman empire, and indeed continued the fight after the Turks officially withdrew in 1912. Since the Sanūsī order was the only institution common to the tribes, it had come to mediate between them and the Turkish government; for the same reason it now provided them with leadership in war.

In this first Italo-Sanūsī war the Cyrenaicans were eventually defeated, largely because in 1916 Aḥmad attacked the British in Egypt. After the end of the world war, however, Aḥmad's successor Idrīs, the future king, was treated by the Italian government as a political leader, even a ruler. In 1922 he accepted an invitation from Tripoli, where a nationalist movement akin to the Vieux Destour in Tunisia had proclaimed a republic, to place himself at the head of a united country. The situation changed abruptly when Mussolini came to power immediately afterwards; Idrīs withdrew to Cairo, the Sanūsī order was destroyed, and the second Italo-Sanūsī war, 1923–33, was fought for the most part by guerrillas for whom Idrīs was no more than a symbolic figure. Yet after resistance was at an end he remained the focus of what might be termed Cyrenaican nationalism, and was in consequence adopted by the British during the Second World War. The Cyrenaican beduin were incorporated into the British army under the Sanūsī flag, and after the war Idrīs was installed as head of a provincial government with the makings of a separate state. In spite of this close identification with a territory jealous of its liberty he was then again invited to lead a Libyan federation by a provisional assembly convoked under the auspices of the United Nations, and in 1951 became king of a united Libya.[57]

This is an instructive tale. Most obviously it shows a traditional religious authority, acting in a traditional capacity in a stateless society, turning under pressure into government, at the head of a modern nation state. In so doing it is seen entering into relations in Tripolitania with the kind of nationalism represented by the Vieux Destour in Tunisia and by the Istiqlāl as described by M. Palazzoli in Morocco, while in Cyrenaica it becomes involved in popular revolt. It is possible to modify and to complete the story, but only in order to make it the more representative. About the critical year 1911, it may be wondered whether Muslim solidarity was indeed the prime consideration of the Beduin as a natural extension of the rules of tribal solidarity – would they not have fought equally, along with the Sudanese, against an invasion of Muslims from Egypt? – or whether much of the lead did not come from Aḥmad al Sanūsī on the one hand and the society of the Ottoman regime in Cyrenaica on the other, touched along with the Tripolitanians by the various currents of nationalism and reform. Of the events preceding independence, it is important that in 1950–1 the most influential party in Tripolitania, the National Congress Party, taking an Arab nationalist line and standing for a unitary rather than a federal structure for Libya, was eliminated as the result of a tactical error from the decision-making process initiated by the United Nations commissioner.[58] The outcome was an essentially conservative solution to the problem of the new state, which in 1969 eventually cost the king his throne. The typical appearance of a military regime, however, seems characteristic of a general need for a leader of sufficient prestige or power, king, colonel or commoner, to hold the political balance.[59] This is by no means static; that the variables are uncertain is no reason to reduce them to functions of a changeless structure – *plus c'est la même chose*. Nor can they yet be seen in terms of a unilinear progression. Conditions vary; options open while others close. With oil, Libya has more freedom of action, with agriculture perhaps less.

This essentially timid conclusion, which could be rendered by the banal image of 'countries at the crossroads', is not perhaps as trite as it may seem. In the Libyan story it is possible to see intertwined not only most of the factors but also most of the problems of interpretation involved in the history of the area as a whole. It is no accident that the intellectual options are as open, and as closed, as the actual. In a diminishing world, they are increasingly the same. The historian may hold fast to the event, in the conviction that it is only there that the possibilities have been and will continue to be revealed, rejected or realized. He will try to construct the present from the past, not the past from the present, aware that 'la révolution était en avance sur les consciences'.[60] Such professionalism will not save him from commitment, from a contribution to the argument over the current agenda of the species. We may usefully turn from Berque's preface to his conclusion to the first edition of *Le Maghreb entre deux guerres*, and note the allegorical reading of the title which he recommends. What refers ostensibly to the period between the two world wars may also, he suggests, be taken to epitomize the situation of a people caught between the war against the external enemy and that against the internal, the jihād against the other and the jihād over the self, to find the mean.[61] This statement of the problem of modernization as an intellectual dilemma cannot, evidently, be taken out of context, without reference to the conditions. Nevertheless it may recall I. M. Lewis' conclusion, 'the paradox is that Islam is gaining its greatest following in the history of tropical Africa at a time when its wider influence seems to be diminishing'.[62] Since the days of Renan, the strong tendency which appears from the foregoing survey is to subordinate the religion to the situation. That it has continued to provide an important means of conceptualization, on the other hand, seems indisputable. That it should continue to do so not necessarily at the level of the new national societies is a fact that may not be without significance even in those countries of northern Africa in which it has been adopted as an expression of national identity.[63] Considering the progress of the 'two wars', we return after all on this point to the first subject of the Symposium, Islamization, the profession of faith. What are the revolutions of which it is not aware?

NOTES

1 Ed. I. M. Lewis, 1966; Introduction.
2 '. . . this totalitarian dogma . . . which satisfies the needs of more than 300 million people . . . in spite of thirteen hundred years . . . still stands.': Guernier, 1950, I, 206 (my translation); cf. Renan, 1883, and Ameer Ali, 1922.
3 '. . . the attitude of a given Algerian woman with respect to the veil will be constantly related to her overall attitude with respect to the foreign occupation': Fanon, 1970; 'The struggle for national liberty has been accompanied by a cultural phenomenon known by the name of the awakening of Islam.': Fanon, 1967.
4 E. I. J. Rosenthal, 1958, 8.
5 D. de Santillana in Arnold and Guillaume, eds., 1931, 294.
6 C. H. Becker, 1924, I, 45.
7 See below, 73–83; cf. also N. J. Coulson, 1964, Chap. 9.
8 Coulson, 1964, Chap. 10.
9 Rosenthal, loc. cit.
10 G. E. von Grunebaum, 1961, 127–40.
11 B. Lewis, 1963, Chap. VI.
12 Cf. von Grunebaum, loc. cit.
13 Cf. E. E. Evans-Pritchard, 1949; E. Gellner, 1969.
14 See below, 49–56.
15 Cf. von Grunebaum, loc. cit.
16 For Ibādī Islam cf. EI², s.v. Ibādī.
17 Rosenthal, 1958, 51–61.
18 Hitti, 1960, 740–1.
19 See below, 57–64.
20 Ibid., 83, n. 4.
21 Exhaustively documented by Ageron, 1968.
22 Ibid., pp. 292–3, 296, 892–908.
23 See below, 123–41.
24 A. Hourani, 1962, 106–7.
25 P. M. Holt, 1966, 192
26 C. H. Churchill, 1867.
27 Hourani, 1962, 194.
28 Ibid., 84–94.
29 Ageron, 1968.
30 J. Brignon, A. Amin, etc., 1967.
31 Hourani, 1962, 130–60.
32 Ibid., 306.
33 For this movement, cf. A. Merad, 1967.
34 See below, 85–95.
35 Ch.-A. Julien, 1972, 130–3.
36 Hourani, 1962, 359–60.
37 Ibid., 201.
38 J. Berque, 1970, 114–17.
39 Fanon, 1970; cf. n. 1.
40 Cf. e.g. S. Amin, 1970, 105–6.
41 Cf. e.g. Oliver and Fage, 1970, 202–4.
42 Cf. L. Behrman, 1970.
43 Cf. Ageron, 1968, 891–922.
44 E. Gellner, in J. Pitt-Rivers, ed., 1963.

45 See below, 97–109.
46 Gellner, 1969.
47 J. Waterbury, 1970.
48 Cf. n. 1.
49 P. Bourdieu, 1961, 95–104.
50 M. Rodinson, 1966.
51 Bourdieu, 1961, 95.
52 Ibid., 35–50.
53 S. Amin, 1970.
54 See below, 111–21.
55 E. E. Evans-Pritchard, 1949.
56 Gellner, 1969.
57 A. Pelt, 1970.
58 The insistence upon the selection rather than the election of members of the provisional council meant that in the event the party was in a minority in the Tripolitanian delegation; cf. Pelt, 1970, 243 et seq.
59 Cf. I. W. Zartman, 1964, 3–18.
60 Berque, 1970, 13.
61 Ibid., 464–5.
62 I. M. Lewis, 1966, 91.
63 See below, 10.

REFERENCES

Ch.-R. Ageron, *Les Algériens musulmans et la France, 1871–1920*, 2 vols., Paris, 1968.
Ameer Ali, *The Spirit of Islam*, London, 1922.
S. Amin, *The Maghreb in the Modern World*, London, 1970.
T. W. Arnold and A. Guillaume, eds., *The Legacy of Islam*, Oxford, 1931.
C. H. Becker, *Islamstudien*, 2 vols., Leipzig, 1924.
L. Behrman, *Muslim Brotherhoods and Politics in Senegal*, Cambridge, Mass., 1970.
J. Berque, *Le Maghreb entre deux guerres*, 2nd ed., Paris, 1970.
P. Bourdieu, *Sociologie de l'Algérie*, Paris, 1961.
J. Brignon, A. Amin, etc., *Histoire du Maroc*, Paris and Casablanca, 1967.
C. H. Churchill, *The Life of Abdel Kader*, London, 1867.
N. J. Coulson, *A History of Islamic Law*, Edinburgh, 1964.
Encyclopaedia of Islam, 2nd ed. (EI²), Leyden, 1955 continuing.
E. E. Evans-Pritchard, *The Sanusi of Cyrenaica*, Oxford, 1949.
F. Fanon, *The Wretched of the Earth*, London, 1967; *A Dying Colonialism*, London, 1970.
E. Gellner, *Saints of the Atlas*, London, 1969.
G. E. von Grunebaum, *Islam*, 2nd ed., London, 1961.
E. Guernier, *La Berbérie, l'Islam et la France*, 2 vols., Paris, 1950.
P. K. Hitti, *History of the Arabs*, 7th ed., London, 1960.
P. M. Holt, *Egypt and the Fertile Crescent, 1516–1922*, London, 1966.
A. Hourani, *Arabic Thought in the Liberal Age, 1798–1939*, Oxford, 1962.
Ch.-A. Julien, *L'Afrique du Nord en marche*, 3rd ed., Paris, 1972.
B. Lewis, *The Arabs in History*, 3rd ed., London, 1964.
I. M. Lewis, ed., *Islam in Tropical Africa*, Oxford, 1966.
A. Merad, *Le Réformisme musulman en Algérie*, Paris, 1967.
R. Oliver and J. B. Fage, *A Short History of Africa*, 3rd ed., 1970.
A. Pelt, *Libyan Independence and the United Nations*, New Haven and London, 1970.

J. Pitt-Rivers, ed., *Mediterranean Countrymen*, Paris, 1963.
E. Renan, *L'Islamisme et la science*, Paris, 1883.
M. Rodinson, *Islam et Capitalisme*, Paris, 1966.
E. I. J. Rosenthal, *Political Thought in Mediaeval Islam*, Cambridge, 1958.
J. Waterbury, *The Commander of the Faithful*, London, 1970.
I. W. Zartman, *Government and Politics in Northern Africa*, London, 1964.

I

The Spread of Islam in Egypt and North Africa

Michael Brett

Religion has so coloured the sources for the history of northern Africa in the Muslim period that it must to a large extent be seen in terms of the development of Islam. The salient fact, the profession of faith, inevitably acquires great significance in relation to what went before and what has been the case meanwhile. For a Muslim thinker in the classical tradition, the spread of Islam marked a break with the past, the final step along the line from creation to judgement. Thereafter the profession of faith marked out the community of true believers from those who still refused to accept the revelation of the Prophet. It was the starting point of a distinctive and necessarily superior way of life which could be defined in contrast to that of the unregenerate.[1] Seen from a European point of view, as a victory of the East over the West,[2] the spread of Islam has been held in varying measure responsible for the transition from Ancient to Medieval history.[3] Naturally it has then been critical for the ensuing estimate of the history of the Islamic lands divorced in this way from Europe, either as one of continual decline from Classical prosperity,[4] or as a tale inverse to that of the Western rival, of superiority giving way to inferiority.[5] Whatever the inflection, the estimate has usually involved a judgement upon the Islamic way of life. Its description is certainly important; its relevance to the Islamic peoples and their history cannot be denied. What is far more difficult is to use its development as an index, as evidence for economic, social and political change. The nature of the relationship is not sufficiently demonstrable for the whole to be inferred in this way from the part, however prominent and pervasive religion may seem to be.

The problem may be represented initially by two questions: why did Christianity disappear from North Africa while it survived to a certain extent in Egypt, and why did Islam succeed so completely? To the first, the answer summarized by Cornevin is that on the eve of the Muslim conquest North African Christianity was demoralized and disunited, whereas Egyptian, Coptic, Christianity, represented by the Monophysite church, was a national religion in rebellion against the persecution of the Imperial government and the Orthodox church.[6] The second, which at the outset begs the question of what Islam may be said to have been during the first two centuries of its existence, has appeared more complicated. The stereotype of a religion preached initially by the sword has long given way to recognition of the fact that the Arab conquerors were more concerned with tribute, and to the conclusion that proselytism was against the interests of the new rulers, since conversion would diminish the number of tax-paying subjects. In the case of Egypt, however, Becker considered that conversion resulted from this situation on a massive scale, so much so that by the first half of the ninth century a majority of the Egyptian population had adopted Islam to claim its lighter fiscal load.[7] In North Africa on the other hand, proselytism has been seen as an adjunct of conquest to obtain the submission of the bulk of the pagan Berber peoples by the first half of the eighth.[8] In Egypt the consequences would have been economic, a flight from the land from which the economy never recovered.[9] In North Africa they would have been political, a revolt in the name of Islam against the tyranny of the state.[10]

None of these arguments is satisfactory. Whatever the state of Christianity in North Africa in the seventh century, the existence of an apparently substantial Christian population in Ifrīqiya, basically modern Tunisia, in the ninth would indicate a measure of adjustment to Muslim rule.[11] The survival of Coptic Christianity as the religion of a specialized minority contradicts the notion of a national faith.[12] It might be thought that in both Egypt and North Africa Christianity survived as the religion of local communities and in particular as the religion of a middle class whose services were of use to the state and to society at large. That Christianity died out in North Africa some time after the middle of the eleventh century might be the result of Almohad intolerance;[13] on the other hand it may have been the result of the steady attrition which has gradually reduced the numbers of the Coptic community in Egypt,[14] but where the metropolitan character of the church may account for a greater tenacity.

In the matter of conversion, any financial incentive was evidently outweighed in the case of the professional classes who remained Christian, and also in the case of the Jews.[15] Applied to the Egyptian peasant, the evidence is that while taxation may have led to evasion and even revolt, at least until the middle of the eighth century there was little conversion, either because the tax in question, the poll tax, represented only part of the total obligation, or because conversion was in fact prohibited.[16] In North Africa the situation with regard to the Christians of Ifrīqiya was doubtless similar. In the case of the

Berber peoples beyond such administrative control, some kind of preaching is plausible in spite of the dubious nature of the evidence, but with reservations about its character, purpose and results.

It is very difficult to say what Islam may have been before the ninth century, and consequently what it may have meant to be or to become a Muslim. There are virtually no sources in the Arabic tradition extant before that date. At least in the important field of law, the system they exemplify is new.[17] From the way in which they contemplate the beginnings of Islam in the light of the end, suspicion may attach to the early history of the faith as a whole.[18] It is certainly the case that the earliest historian of Egypt and North Africa to have survived, the ninth-century Egyptian ibn ʻAbd al Ḥakam, is demonstrably concerned to establish points of law to an extent that invalidates a great number of specific statements, and colours the whole with the outlook of a later age.[19] If this renders it impossible to argue from the logic of the new faith, on the other hand it becomes possible to suggest how the Muslim community originally grew, without going far beyond the basic meaning of which Islam is the noun, Muslim the active participle, aslama, 'to submit'.

The first Muslims were Arabs. To what extent they were already the result of assimilation may be unknown. It is certain, however, that from the period of the conquests, Arabization, not necessarily of language, but in the form of association with Muslim Arab society, was a feature of the spread of the new religion. This association seems fundamental. The name of the new Muslim in the early period was mawlā, pl. mawālī, 'client', from the status he acquired at conversion in relation to a Muslim member of an Arab tribe by the procedure of muwālāt, as a man might acquire a master, or a slave the duties of a freedman to his former owner.[20] Since the early references to mawālī are almost all to actual retainers, in the service of individuals or the state,[21] it might be thought that conversion was inseparable from recruitment to a largely military following for the new regime and its increasingly wealthy aristocracy. Such recruitment was perhaps by voluntary commendation, but was probably dependent to a large extent upon the slave trade organized initially out of the wars and raids of conquest.[22] It would explain the absence of general conversion in Egypt up to 750. On the other hand it leaves the problem of that conversion intact.

To some extent conversion may be attributed to a natural increase in the Muslim population by marriage and descent. This is plausible in the cities, especially in the new capital Fusṭāṭ, the origin of modern Cairo. In the countryside, however, it is possible that the necessary condition was provided by a return to Byzantine circumstances[23] in the form of great estates, whose encroachment upon the public domain by the ninth century had led to the appearance of a 'feudal' regime in Egypt.[24] There is evidence for a settlement of Arab beduin as peasants upon agricultural land from the first half of the eighth century.[25] In the ninth, ten beduin 'of my lord' appear listed alongside peasants with Arabic names.[26] The spread of 'feudal' conditions in the countryside, without requiring conversion, may have circumvented the original reluctance of the regime to give permission, and created a rural society in which it was a practical possibility. Hence perhaps the statement of al Kindī transmitted and apparently developed by Maqrīzī, to the effect that after 832 the Copts (Qibṭ) were incapable of resistance, and the Muslims in possession of the villages; the Arabs were settled as agriculturists on the land, while the Copts had accepted Islam at least in appearance, thereby mingling with the Muslims to the extent of taking Muslim wives.[27] The process was slow, and Christians remained a majority at least until the tenth century.

Among the Berber peoples of North Africa, the formation of a military class of mawālī is a salient feature of the period before 739.[28] It is in connection with their recruitment about 700 that the principal references to a preaching of Islam occur,[29] and it is in this sense that they are best understood. At the same time Islam may have been exacted from the tribes as a sign of submission. In this way it is possible to explain that the revolt of the mid-eighth century took place within Islam and not against the new religion. Over the first five or six years at least, the leaders appear mawālī, some perhaps Arabs, at the head of Muslim followers, who obtain the support of Berber tribes.[30] For this reason it seems incorrect to think in terms of a national Berber reaction to Arab rule.[31] Equally it is unnecessary to invoke the egalitarianism of the Khārijī Islam with which the rebels are associated, and to see in this a religious expression of Berber solidarity.[32] It is a question in the first place of a revolutionary movement within the Muslim society of the aristocracy, the army and the allies, which in contrast to that of the 'Abbāsids operating from the eastern extremity of the Muslim world, enjoyed a merely local success. The nature of that success, the appearance of independent Muslim states among principally Berber peoples, is best seen as the outcome of the ability of the Muslim aristocracy and subsequently of the 'Abbāsid government to retain its hold upon Ifrīqiya. The development of the Islam of those states as a form of unorthodoxy associated with Berber-speaking peoples[33] would arise from their political separation from the original Muslim society now centred on Baghdad.

From this discussion of the early period of Islam from the seventh to the ninth century, characterized by a lack of contemporary authors and a consequent uncertainty about the content of the new religion, the problem presented by the spread of Islam becomes clear. The danger of drawing conclusions from belief and practice is particularly apparent; it is more profitable to concentrate more simply upon the profession of faith. This can be seen to have served a number of political and social purposes for the new Muslim as well as for the old. Even with this limited definition of Islamization, however, difficulties remain. The 'worm's eye view' is lacking. What these purposes may have been for the population at large is to a great extent obscured by affairs of state on the one hand, the assumptions of the sources on the other. This remains true of the following centuries, when the question of mass conversion is disguised rather than revealed by the circumstances under which Islam can be said for the first time to have acquired an identifiable religious content. In the history of the 'Abbāsid caliphate, the ninth century is distinguished in this respect by the failure of the ruler to obtain the power to legislate in matters of faith, or even to procure a system compatible with administrative efficiency. Instead, Islamic law in particular became the preserve of scholars, and government the preserve of the sulṭān, the (man of) power, in a relationship torn between mutual support and mutual opposition. In Egypt the ninth century saw on the one hand the consolidation of the Mālikī school of jurisprudence, and on the other the establishment of the independent Ṭūlūnid dynasty, a process repeated in Ifrīqiya with the development of Qayrawān as a centre of religious learning, and the rise of the Aghlabid dynasty. At the same time the definition of Islamic orthodoxy in North Africa by the schools of Qayrawān produced a theological opposition to Khārijī Islam, represented chiefly by the Ibāḍī sect.[34]

The importance of Ibāḍī Islam in the ninth century was not, however, that it represented any notably different principle. What it can be said to have done is to have duplicated the religious authority of the orthodox schoolmen, the 'ulamā',[35] and to have revealed its political possibilities in a society lacking the structure of a centralized state.[36] The Ibāḍī Imamate of Tāhart was a theocracy which commanded the nominal allegiance of communities as far away as Tripolitania, grouped around the scattered shaykhs of the sect. It is possible that these reproduced in the countryside an earlier pagan type, already familiar in local society. This may partially account for the initial success in the tenth century of a third variety of Islam, that which looked to the descendants of the Prophet's son-in-law 'Alī, the fourth caliph, to provide the hereditary leadership of the Muslim world. In theory the Fāṭimids appealed to the mass of Muslims everywhere, in practice to particular societies. Their attempt to capture the Muslim world from the west as the 'Abbāsids had taken it from the east began with the activity of their representative among the Kutāma people of the central Maghrib.[37] Overthrowing the Aghlabids in 909, they went on to capture Egypt in 969, where their caliphate lasted until 1171.

Despite their claims, in North Africa and Egypt the unorthodox Ismā'īlī Islam of the Fāṭimids seems never to have been much more than the cult of their dynasty, and to have disappeared from the area with their power. In North Africa they provoked a strong reaction, beginning with the 'ulamā' of Qayrawān, one consequence of which from the eleventh century was the steady elimination of the earlier heterodoxy, Ibāḍī Islam, until it survives today only among small and isolated communities.[38] Associated with, and conceivably a more immediate consequence of this reaction, was the movement of the Murābiṭūn, the Almoravids, in the west, which in many respects repeated on behalf of orthodox Islam the history of the Fāṭimids farther to the east. Thus the appeal of the holy man ibn Yāsīn to the tribes of the Sahara yielded an army capable, in the hands of an ambitious monarch, Yūsuf ibn Tashfīn, of going on to the conquest of Morocco and Muslim Spain. The process, however, was not complete, for in the twelfth century the new empire was taken over by yet another such movement, that of the Muwaḥḥidūn, the Almohads, who extended it to include the whole of the Maghrib at a time when the Fāṭimid caliphate itself was giving way in Egypt to pressure from Syria. Saladin's seizure of power in Cairo in 1169 and the Almohad expansion were both to some extent provoked by Christian aggression in Spain, North Africa and the Levant. For the present purpose it is more important that in their different ways both Saladin and the Muwaḥḥidūn derive from the scholarship developed in the Middle East from the second half of the eleventh century, commonly associated with the Niẓāmīya university in Baghdad, and with the name of al Ghazzālī.[39]

This scholarship has been seen as a watershed. On the one hand a systematic formulation of orthodoxy would have disposed of the challenge of heterodoxy; on the other a generous catholicism would have reconciled the legalism of the jurists with the spiritualism of the mystics.[40] In the matter of Islamization, attention is thus directed away from heresy towards the widespread pietism called Ṣūfism, which from about this time gradually acquired institutional form, as pupils and followers gathered for purposes of instruction and devotion around a notable master, to be perpetuated after his death in congregations which might run to many thousands and spread throughout the Muslim world under the leadership of his successors.[41] Ṣūfism, in effect, appears as the equivalent of Christian monasticism, with the same enormous variety, but with a much larger lay following than has been customary in western Europe since the sixteenth century. Certainly it has been prominent in Egypt and North Africa.

In this way a long period, from the ninth to, say, the fifteenth century, is broken in two. In the earlier portion, the attention continues to be held by politics, and it might be thought that an important factor in the spread of Islam beyond the original ruling group was the proliferation of rivals in competition with each other for support, in other words by propaganda. The Fāṭimids provide the most notable example of missionary effort, but it could be argued also for the Ibāḍīs, the Almoravids and the Almohads. The difficulty is to envisage the character of such groups and the nature of their appeal. They have been seen as expressions of national, social and economic discontent and ambition in a rich and still expanding Muslim world.[42] In the area under discussion, however, the correlation in any given case is hard to establish. It might be better to see them as initiatives which acquired a political and social history according to circumstance. Frequently they became exclusive. While they may be taken as symptomatic of an increasing profession of faith on the part of peoples throughout the area, it is impossible to be categoric about the relationship, or the extent to which their propaganda and their achievements were a major cause.

It is, for example, the implication of at least one view of the later portion of the period that their activities in this respect were superficial. The problem centres around the intellectual developments about the year 1100, to decide in what way these were indeed critical, and the subsequent proliferation of Ṣūfī groups in consequence significantly new, extending the profession of Islam while bringing about a transformation of the existing Muslim community. For the Muslim world as a whole, it was Gibb's contention that the triumph of orthodoxy imposed a spiritually unsatisfying uniformity upon an Islam that was still essentially urban and upper class, that the spread of Ṣūfism, achieved by proselytism among the masses, was the means whereby Islam itself was extended beyond the radius of urban civilization, and that taking place against the decline of that civilization from the eleventh century onwards, it came to provide a replacement for the original scholasticism of the 'ulamā' as the dominant form of Islam.[43] Even more than in the case of the earlier competition, therefore, the course of history in the Islamic lands is invoked to explain the spread of religion in terms of far-reaching social and economic change, the reverse of previous trends, decline instead of expansion.

In North Africa and Egypt the proposition is doubtful; it seems unlikely that nomads wrought the havoc commonly ascribed to them.[44] It is at least curious that in western Europe a contemporary development towards more emotive forms of piety has been considered symptomatic of social and economic growth.[45] Nor is it helpful to insist upon a dichotomy between two kinds of Islam, as previously between orthodoxy and heterodoxy. The inference of an historical division into a period of urban followed by rural propagation, although advanced by Bel specifically in the case of North Africa,[46] seems falsely to impose upon a continuous evolution. For the whole of the period from the ninth to the fifteenth century it seems equally advisable to leave aside questions of belief and practice and of the corresponding groups, to concentrate instead upon a common denominator of fundamental importance.

This is the authority already referred to, that of the individual master of piety and learning. It was clearly established by the time of the ninth century formulation of Islam, and was indeed the means by which that formulation was brought about. It depended on reputation, was carried on by pupils, and was exercised through consultation. Although it may first have been prominent in connection with law it was duplicated in other matters of learning as well as in that of simple piety. In all its forms it seems to have been quickly common to all the Muslim societies under discussion, perhaps because it arose from and was assimilated to various existing types, priest, rabbi, hermit, soothsayer, pedagogue, scholar. Orthodoxy or unorthodoxy is irrelevant for this purpose, likewise the particular function, especially since one man, for example the jurist, might exercise the role of saint, the pious mediator between man and God represented by the ascetic murābiṭ of ninth century Ifrīqiya and subsequently by the Ṣūfī shaykh.[47] Conversely, in later centuries the Ṣūfī was frequently a scholar, often in effect a jurist.[48] What is important is that the establishment of this kind of authority might be taken to represent the emancipation of Islam, first in principle and then in practice, from allegiance to the original Arab ruling class, and that it is possible to see the development of Muslim society as an assortment of separate regional communities in terms of the demands it made and the demands it fulfilled.

In this way a measure of autonomy is conferred upon the subject. On the one hand it avoids too great an identification of the religion with the social and economic background, whose character may still be uncertain. On the other it excludes an evaluation of the quality of the religion as a significant feature, either as a determinant[49] or as a yardstick by which to measure the extent and therefore the stages of Islamization.[50] This is important for the final period before the impact of Europe in the nineteenth century, the period from the sixteenth to the eighteenth century, when the character of religious authority has been seen as equivalent in large measure to the content of the faith in an age of spiritual, social and economic atrophy.[51] The judgement is doubtful as a conclusion to the proposition that Islam descended the social scale in stages commensurate with the decline of its civilization.[52] The fact is that the Muslim 'man of God' has been an effective figure in town and country from an early date, a prominent feature of the Muslim way of life in which the sources take such conscious pride. For that reason, of course, he is not an objective phenomenon. He is the stuff of the sources, the subject of the endless biographies and hagiographies from which so much of our historical information is derived, but his position, functions, attributes and actions are largely cast in stereotype. From the ninth century, for example, he operates in a Muslim world; in other words, in the matter of Islamization, the conversion of the bulk of the population of Egypt and North Africa is largely assumed. Even where missionary activity is in question, it is after the manner of the Old rather than the New Testament; either there is an invitation from the people to improve the quality of their Islam, as with the Fāṭimid dā'ī Abū 'Abd Allah, or the Almoravid ibn Yāsīn, or what is preached is a reformation or revival, as with the Almohad ibn Tūmart. After making all allowances, however, it seems reasonable to see in his type of authority an indicator and an agent of an undramatic but cumulative process continuing in accordance with circumstances down to the present day.

The significance of this process should not be exaggerated at the expense of other factors. Considering for example the way in which Islamization has continued in the sense of a distinction from the non-Muslim world, within this area of northern Africa it has served to define the position of the Christian and the Jew by limiting the permissible relationships between these and the Muslim. The same has applied to the foreigner, most obviously the European, from without. On this understanding, symbiosis has been the rule, despite the fastness of the barrier.[53] Moments of intolerance have been exceptional, and not always common to society at large. Military hostility, from the time of the Crusades, has arguably made little difference. It is perhaps the barrier in the European mind which has been more fateful, at least since the Napoleonic wars. A case could be made out that the religious distinction was instrumental in bringing about the difference in treatment of lands to the north and south of the Mediterranean which on other counts were very similar. Whereas Greece and Sicily for example were encouraged towards independence and democracy within the community of Europe, the African shore was deemed fit for subjection, not merely because of the ingrained assumptions of European opinion, but because the various protectorates, in Egypt, Tunisia and Morocco, developed out of the protection of European nationals in the countries concerned on the basis of the traditional *modus vivendi* between Muslims and non-Muslims. In the special case of Algeria, conquered and colonized by France, Islam came to be the criterion employed to discriminate between the *colon* and the *indigène* in matters of civil and political rights, especially after the Crémieux decree of 1870 abolished the anomaly of the native Jewish community by naturalization.[54]

It is as a reaction to such treatment that the association of Islam with nationalism may be considered a modern application of a traditional category to a traditional purpose. Its use in this way has been sharpened by the creation of the state of Israel in 1948, which has provoked a wholly new intolerance of the native Jewish communities leading to the substantial emigration of the indigenous Jewish populations. This exodus of Jews, and of Europeans from the North African countries since independence, has been in effect the latest stage in the process of Islamization, leaving the area, with the exception of the Coptic community in Egypt, more solidly Muslim than ever before. At the same time, however, modernist legislation has invaded the sphere of traditional religious authority, considerably modifying many of the ways of the Muslim community itself. The influence of the individual local personality has been reduced or diverted into new activities like electoral politics. On the other hand it has been supplemented for religious purposes, and to some extent replaced, by that of thc many as a result of modern communications, roads, railways, and radio. Where in tropical Africa the outcome appears as a great increase in the spread of Islam,[55] in North Africa in particular there has occurred along with the increasing use of Arabic by the Berber-speaking population, a growing standardization of religious knowledge and practice.[56] It would seem that at the present juncture Islamization, the profession of faith, entails, if it does not actually mean, increasing conformity within societies organized on a national scale. While this may tend to enhance its value as an expression of national identity and unity, its value in other respects may be permanently diminished by the secularization of everyday life. How it would fare if the consensus which prevails in the present age of Presidential regimes were to break down into a radical confrontation of Right and Left, is a matter for speculation.

NOTES

1 Cf. e.g. G. E. von Grunebaum, 1961, 31–57.
2 Cf. e.g. R. H. C. Davis, 1957, 107.
3 Notoriously so in H. Pirenne, 1937.
4 For Egypt cf. e.g. C. H. Becker, 1902–3, II, 136.
5 Cf. e.g. H. A. R. Gibb, 1962, 3–33.
6 R. Cornevin, 1962, 227, 237.
7 Cf. Becker, 1924, I, 153–5.
8 Cf. e.g. G. Marçais, 1946, 35–40.
9 Becker, 1924, I, 167, 210–11.
10 Marçais, 1946, 43–53.
11 Ibid., 70–3.
12 For the Coptic community, cf. E. W. Lane, 1860, 535–57.
13 Marçais, 1946, 270.
14 Lane, 1860, 535.
15 For the Jews, cf. S. D. Goitein, 1967.
16 Cf. D. C. Dennett, 1950, 3–13, 65–115.
17 Cf. J. Schacht, 1950.
18 This is evidently controversial; however, cf. J. Wansbrough, 1970, 264 and n. 77, 613–15.
19 Cf. R. Brunschvig, 1942–7, 108–55.
20 Cf. Schacht, 1950, 161, 173.
21 Cf. al Kindī, 1912, 38, 51, 52, 70, 84, 87, 96; ibn ʻAbd al Ḥakam, 1948, 66, 74, 76, 96, 112.
22 Cf. e.g. M. Talbi, 1966, 25–33.
23 Cf. e.g. H. I. Bell in S. R. K. Glanville, ed., 1942, 332–47.
24 Cf. Becker, 1902–3, II, 136 ff.
25 Ibid., II, 125–9.
26 Ibid., II, 130.
27 Ibid., II, 120–1, 135.
28 Ibn ʻAbd al Ḥakam, 1948, 74, 76, 78, 96, 112, 114.
29 Cf. e.g. ibn ʻIdhārī, 1948, 42; al Nuwayrī, 1917–19, II, 23.
30 Cf. ibn ʻAbd al Ḥakam, 1948, 122–44, passim.
31 Marçais, 1946, 46.
32 Ibid., 47, 48.
33 Ibid., 101–16.
34 Cf. H. R. Idris, 1962, 743–5.
35 Cf. Marçais, 1946, 105, 107.
36 Ibid., 106–7.
37 Ibid., 133–4.
38 Cf. M. Brett, 1969, 360.
39 For the Almohads and their intellectual origins, cf. Marçais, 1946, 253–75; for an estimate of Saladin, cf. e.g. Gibb, 1962, 91–107.
40 Cf. Gibb, 1962, 3–33.
41 For Ṣūfism and its history, cf. J. Spencer Trimingham, 1971.
42 Cf. B. Lewis, 1964, 99–114.
43 Gibb, 1962, 27–32.
44 Cf. e.g. Brett, 1969, 347–64.
45 R. W. Southern, 1953.
46 A. Bel, 1938, 361–5.
47 Cf. e.g. ibn Rashīq, Lament for Qayrawān, in ibn Nājī, 1320H, 15–18, 11. 1–17.
48 Cf. e.g. the sixteenth-century Egyptian al Shaʻrānī, Trimingham, 1971, 220–5.

49 Cf. e.g. E. Guernier, 1950, I, 203–46; above, xi, n. l.
50 Cf. e.g. J. Wansbrough, 1968, 645; G.-H. Bousquet, 1957, 98.
51 Cf. Gibb, 1962, 213–17; P. K. Hitti, 1960, 719–20; Ch.-A. Julien, 1952, II, 303–9.
52 Cf. also Trimingham, 1971, 103.
53 Cf. e.g. Lane, 1860, 111–12; Bousquet, 1957, 100–1.
54 See above, xvi.
55 I. M. Lewis, ed., 1966, 81–2.
56 Cf. e.g. Bousquet, 1957, 99.

REFERENCES

C. H. Becker, *Beiträge zur Geschichte Ägyptens*, 2 vols., Strassburg, 1902–3; *Islamstudien*, 2 vols., Leipzig, 1924.
A. Bel, *La Religion musulmane en Berbérie*, Vol. I, Paris, 1938.
M. Brett, 'Ifrīqiya as a Market for Saharan Trade', *Journal of African History*, X, 3, 1969, 347–64.
G.-H. Bousquet, *Les Berbères*, Paris, 1957.
R. Brunschvig, 'Ibn Abdalh'akam et la conquête de l'Afrique du Nord', *Annales de l'Institut des Etudes Orientales*, Algiers, VI, 1942–7.
R. Cornevin, *Histoire de l'Afrique*, Vol. I, Paris, 1962.
R. H. C. Davis, *A History of Mediaeval Europe*, London, 1957.
D. C. Dennett, *Conversion and the Poll-Tax in Early Islam*, Cambridge, Mass., 1950.
H. A. R. Gibb, *Studies on the Civilization of Islam*, London, 1962.
S. R. K. Glanville, ed., *The Legacy of Islam*, 1st ed., Oxford, 1942.
S. D. Goitein, *A Mediterranean Society*, 2 vols., Berkeley and Los Angeles, 1967–.
G. E. von Grunebaum, *Islam*, 2nd ed., London, 1961.
E. Guernier, *La Berbèrie, l'Islam et la France*, 2 vols., Paris, 1950.
P. K. Hitti, *History of the Arabs*, 7th ed., London, 1960.
H. R. Idris, *La Berbèrie orientale sous les Zīrīdes*, Paris, 1962.
Ibn 'Abd al Ḥakam, *Conquête de l'Afrique du Nord et de l'Espagne*, ed. and trans. Gateau, Algiers, 1948.
Ibn 'Idhārī, *Al Bayān al Mughrib*, ed. Colin and Lévi-Provençal, Vol. I, Leyden, 1948.
Ibn Nājī, *Ma'ālim al Īmān*, Tunis, 1320H.
Ch.-A. Julien, *Histoire de l'Afrique du Nord*, 2nd ed., 2 vols., Paris, 1952.
Al Kindī, *Governors and Judges of Egypt*, ed. Guest, Leyden and London, 1912.
E. W. Lane, *Manners and Customs of the Modern Egyptians*, 5th ed., London, 1860; Everyman, n.d.
B. Lewis, *The Arabs in History*, 3rd ed., London, 1964.
I. M. Lewis, ed., *Islam in Tropical Africa*, Oxford, 1966.
G. Marçais, *La Berbèrie musulmane et l'Orient au Moyen Age*, Paris, 1946.
Al Nuwayrī, *Historia de los Musulmanes de España y Africa*, ed. and trans. Remiro, 2 vols., Granada, 1917–19.
H. Pirenne, *Muhammad and Charlemagne*, London, 1937.
J. Schacht, *The Origins of Muhammadan Jurisprudence*, Oxford, 1950.
R. W. Southern, *The Making of the Middle Ages*, London, 1953.
M. Talbi, *L'Emirat Aghlabide*, Paris, 1966.
J. S. Trimingham, *The Sufi Orders in Islam*, Oxford, 1971.
J. Wansbrough, 'Majāz al Qur'ān', *Bulletin of the School of Oriental and African Studies*, XXXIII, 2, 1970; review, ibid., 3, 1970, 613–15.

II

The Islamization of the Nilotic Sudan

P. M. Holt

School of Oriental and African Studies
University of London

1. *The Nubian Kingdoms and their Overthrow*

At the time of the conquest of Egypt by the Muslim Arabs (A.D. 639–641), three Nubian kingdoms extended up the Nile valley, south of Aswān. The two northernmost, Nobatia and Mukurra, united about this time to form the state known to Arab writers as al Muqurra, which stretched from the First Cataract probably to a district lying south of the confluence of the Atbara with the Nile. Southwards lay the third kingdom, called 'Alwa by the Arabs. The kingdoms had recently been converted to Christianity, Nobatia and 'Alwa by Monophysite, and Mukurra by Orthodox missionaries. In the hill-country between the river and the Red Sea, lived the nomadic Beja tribes, free from the control of the sedentaries of the Nile valley.

The first armed clashes between the Arabs and Nubians followed hard on the Muslim conquest of Egypt; and an Arab army besieged Dongola, the northern capital, in 651–2. Our information about these events is derived solely from later Arab sources, which represent the Arabs as victors, imposing an annual tribute of slaves (the baqṭ) on the Nubians. More probably, it would seem, an attempt at conquest proved abortive, and agreement between the two parties resulted in the re-establishment of barter-trade. With occasional periods of tension and warfare, this co-existence of Christian Nubia and Muslim Egypt continued until the establishment of the Mamluk Sultanate in the later thirteenth century.

During this period of six hundred years, the great but insidious threat to the Nubian kingdoms came, not from military enterprise by the rulers of Egypt, but from the spontaneous and unorganized penetration of Arabs into al Muqurra. The ninth century was a critical era. It witnessed a 'gold rush' to the mines in the Red Sea Hills, resulting in the formation of an Arab frontier-society in Beja territory – a development which had repercussions upon both al Muqurra and Egypt when an Arab adventurer, al 'Umarī, made himself virtually the independent ruler of 'the Land of the Mines'. An Arab clan which subsequently gained control of the mines, and intermarried with the Beja, became dominant in the Aswan region. Its chief, who captured a rebel against the Fāṭimid caliph, al Ḥākim, received the honorific of Kanz al Dawla (1007). This was borne by his successors, who were in effect marcher-lords on the frontier of Islam. Meanwhile Arab tribal movements southwards into Upper Egypt and Nubia had been stimulated when the 'Abbāsid caliph, al Mu'taṣim (833–42) ended the payment of salaries and pensions to Arab tribal warriors. The effect of these developments was gradually to erode the control of al Muqurra in the north.

Intervention in the dynastic quarrels of al Muqurra was practised by the Mamluk sultans, who on several occasions sent expeditions into Nubia in support of pretenders, one of whom (in 1317) was the contemporary Kanz al Dawla. From the late fourteenth century, Nubia enters a dark age. Nothing more is heard of the kings of al Muqurra, and ibn Khaldūn, writing at that time, says, 'So their kingdom fell to pieces and their country was inherited by the Arabs of Juhayna'. The southern kingdom of 'Alwa probably still survived: indeed, according to Sudanese tradition (not recorded until long after the event), its capital of Sūba on the Blue Nile fell to the Arabs early in the sixteenth century. Another tradition speaks of the Arab town of Arbajī on the Blue Nile (about 90 miles from Khartoum) as having been founded in 1475–6.

The process so far described was essentially one of arabization – the penetration of Arab tribesmen into Nubian territory, intermarriage with Nubians and Beja, and, ultimately, the establishment of Arab political ascendancy over the fragmented remains of the former kingdoms. To what extent did this accompany or initiate a process of islamization? Our information is extremely sparse. A fifteenth-century account of the baqṭ agreement of 652 refers to 'the mosque which the Muslims have built in the centre of your city', but this is almost certainly a late elaboration. The present mosque in Dongola was originally a church, and contains the Arabic inscription commemorating its conversion in 1317 by a Nubian pretender sponsored by the Mamluks. Although the reign of this ruler was neither long nor distinguished, he was significant as being the first Muslim king of al Muqurra. The degree to which the population had become Muslim cannot be known: a Christian bishop of Ibrīm and Faras (both towns in the north of the kingdom) was consecrated in Cairo in 1372. It is unlikely that the Arab tribal warriors and frontiersmen who infiltrated into Nubia made any great contribution to the Islamization of the peoples whom they conquered, and with whom they intermarried. Effectively this was the work of holy men coming to the Nilotic Sudan from the older Muslim lands. Hardly any of these have left any record in tradition before the establishment of the Funj Sultanate in the sixteenth century. One of them, Ḥamad Abū Dunāna is said to have settled in Berber district in 1445, and to have introduced the Shādhilīya ṭarīqa. Another, Ghulāmallāh ibn ʻĀ'id, is rather better documented. His father came from the Yemen, and he himself 'went out with his sons to the land of Dongola, because it was in extreme perplexity and error for lack of scholars. When he settled there, he built the mosques, and taught the Quran and the [religious] sciences'. Since Ghulāmallāh can be dated approximately to the early fifteenth century, the passage quoted (although written much later) throws some light on the religious situation in al Muqurra after the passing of the kingdom. A third holy man, ʻAbdallāh Jammāʻ, who married a daughter of Ḥamad Abū Dunāna, is remembered as the Arab chief who took Sūba. Descent from the family of the Prophet was claimed by (or ascribed to) all three of these holy men.

2. *The Funj Sultanate*

Early in the sixteenth century, the outlines of new political groupings can dimly be seen. The Arab immigrants appear to have intermarried with the sedentary Nubian communities along the main Nile, producing in the region between the confluence of the Atbara and the Sabalūqa gorge the quasi-tribal group known as the Jaʻalīyūn. South of the Sabalūqa gorge, in the territory around the confluence of the Blue and White Niles, the paramountcy over the Arabs, both sedentaries and nomads, was held by ʻAbdallāh Jammāʻ, and passed to his descendants, the ʻAbdallāb. The southward drift of the Arabs was, however, sharply arrested in the vicinity of Arbajī by the extension northwards, down the Blue Nile, of another group, the Funj, who may have co-operated with the Arabs in overthrowing Sūba. However this may be, relations between the two groups was by no means wholly peaceful, although on the whole the Funj maintained their ascendancy over the Arabs.

The prehistory of the Funj has long been a subject of controversy and somewhat unprofitable conjecture. What is clear is that at the outset they were neither Muslims nor Arabs. Their first historical ruler, ʻAmāra Dūnqas, is said to have founded Sinnār (which became the dynastic capital) in 1504–5, and to have appointed ʻAbdallāh Jammāʻ as a subordinate ruler. Conversion to Islam soon followed, although traditional and non-Islamic rites continued to be practised at the installation of a new Sultan. At the height of its power, in the seventeenth century, the Funj dynasty exercised a species of high-kingship over the ‘Abdallāb and other subordinate rulers from the foothills of Abyssinia northwards to the Third Cataract, and westwards across the Gezira to the White Nile. Control over the remoter areas subsequently weakened, and in 1762 power at Sinnār passed to a family of hereditary regents who were neither Funj nor Arab by origin. The last decades of the Sultanate were a time of growing anarchy in the Funj and ‘Abdallābī territories proper. The Ja‘alīyūn and other groups along the main Nile became in effect independent tribal kingdoms, until the Turco-Egyptian conquest in 1820–1 brought the whole of the former Sultanate under the rule of Muḥammad ‘Alī Pasha.

The three centuries of the Funj Sultanate were a period of decisive importance in the effective Islamization (as compared with the more superficial Arabization) of what is now the northern Sudan. The sixteenth century witnessed the arrival of several holy men from the outside Islamic world, while a few people from the Nilotic Sudan went to Egypt to study and then returned to teach in their homeland. Notable among these last were Maḥmūd al ‘Arakī, a jurist, who established a fortress on the frontier of Islam on the White Nile, and the four Sons of Jābir, who founded a successful school in the territory of the Shāyqīya tribe in the north. Not all the holy men were teachers of religion and the Holy Law. A visitor, originally from Baghdad, introduced the Qādirīya Ṣūfī ṭarīqa, which gained many adherents and produced local leaders throughout the Funj territories. From the late sixteenth century, the Islam of the Nilotic Sudan was self-supporting and self-perpetuating, although a trickle of immigrant teachers and jurists can be traced, and there were contacts with the older centres of Islam, especially through the Pilgrimage.

Nevertheless, Sudanese Islam developed on the fringe of Muslim Africa, in a region geographically remote and politically detached from the Muslim heartlands. In these circumstances, it is not surprising that the characteristic institutions of the great Islamic states – the congregational mosque, the official hierarchy of cult officials, the formal establishment of qāḍīs and muftīs – played little part in the Islam of the Funj Sultanate. Certainly these were royal mosques in Sinnār and Ḥalfāyat al Mulūk (the later capital of the ‘Abdallāb), and there are indications in the literary sources and in charters of the appointment of qāḍīs and other officials. More characteristic of the Sudanese Islam of the period, however, was the holy man, the fakī, holding no official appointment but playing an important part in the community by teaching the Quran and the elements of the Holy Law according to the Mālikī madhhab, by acting as an arbitrator in cases submitted to his judgement by the parties concerned, or by providing initiation and leadership in the devotional practices of the

Qādirīya ṭarīqa. While some of the fakīs were primarily teachers and jurists, others primarily Ṣūfī leaders, there was no rigorous division of functions in practice. The very real influence, and indeed authority, enjoyed by the fakīs was not simply a consequence of their services to the community, but reflected the general belief (not, of course, peculiar to the Nilotic Sudan) that they were vehicles, in life and in death, of supernatural power (baraka) which could be communicated to the objects they used, the tombs in which they were buried, and their offspring after them.

Hence, the holy men were often founders or members of holy families. An instance is provided by the Sons of Jābir, already mentioned. Ibrāhīm al Būlād ibn Jābir, on returning from study in Egypt, started his school about the year 1570. It was continued after his death by two of his brothers in succession, then by a nephew, who married a queen of the Shāyqīya and allowed the school to die. Another nephew, Ṣughayyirūn, moved to the territory of the Ja'alīyūn (c.1612) and founded another school, which flourished under his descendants at least until the mid-eighteenth century. Other branches of the family formed clans of holy men elsewhere in the Funj territory. An example of a holy family connected with a Ṣūfī order is given by the Ya'qūbāb. The founder of the family, Bān al Naqā al Ḍarīr, was related through his mother to the Funj, and had himself been an officer at the Sultan's court. One of the first Sudanese initiates into the Qādirīya ṭarīqa in the later sixteenth century, he established a hereditary leadership of the order, and his home district, near Sinnār, became a centre of Ṣūfī teaching.

The social significance of the holy men and their families sometimes extended far beyond their religious functions. Ḥasan b. Ḥassūna (d. 1664), the grandson of a Maghribī immigrant, established himself as a horse-trader in the Buṭāna, a nomadic area, east of the main and Blue Niles. There, through his religious prestige and his wealth, he became the patriarchal head of a large community, with a considerable slave-retinue and a household modelled on the Funj court. In the early nineteenth century, the Majādhīb, a learned and holy family whose centre was at al Dāmir in Ja'alī territory, had acquired great influence over the Beja, which helped to ensure the safety of caravans passing between the Nile and Sawākin.

The relations between the holy men and the rulers were not uniform. Fakīs frequently served as mediators – a traditional function of the Muslim 'ālim, perhaps rendered more efficacious in the Nilotic Sudan by the general belief in baraka. Unlike the 'ulamā' in most Muslim states, however, they did not show a habitual deference to the holders of political power. Ismā'īl b. Jābir, for instance, would not use water coming from the irrigation-ditches of the Shāyqīya, since the oxen which raised it had been taken by force. A more ominous figure was that of the ascetic, Ḥamad al Naḥlān called Wad al Turābī (d. 1704), who claimed to be the Expected Mahdī (always an indication of tension within the Islamic community) and laid a powerful and effective curse on the tax-gatherers of Sultan Bādī III. Nevertheless, relations between the fakī and the rulers were not always hostile. Ṣughayyirūn left home after a quarrel with a king of the Shāyqīya, but was given land by Sultan Bādī I (*c.* 1611–12). At a later date, land-grants were made by formal charters of an elaborate and stereotyped form. The earliest of these known to be extant date from the reign of Bādī IV (1742–62), and may represent an attempt of that Sultan to gain the support of the holy families, as he did that of other groups, against a branch of the dynasty whom his father had displaced.

In the last half-century of the Funj Sultanate, certain religious developments took place which indicate a greater response in the Nilotic Sudan to movements in the wider Islamic world. The eighteenth century was a period of Islamic revival. Apart from the rigorist Wahhābī movement in Arabia (which at the outset produced a schism within Islam), important forces were at work in the Ṣūfī ṭarīqas. The Naqshbandīya, orthodox in its teaching, gained considerable prestige in the Arab lands, while the Khalwatīya lost its original taint of heterodoxy and increased its adherents. A Khalwatī leader, Muḥammad ibn ʻAbd al Karīm al Sammān (1718–75), established in the Ḥijāz what became an independent order, the Sammānīya. A Sudanese belonging to a holy family, Aḥmad al Ṭayyib ibn al Bashīr became an adherent of the Sammānīya while living in the Ḥijāz, and on his return home, probably about 1776, propagated the new order with considerable success. After his death in 1824, the leadership of the order in the Sudan passed to his descendants.

Rigorism and Ṣūfism met in the person of the Maghribī, Aḥmad ibn Idrīs al Fāsī (1760–1837), the teacher of Muḥammad ibn ʻAlī al Sanūsī and Muḥammad ʻUthmān al Mīrghanī, both of whom founded orders which combined these two elements. Al Sanūsī's influence in the Nilotic Sudan was negligible, but al Mīrghanī visited the Funj territories on his master's behalf in 1816–17. He made a tour through Dongola, Kordofan and Sinnār, where he met with opposition. By a Sudanese woman whom he married, he had a son, who succeeded him in 1853 as head of the order, known as the Khatmīya, which he had established. Thus, although the Funj Sultanate had virtually disintegrated before the Turco-Egyptian invasion, the characteristic institution of Sudanese Islam, the holy family, was proving both durable and responsive to new currents of Muslim thought and practice.

3. *After the Turco-Egyptian Conquest*

The last century and a half has witnessed four major political changes in the Nilotic Sudan. The invasion by the troops of Muḥammad ʻAlī Pasha in 1820-21 extinguished the Funj Sultanate and brought the tribal kingdoms of the Nile, as well as the province of Kordofan (wrested from the sultanate of Darfur), under Turco-Egyptian rule. Other acquisitions, principally in the reign of Khedive Ismāʻīl (1863–79), expanded the Egyptian Sudan to a wider territory than the modern republic, extending from the frontier of Egypt proper to the equatorial lakes, and from the Red Sea to the boundary of Darfur and Wadai. A centralized administration imposed on the heterogeneous peoples of these diverse regions a greater uniformity than they had ever previously known. Between 1881 and 1885, Egyptian rule was overthrown by a revolutionary millenarian movement, the Mahdiya, which subsequently re-established a centralized administration over a large part of the former Egyptian Sudan. The Mahdist state in turn succumbed to an Anglo-Egyptian invasion in 1896–8, and was superseded by the so-called Condominium, which in effect (although not in legal theory) set up a British colonial administration. The tripartite tensions, between Britain, Egypt and the Sudanese, were finally resolved when, on 1 January 1956, the Sudan became an independent republic.

The Turco–Egyptian invasion had from the outset religious implications, since it was an attack on Muslim territory by a Muslim army. To avoid censure for thus disregarding the Holy Law, Muḥammad ʻAlī sent three ʻulamāʼ with his troops, to urge the Sudanese to submit peaceably to the representative of the Ottoman Sultan. In the long run, the conquest had two major consequences for Sudanese Islam. Since the establishment of the Funj Sultanate in the sixteenth century, the frontier of Arabization and Islamization had run from the Abyssinian foothills and across the Gezira, to the White Nile at about lat. 13° N. By the middle of the nineteenth century, this had been broken through; the Upper Nile and the Baḥr al Ghazāl were open both to trade and to cultural influences from the Muslim north. Since these developments are considered in other papers, they will not be further examined here.

For the older Islamic territory of the northern Sudan, Turco–Egyptian rule brought important changes. Islam was officially sponsored by the new regime. Mosques were built, a salaried hierarchy of ʻulamāʼ was established, and, with the political unification of the Nilotic territories, the road to al Azhar became easier for

Sudanese students. Thus there came to co-exist in the Sudan two Islamic institutions, derived from different traditions. The fakīs and the holy families represented the syncretistic fringe-Islam which had grown up during the Funj Sultanate. The 'ulamā' of the orthodox hierarchy were both the servants and the spokesmen of a new and alien administration. There was thus a potential schism between the traditional and official establishments. Nevertheless, the Turco–Egyptian administrators, like the earlier Funj and 'Abdallābī rulers, patronized individual holy men and subsidized their schools, while the line of demarcation between the two groups was sometimes blurred. Thus, of the two sons of Ismā'īl al Walī, a holy man of Kordofan, one succeeded his father as head of the local ṭarīqa, while the other studied at al Azhar and rose high in the judicial hierarchy of the Egyptian Sudan. When the Mahdiya began, the former became an adherent of the Mahdī, whom the latter denounced in an orthodox manifesto.

The Mahdiya began as a twofold reaction against the developments of the previous sixty years. From one point of view, it was a revolt of the fakīs. Its organizer, Muḥammad Aḥmad ibn 'Abdallāh, a descendant of a minor holy family, had received a traditional education in the religious schools of the Sudan, and was already eminent as an ascetic, a worker of miracles, and a leader in the Sammānīya ṭarīqa before he declared himself to be the Expected Mahdī. The claim itself, as well as much of the imagery in his writings, indicates how deeply he was imbued with the indigenous Ṣūfism of the Sudan, and his earliest adherents were men of a like background to his own. On the other hand, the revolt was also against the modernizing tendencies of the Turco–Egyptian administration, which had diminished the role of the 'ulamā' in the Muslim community, circumscribed the application of the Holy Law, and given authority to non-Muslims. Since the Mahdī set up against the innovation (bid'a) of the age the good practice (sunna) of the Prophet and his Companions, his movement, like that of the Wahhābīs, had a rigorist character. It is the fusion of these two strains, the intense religious emotion drawn from Ṣūfism, and the equally intense rigorism, that gives the Sudanese Mahdiya its particular character, by virtue of which the Mahdī and his followers envisaged themselves not as reformers or revolutionaries – and certainly not as Sudanese nationalists – but as primitive Muslims re-enacting in the end-time the life of the original Islamic community. This intensity did not long survive the death of the Mahdī in June 1885. Under his successor, the Khalīfa 'Abdallāhi, the maintenance of a territorial state in part of the former Egyptian Sudan taxed to the full the capacity and resources of the ruler. That the Mahdist state was finally overthrown only by superior military force from without indicates the measure of his success, but the Khalīfa contributed little or nothing to the Islamization of the Sudan.

The administrators of the Condominium were at the outset haunted by the fear of a resurgence of Mahdism, whether the militant movement which had so recently been defeated, or a new Islamic millenarianism appealing to the disaffected. Like their Turco–Egyptian predecessors, therefore, they endeavoured to build up an orthodox Muslim establishment. Apart from reviving the hierarchy of 'ulamā', encouraging the building of mosques, and facilitating the Pilgrimage to Mecca (which had been forbidden by the Mahdist state), Wingate, who was governor-general from 1899 to 1916, set up the Board of Ulema, in order to associate the 'ulamā' with governmental decisions on Islamic matters. While thus favouring orthodoxy, Wingate and his subordinates were extremely suspicious of Ṣūfism, and regarded the ṭarīqas as potential seed-beds of subversion and fanaticism. Only the Khatmīya, which had been closely allied with the Turco-Egyptian administration and had consistently opposed the Mahdiya, received preferential treatment. The Anṣār, as the followers of the Mahdī were called, were particularly mistrusted. There was, in fact, no neo-Mahdist revolt, although there were several sporadic millenarian risings between the Reconquest and the First World War. The War itself contributed to a change in the relations between the government and the Ṣūfī leaders, since the outbreak of hostilities between Britain and the Ottoman Sultan-Caliph made Wingate anxious to conciliate all influential Muslims in the Sudan. A beneficiary of this relaxation of policy was Sayyid 'Abd al Raḥmān, the posthumous son of the Mahdī, who found his father's invective against 'the Turks' suddenly congenial to the new masters of the Sudan. He was thereby launched on the career which made him the rival of Sayyid 'Alī al Mīrghanī, the leader of the Khatmīya, and turned their respective religious followings into the raw materials of nationalist political parties.

Under the Condominium, the tendencies towards modernization and westernization, which had first shown themselves under the Turco–Egyptian administration, and which had helped to provoke the Mahdist reaction, dominated the administration and the educational system. Although education was largely restricted to a town-dwelling *élite*, its consequences were far reaching, especially when in the inter-War period, it was reinforced by the radio and the cinema. Influences from Britain and from a highly westernized Egypt combated the fringe-isolation which had characterized the culture of the Nilotic Sudan throughout the Funj period, and which had been briefly restored during the Mahdiya. Placed at the point of tension between traditional and westernized cultures, the Muslims of the Nilotic Sudan became conscious, as did other Muslim communities in the previous century, of the predicament of Islam in the modern world.

BIBLIOGRAPHY

Further information on topics considered in this paper may be found in the following:—

Y. F. Hasan, *The Arabs and the Sudan*, Edinburgh, 1967.

P. M. Holt, *The Mahdist state in the Sudan,* 1881–1898, 2nd edn., Oxford, 1970.

Holy families and Islam in the Sudan (Princeton Near East Papers, No. 4), Princeton University, 1967.

"Modernization and reaction in the nineteenth-century Sudan, in William R. Polk and Richard L. Chambers, *Beginnings of modernization in the Middle East – the nineteenth century*, Chicago and London, 1968; pp. 401–15.

J. S. Trimingham, *Islam in the Sudan*, London, 1949.

Gabriel Warburg, *The Sudan under Wingate*, London, 1971.

There are useful articles in *Sudan Notes and Records*, Khartoum, 1918–22.

III

Hassebu: Islamic Healing in Black Africa

Humphrey J. Fisher
School of Oriental and African Studies
University of London

The magic spell worked and the Sultan was made well again. All the people said that Hassebu was the cleverest doctor ever to be known in Zanzibar. His friends were given their freedom, and the Sultan wanted to make Hassebu rich and famous.[1]

The association between the penetration of Muslim traders into Sudanic Africa, and the introduction there of Islam, has been frequently affirmed, as for instance in this recent generalization:

> It is today well established that the most active agent spreading the Muslim faith was the trader, Berber or Black: black Islam is a trader's Islam.[2]

No doubt the association is of great importance, but it has perhaps been overstressed. There are even signs of a tendency to translate all early Muslims in black Africa into traders. Here is a modern comment on ancient Ghana:

> Indeed, as early as the eleventh century merchants from Barbary and the Mzab were frequenting the slave market of Kumbi, the capital of the original Ghana . . .[3]

Our only detailed authority for the Ghana capital in the eleventh century, al Bakrī, does mention influential Muslims there, but he does not say they were merchants, nor does he refer to any market. Rather, he singles out for special mention those Muslims who served the Pagan king as ministers, wazīrs. Examples might be multiplied: a recent observation on Jimma, the Galla kingdom now within Ethiopia, tells how '. . . Muslim traders from the north came to Jimma, and some of them . . . were given land in return for their services as teachers'.[4] Of course, some individuals may well have combined mercantile and clerical professions, or have changed from one to the other – but even allowing for this, it seems that the title 'merchant' is being too widely bestowed.[5]

What were these ministers and teachers, and the whole range of people whom we may conveniently classify under the heading 'clerics', actually doing? We shall probably never know, in so distant a case as ancient Ghana, but it is more than likely that the Ghana monarch's ministers were performing the same roles as are described in Mervyn Hiskett's paper for the early period in Hausaland – '. . . such roles as court astrologers, religious teachers, scribes . . . rain-makers, military advisers, physicians. . . .'[6] They were, in the words of Rex O'Fahey's paper, 'holy men and occasionally miracle workers';[7] and it was such holy men, as Peter Holt's paper affirms for the Nilotic Sudan in particular,[8] who were the most effective agents of Islamization in black Africa. In fact, if we take into account also the 'man of God' of Michael Brett's paper,[9] it seems that the sea of faith is once more at the full, and round this symposium's shore lies like the folds of a bright girdle furl'd. The cleric has come again into his own; the merchant-missionary, darling of the economic determinists, though not unhorsed, has lost pride of place.

I have tried, in this paper, to explore one aspect of clerical activity, that of healing. There are two preliminary questions to be asked and, if possible, answered. First, is it sensible to take a particular theme such as healing, highly susceptible to variations in local circumstances, and to try to make that theme, rather than an area, a people, or a period, the framework of the discussion?[10] I think it is; indeed, such an approach seems cardinal in any study of the history of Islam, as contrasted with the history of Muslims lands and peoples. For many areas, peoples and periods, there will be special factors to be taken into account, which will modify the generalizations of the historian of Islam; but, on the credit side, he will be suggesting comparisons, and common elements, the importance of which the local specialist might otherwise overlook. The extent of the common elements may be greater than we realize; many papers of this symposium draw attention to the remarkable mobility of men and ideas within the Muslim world – holy men migrating to the Nilotic Sudan from older Muslim lands, or attracted to the Islamic frontier in Darfur, and so on – a mobility which sustains such common elements over vast areas.

The second question is, why healing rather than any other activity, for example divination, particularly since healing is often only artificially separable from a cleric's other responsibilities? I confess that my notes on healing are very fragmentary. I have borrowed it, as a theme, from the history of Christianity in black Africa. Two recent studies of separatist churches in West Africa attach the greatest significance to faith healing, which one calls 'the main occasion for the emergence of the Aladura churches'.[11] It seems almost certain that, in the interaction which has taken place in black Africa between the indigenous tradition and the incoming world religion, whether Islam or Christianity, changes have come about which bring these two religions into closer resemblance with one another. It is conceivable that that common experience of Islam and Christianity in black Africa might provide the material for some future symposium such as this one.[12] If healing is so powerful in black African Christianity, the same is likely to be true in black African Islam. That it does not at once strike the observer may simply be the result of not asking the right questions. I am deeply suspicious, in the exploration of oral tradition, of too many specific questions; but the right question, which sets people talking spontaneously and at length may very well open most interesting windows on to the past. When I was last in Africa healing was not in my mind as such a question; next time it will be. Meanwhile, a good deal can be gleaned from written records.

To attempt to embrace the whole range of Muslim healing in black Africa within a single paper would be extravagant, for both natural and supernatural procedures and remedies are involved. Surgery is represented: in operations for cataract, in castration of slaves intended as eunuchs, and in the 'surgery of punishments',[13] to name only three of the commonest examples. Medicine appears in herbal potions and many other concoctions. Specific practices on which a considerable literature already exists, and/or which might well repay further study, include vaccination or inoculation against smallpox,[14] the treatment of guinea-worm,[15] dealing with gun wounds,[16] and the medical care of horses[17] – both these last providing new vantage points from which to view central themes in African history. It might also be possible to examine the strictly medical literature of black Africa, though this seems likely to prove a stony meadow. One Fulani cleric, who died about 1776, wrote a verse treatise on the diagnosis and treatment of haemorrhoids.[18] Although certain other minor medical texts await examination, medicine was apparently not included in the formal curriculum of scholarship even in the Sokoto caliphate.[19] In Somaliland, it is Arabic books of astrology, such as the *Kitāb al Raḥma* of al Suyūṭī which are most in demand by clerics in treating illness.[20] My primary concern in this paper, though I do not entirely exclude secular remedies, is with faith healing, through prayer, amulets, and other such religious and/or magical resources. The dividing line between the two is sometimes unclear, and I have found no trace in black African Islam of that strict division between faith healing and ordinary medicine, occasionally to the utter exclusion of the latter, upon which some Christian churches insist.[21]

I have already mentioned mobility, of people and ideas, as an outstanding characteristic of Islam in Black Africa, and indeed when we consider the immense distances which separated these frontiers from the Islamic heartland, and the grave dangers and difficulties which confronted the traveller, it is remarkable that the purity of Islam in black Africa was sustained as well as it was. Individuals in remote parts journeyed to Muslim centres in black Africa, or to North Africa and the Middle East, and were able to observe the practice of Islam here; pious and relatively experienced Muslims visited the most distant villages, and found time to exhort and reprove there. It is perhaps in seeking to explain this mobility that scholars have been led to place great stress on trade, which is such an important element in it. But healing, and many other clerical activities, may also contribute substantially to mobility.

Healing helps, for example, in a purely practical manner, caring for travellers along the way: the Uhabīr, or so-to-speak captain, of a trans-Saharan caravan should know, among many other things, the remedies for various illnesses, how to set broken bones, and to deal with snake and scorpion bites.[22] I should like, however, to stress particularly two other features of the interrelationship between healing and mobility; one is the almost universal mobility of doctors, the other is the fear which those who control disease may inspire.

Medical practitioners, in nearly every part of the world, and at every time, have enjoyed almost unrivalled facilities for travel; Indian doctors coming to Britain today, or British doctors leaving for America, are contemporary examples of an ancient tradition. In the time of King Jesus I of Ethiopia, 1680–1704, when that country was still influenced by anti-Roman Catholic reaction, the druggist Poncet, taking with him a Jesuit disguised as his personal servant, was able to visit the king, who had indeed sent to Cairo seeking someone able to cure his skin complaint. Poncet succeeded in this, and returned safely to Europe. The next emissary, in 1705, was murdered.[23] Barth, though not a doctor, often benefited from his medical knowledge and supplies. Reporting on his brief visit to Yola, in 1851, whence he was summarily dismissed and where, I suppose, he might have suffered a worse fate, he said:

> Monday passed quietly, with the exception of a great many people calling for 'laiya' or charms, and for medicines.[24]

and again, stopping on his way back from Yola:

> . . . Although I was unable to alleviate the pains suffered by my host from an arrow-wound in one of his eyes, or to give him a charm to prevent the death of his cattle, I was so fortunate as to effect a splendid cure on one of his sons, which procured me great fame.[25]

Nachtigal, Barth's successor, and the first European to visit the unusually hostile country of Tibesti, or to travel through Wadai and Darfur, was immensely helped by being a doctor. When in 1893 the Sultan of Morocco was travelling to Tafilet, in the south of his kingdom, he sent back all the Europeans in his party, save only his French doctor.[26] A special entrée was reserved even for slaves; medical men captured by the North African corsairs were the best treated of all slaves, and we have the account of a French naval surgeon captured in 1668, who subsequently served the ruler of Tripoli.[27] The multiplication of European examples might proceed indefinitely; this is not because European Christians were more numerous, as itinerant healers, than were Muslims, but rather because our documentation for the former group is superior. Passing references show Muslims enjoying the same welcome; one of the first Muslims reported in Freẹtown, for example, was a Mandinka 'country doctor' practising in Charlotte Street in 1831.[28]

Not only have foreign methods of healing spread into black Africa in this way, but black Africa has exported its own expertise. An early recorded instance is of the North African shaykh, in the ninth century A.D., who specially ordered an eye medicine from the Sudan.[29] In the western Sahara one man was esteemed for his ability to cure the bite of a peculiarly lethal snake, a snake against which even the most powerful amulet was in vain, and this ability he had learnt from a Negro from Likwar in the Sudan.[30] Among the Chaamba Arabs of Algeria, Negroes and their descendants are celebrated for the manufacture of amulets, love potions, poisons and spells.[31] Throughout North Africa, organizations and rituals derived from the Sudan have been kept alive by slaves and their descendants, many of these procedures – often closely linked with *bori*, or spirit possession cults – have healing among their purposes. When Richardson was ill and dispirited, in Ghadames, Sudanese there diagnosed his difficulty as concerned with *bori*.[32] In the Hansa folktale of the doctor and his two servants, one servant vaunts that his master had been to Murzuq, there to cure the king of a disease which none else could cure.[33] Patterns of Sudanese religious influence on North Africa might provide an interesting research theme.[34] There are even more distant repercussions; in the seventeenth century, when doctors attending the Mongol Hulagu Khan and bleeding him opened an artery by mistake, it was an Ethiopian nobleman, 'who was not without perception and sense', who probably saved the Khan's life by suggesting a tourniquet arrangement.[35] It is reported, in a charming tale, that when Anselm d'Isalguiers of Toulouse returned across the Sahara in the early fifteenth century, he brought with him several Negro slaves, one of whom, a eunuch named Aben Ali, set himself up in medical practice in Toulouse, and succeeded in curing the Dauphin Charles, later crowned Charles VII by Joan of Arc. The tale, alas, now seems to have been a fable.[36] There may even have been some elements of Saharan origin in the medical lore of Elizabethan England. It was held in England that a scorpion's bite could be cured 'by saying to an ass secretly, and as it were whispering in his ear – I am bitten with a scorpion'.[37] It was a common western Saharan belief that to mount an ass facing its tail gave prompt relief from a scorpion's bite, though our reporter, having once tested the hypothesis himself, had quickly perceived its falsity.[38]

Fear of the healer is the second point I wish to stress about mobility. This is healing in reverse; he who administers medicine may substitute a poison, the cleric who prays for your recovery may as effectively call down upon you some frightful disease in a curse. Wherever the danger of such retaliation was recognized, the implicit threat served to protect individuals and groups who might otherwise have seemed, in some cases, exposed and helpless. The first Muslims in Kano, in the fourteenth century, cowed their opponents by praying successfully against them, so that they were all struck blind, they and their womenfolk also.[39] The episode in Rex O'Fahey's paper[40] about the dissident Keira princes blinded by a cleric, is reminiscent of this. There are many Saharan stories about horrible diseases coming upon those who abused men of religion, often members of the Zwāya or clerical clans, diseases which the inflicting cleric removed only after full repentance and recompense.[41] When, early in the nineteenth century, Da the Bambara king of Segu, despite the warnings of a sharīf, or descendant of the Prophet, began to oppress the Muslims in his region, he was suddenly smitten with illness. He appealed to a cleric for healing, but the cleric instead prophesied three evils for Da: that in the same year his power would be checked, that his favoured son would not succeed him, and finally that he would never be cured.[42] Sometimes inflicted illness was not the defence of the pious in danger but simply a weapon of in-fighting among the faithful, as for example when the Eastern Sudanese saint, Walad Abū Ṣādiq, whose marital irregularities had been criticized by a judge, cursed the judge with skin disease.[43]

Punitive illness was wielded by non-Muslims as well. In Ethiopia, for example, no Amhara would kill a Galla *kalicha* – among whose main functions are exorcism and healing – under any circumstances, for fear of his dying curse.[44] Slaves might carry such Pagan powers into a Muslim setting. A fifteenth-century source, perhaps from the Agades region, remarked:

> Some of the women say that among the khadam [slaves or servants] are those who kill and if one touches you, you fall sick.[45]

Similarly, in the Mauritanian town of Tidjikdja, a slave owner who beat a slave would fall ill after one or two days, and soon die. A sorcerer slave always looked at the chest of a person, catching his heart and hiding it in the ashes, so that it became a ram; a man thus bewitched would not die as long as that ram was not slaughtered. This, as the chronicler recording these tales commented, is no doubt nonsense; but, he continued, it is true that if the sorcerer slave, threatened with death by the family of the bewitched, lays his hand on the breast of the bewitched person, he is loosed from the spell, and the same is true if the sorcerer dies. The people of Tidjikdja, distressed by these perils, contemplated killing their slaves, but desisted since there would then be none to care for the palm trees. So they brought instead, for a handsome fee, an expert from the Sudan, who gave the slaves something to drink. The expert departed, but the sorcery continued, until the people began killing all slaves suspected of it, and it decreased appreciably.[46] Even in recent times, a booklet of Yoruba traditional medicine includes a section on 'Medicine to bring to pass any curses which you may utter'.[47]

To be welcome, to be feared, are characteristics of the healer no doubt highly useful to himself, but you cannot live without an income, and healing has often supplied an important part of the healer's livelihood. Of Upper Dahomey, it was said earlier this century that both Pagan and Muslim practitioners drew a good income.[48] A Bolanchi tale of a man who healed with certain leaves the blindness of a chief's daughter tells how he gained not only the daughter as his bride, but also clothes, riches, and slaves, so that he in his turn might bestow lavish alms; I do not know if this is a Muslim or a Pagan example.[49] Among the few accounts which have come down to us from the healers themselves is that of el-Tounsy, who was stranded in Sokna, on the Fezzan-Tripoli road, without provisions. An old woman, whose daughter had lain ill for a year, came to him, begging him to write some Quran lines as invocation and blessing. That night, having performed his ablutions, and the evening and night prayers, el-Tounsy wrote the paper. Next morning he gave it to the anxious mother; and the day after she and her companions returned, bearing baskets of food in gratitude for the daughter's restored health.[50] From Liberia comes an account of preventive medicine, applied by Muslim clerics on behalf of the new-born children of local people; the price here may be quite high, but it is payable only after the child has successfully survived the critical period, four years for a boy, three for a girl.[51] Payment by results in this way, which may be applied in the case of teachers as well as of doctors, is approved in Muslim religious law.[52] Burton, in Cairo as an intending pilgrim, built up a lucrative medical practice; one of his triumphs was to cure slavegirls of the price-reducing habit of snoring. He used hypnosis rather than faith, however.[53] Sir John Chardin, writing in 1668 of Roman Catholic missionaries in Persia, though he is geographically far from black Africa, gives a good description of the high income bracket of doctors:

> They have permission from the Pope to take Money for their Cures, and they make good advantage of it, Physick being their chiefest Subsistence: they are generally paid in Wine, Meal, Cattel, and young Slaves; and some there are that give 'em Horses; all of which they sell whatever they have no need of, or whatever they have to spare.[54]

There is occasionally some feeling among African Christians that faith healing should not be the cause of material benefit to those who have received the grace to practise it. Thus James Johnson, West African patriot and Anglican bishop, approved the early work of the prophet Garrick Braide, in Eastern Nigeria, who for seven years healed the sick without taking a penny in return.[55] Something of the same scruple may be traced in black African Islam; among the Murīds of Senegal, for instance, when the Khalīfa-General prepares a healing charm, no payment is demanded, although a gift is customary. The specialist healers of the Murīds are usually not the great shaykhs of the order.[56] It has been suggested that some Murīd clerics have resisted the introduction of modern medicine because of the danger of competition in their lucrative healing work.[57]

In addition to payment for services rendered, clerics who engaged in healing might also find opportunities to trade – for it would be a grave over-simplification to regard these and other various categories of Muslim employment as mutually exclusive. Many medicinal supplies were also important trade goods. One such category comprises perfumes, widely esteemed medically in the Muslim world, as Doughty's comment on the Arabian beduin indicates:

> good odours they esteem comfortable to the health, and so our old physicians held them (that which we perceive in smelling to sweet roses). The Aarabs make therefore nose-medicines, little bunches of certain herbs and odours, to hang a day or two in their nostrils, and in the nostrils of their camels.[58]

Camphor is particularly popular, and not among Muslims only. Some Yoruba Christians combine camphor and the Psalms in amulets to protect children.[59] De Chateaubriand, travelling in the Middle East early in the nineteenth century, carried camphor with him as a preventive against the plague.[60] Nachtigal, in Kuka in 1872, had kept back considerable quantities of camphor, partly for his magic lantern, and partly because he realized its therapeutic and magical repute among local people.[61] It is still today a valued present in West Africa; it is a little difficult to procure in London, but I discovered a chemist with some from Hong Kong. Early in the summer of 1971 correspondents in the *Daily Telegraph* of London dwelt upon the utility of camphor in treating cholera, advising that it be included in supplies sent to the refugees from East Pakistan.[62] That scents may have such medicinal properties reinforces the importance which perfume in any case has as an approved luxury in the Muslim world. Perfume as a trade item in Muslim Africa might well repay closer study; Leo Africanus gives the price of a civet cat in Fes, early in the sixteenth century, as 200 ducats, for which you could have bought five eunuchs, or ten good male slaves, or (receiving some small change as well) thirteen women slaves.[63]

Other trade goods sometimes used as medicaments include kola ('a rare medicine against the Dropsie'),[64] natron (which Clapperton in 1826 saw exported from Bornu to Yoruba and then distributed to all parts of the coast to mix with snuff and as a medicine),[65] and kohl, an eye-black cosmetic believed to guard against ophthalmia and also to be useful in cases of smallpox.[66] Coral, highly valued in Sudan trade, was occasionally used medically, but my only specific reference is from sixteenth-century Persia, where it was one of twenty-one ingredients in a specific against miscarriage.[67]

Thus far in our consideration of the cleric as healer, we have seen how his role gives him a mobility quite comparable to that of a trader, winning him a welcome and an entry in strange places, surrounding him with a mysterious and dreadful aura of divine protection, and supplying him with a livelihood. The single most outstanding example of mobility within the Muslim world, however, is neither in trade nor in healing, nor in education nor in any other such sphere, but in the pilgrimage. We may trace a healing strand frequently interwoven here. Material aids circulate, among other trade goods, through the medium of pilgrimage. Among such curative commodities which the pilgrim-healer might bring back with him are sacred water from the well of Zamzam, and perfumes. The representative of a Geneva-based cosmetics company recently told me that about 60 per cent of their annual perfume sales to Saudi Arabia are at the time of the pilgrimage each year. That this is primarily for redistribution through returning pilgrims is suggested by the fact that the religious law requires the abstention of pilgrims from perfume among other indulgences for the duration of the pilgrimage.[68]

As well as material aids, the pilgrim may acquire technical skill. One leading family of Mandingo leeches in Liberia descends from a pilgrim who while away learnt the Arab art of needling for cataract.[69] And finally, aids and skill are underlined by the enhanced reputation of the pilgrim. In Hausaland, every returned pilgrim is believed to have in some measure the power of preparing written charms to curse or cure, and such power is proportionately increased in those who have made the pilgrimage more than once.[70] We have a description of a traditional bone-setter at work among the Tubu, repairing the broken leg of a boy; then a pilgrim was invited to take part, and partly disarranged the leg, much to the bone-setter's distress; finally the boy's father also quarrelled with the pilgrim, who none the less received ten francs for his trouble.[71]

The pilgrimage has also provided a channel for the export of medical expertise from Africa. Doughty remarked that the Maghrībīs, i.e. the North Africans, were 'esteemed in Arabia, the best scriveners of these magical scriptures', that is to say of amulets to be used in place of medicaments.[72] In the Eastern Sudan, West Africans may have the same esteem:

> The reputation of Fellata as people with special powers to do miracles or to make cures by special medicines and to make spells of a potent character is widely spread in the Sudan, and indeed some Fellata have had a large clientele among Egyptians in the Sudan.[73]

Al Ḥājj 'Umar, later founder of the Tokolor empire on the upper Senegal and Niger, visited Syria while on pilgrimage in the early nineteenth century. His renown had preceded him thither, and some leading men asked him to exorcise the son of one of them, possessed of an incurable madness. This al Ḥājj did, enhancing his repute among the people of the east, and earning many rich gifts.[74]

Local pilgrimage – the Arabic term would be ziyāra, not ḥajj – may also have had a healing function. This is very common in North Africa; for one among myriad examples, to spend the night at one particular tomb in Tunisia is sure to extract a leech which all medicines have failed to budge.[75] It is chiefly in the Songhay region, most clearly influenced by North Africa, that in the West and Central Sudan we find parallel instances;[76] the tomb of 'Uthmān Daramī, qāḍī of Tendirma in the sixteenth century, is a case in point, for wishes made at this tomb were always fulfilled, the sick brought here were healed.[77] For a more modern instance, the well of Dien, which appeared in September 1957, has since attracted many people, perhaps even thousands, daily for healing.[78] Farther east, cults of holy and healing places flourish, especially in Ethiopia. At the convent of Abba Garima near Aksum, many sought healing in the cave where the Greek king had done penance[79]; earth gathered round the shrine of Sehotc, a prophet figure of the Gurage and throughout southwest Ethiopia, is said to provide a potion of spiritual and curative powers;[80] earth is carried from the great shrine at Debra

Libanos to be used in healing.[81] Similarly handfuls of earth are taken from the tombs of the Sulṭans of Wadai, buried at Wara – whither even today the reigning Sulṭan goes each year to sacrifice just before the rains – and are used to heal the sick and the barren.[82]

Before we finally leave the pilgrim of powerful repute, it may be appropriate to mention one other special category of Muslim religious figures who may be notable for healing, the sharīfs, or descendants of the Prophet. El-Tounsy, when he arrived in Wadai in the mid-nineteenth century, found a sharīf, Aḥmad of Fes, already well-established there. El-Tounsy heard him give a remarkable lecture on the anatomy of the eye. 'Ce chérif avait reçu de Dieu de marveilleuses dispositions, mais il était irascible et haineux'. Finally he was murdered in Wadai.[83] Another sharīf, who guided Harris on his visit to Tafilet in southern Morocco in the 1890s, boasted an hereditary knowledge in medicine, and rather resented the implied mistrust when Harris refused to supply him with chloroform and a suitable knife for his favoured operation, for cataract.[84]

Let us now turn to the principal therapeutic devices of faith healing in Muslim black Africa. Amulets easily lead the field. Marty, speaking of the Timbuktu area, says that amulets are very popular here, every illness or difficulty having its specific counter amulet.[85] References to amulets abound like the sand of the sea; we may be content with a few medical examples. Here is a passage from the seventeenth century, describing Muslims on the Gambia:

> . . . and this more I have taken notice of, that if any of them be possest of any malady, or have any swelling or sore upon them, the remedy they have, is onely by placing one of these blessed Gregories [i.e. greegree, or amulet] where the griefe lies, which they conceite will helpe them; and for ought I can perceive, this is all the Physicke they have amongst them . . .[86]

Amulets may equally be protective or preventive, and the necessity of action in good time is reflected in the Libyan proverb: after he died they hung an amulet on him.[87] There are indications that amulets were preferred even when other medicines were also available:

> Les tobba (médicins) du Touat sont, au reste, très-renommés; ils ont des remèdes contre toutes les maladies, et savent même atténuer [par inoculation] les terribles effets de la petite vérole . . . Mais ce qui vaut mieux que leurs remèdes, ce sont les amulettes de leurs marabouts; car beaucoup d'entre eux sont de grands saints, et *Dieu est meilleur médecin que les hommes*.[88]

A similar comment comes from Doughty, concerning the beduin of Arabia:

> All the Aarab would have hijabs (charms, amulets) sooner than medicaments, which they find so unprofitable in the hands of their hareem. . . . The same men catch after charms, that will not pay for medicine; every wiseacre of them would purchase a hijab with reals, even were they the last in his slender purse . . . and before other they would have philters of dishonest love.[89]

Such a preference may have important implications for the faith healer, as opposed to the retailer of natural medicines. Muslim amulets may be made of various materials; in the western Sahara one to protect a child against scorpions was prepared containing the ash of a scorpion, which had been burnt, after head, tail, and poison had been cut off.[90] But the overwhelming majority are prepared from verses of the Quran.

The Quran figures even more prominently in the preparation of the other standard specific, slate-water, the water which has been used to wash clean a slate upon which some verses of Scripture had been written. Only rarely is other writing used; some Hausa substitute the names of seven liars, and thus secure an immediate remedy against hiccoughs.[91] Slate-water may be drunk, or applied as a local medicine, or used, so-to-speak, in the bath. In April 1827, Sultan Bello of Sokoto, wounded in the neck by a poisoned arrow while on expedition, was healed by such a drink.[92] A few years earlier Clapperton's servant's mother was healed in the same way; her case was particularly interesting, in that several clerics had prepared slate-water for her without avail, and at the last only a pilgrim succeeded – and part of the healing process was the woman's confession of some wrongdoing.[93] In Darfur water, particularly for bathing eyes infected with ophthalmia, is prepared by dissolving the ashes of a rosary, made of rushes, over which the words, There is no god but God, have been told ten thousand times.[94] Ashes of burnt paper, inscribed from the Quran, were drunk in eighteenth century Tripoli against plague.[95] Slate-water may have been involved when Sufi Sahib, a popular Muslim saint in South Africa, travelling by ship from Bombay to Durban in 1895, checked an epidemic of dysentery among those on board by specially preparing drinking water, though my source does not specify exactly in which way the water was treated.[96] Innumerable further instances might be marshalled.[97] One observer has even suggested that the ink in slate-water, made by boiling down an infusion of certain plants, was probably not without real value as a remedy, aside from its supposed sacred power.[98]

The preparation of amulets and slate-water are two important clerical functions; the interpretation of dreams is another, and in all three instances, although many different purposes may be in mind, the task of healing is often prominent. Dreams may supply specific prescriptions for an illness, or they may offer general advice about what to do. The entire Aladura movement of West African Christianity probably derives from Joseph Shadare, who during the world influenza epidemic in 1918 was guided in dreams to form prayer groups;[99] at least one other dream cure has been reported from West Africa at this same time.[100] To carry further the balance of medicine and poison, prayer and curse, so against dreams of healing and other trustworthy portent must be set bad dreams, which are indeed among the commoner ailments.[101] Some further dream references are gathered in a recent seminar paper at the School of Oriental and African Studies in London.[102]

That so much faith is pinned upon the words of the Quran, in amulets and slate-water, is hardly surprising, for it is the Word of God in Islam in the same central way that Christ is the Word in Christianity. Prayer is also clearly involved, in the cases cited above, for example, when el-Tounsy wrote the charm for the sick daughter in Sokna, or in the Darfur rosary ash. Further illustrations might be cited, as in the following passage, which is additionally interesting for the way in which the cleric brings the local people also into the act of prayer:

> One day while I was in Bolahun [in Liberia], a little girl had a fit in the morning, and the people thought she had an evil spirit. We were told that a Mahommedan doctor had prayed for her, muttering some incantation, to which the people had responded Amina (Amen). The little girl recovered in the afternoon and went to a rice farm to work.[103]

Whether as an act of healing, or as a token of last rites, a Fezzan Arab tried to pray with Clapperton as he lay dying in Sokoto in 1827, but the offer was refused.[104]

Nevertheless, despite the fact that other such cases might be found, it is a little surprising to me that there are not more, particularly since prayer is so central to Christian healing in black Africa, as in this description of Garricke Braide, who healed

> . . . either through his prayers or through the use of a few words of prayer dictated to them by him, or through a mere touch of his hand upon them. . . . His prayers produced quick and visible result, healing diseases at a rate greater than that of native or European medical science.[105]

Doughty, speaking of Arabia, offers an interesting suggestion which may partly explain why prayer is not so prominent a part of the Muslim healing process:

> Moslems, whether in sickness or health, if the body be sullied by any natural impurity, durst not say their formal prayers. Many patients

have come to me lamenting that, for an infirmity, 'they might not pray'; and then they seem to themselves as the shut out from grace, and profane.[106]

Something of the same sort may be hinted at in the story of a saint of the Jabal Nafūsa, in Tunisia, who, when he was ill, found that health returned to him at the appointed hours of prayer, so that he might fulfil his devotional duties properly.[107] But though hesitation may be popularly felt about praying while ill, this is not well founded in the law, which on the contrary lays down with care the correct way to pray when under various disabilities of ill health. Nor have I found explicit mention of such hesitation in my reading about black Africa. In one passage, where ibn Baṭṭūṭa described his arrival in Mali in the fourteenth century, he said that he and his companions all fell ill and one died, but that despite his illness he went himself to the morning prayer, and fainted. Whether or not his infirmity interferes with a patient's own prayers, there seems no reason why he should not enlist a cleric's prayers on his behalf, and it is the absence of references to this kind of thing that I find puzzling.

Having surveyed these four principal methods of Muslim faith healing in black Africa – by amulet, slate-water, dream and prayer – let me insert a note on one important element of medical practice: the provision of love philtres, aphrodisiacs, and, more soberly, of cures for barrenness. In Herrick's words, himself a cleric:

> Old I am, and cannot do
> That, I was accustom'd to.
> Bring your Magicks, Spels, and Charmes,
> To enflesh my thighs, and armes;
> Is there no way to beget,
> In my limbs their former heat?

Al Bakrī, in the eleventh century, mentions a Pagan West African king in whose territory grew a root of surprising aphrodisiac qualities. This root was a royal monopoly, and allowed the king to content an enormous number of wives. Upon a neighbouring Muslim king sending a lavish gift and requesting a cutting, the Pagan returned a gift of equal value, but explained that such a stimulant would tempt the Muslim to excesses reproved by his religion. He sent, instead, a plant to cure sterility.[108] Of course, the privilege of keeping concubines well beyond the limit of four legal wives meant that wealthy Muslims were not necessarily beyond the need of such assistance, particularly when, as sometimes happened, old men found themselves with young wives or concubines.[109] Early European travellers in the Sudan were repeatedly asked for appropriate medicines, as Barth recounted of the governor of Katsina:

Bello received me in his private apartment, and detained me for full two hours while I gave him complete information about the use of the medicines [which I had given him]. He wanted, besides, two things from me, which I could not favour him with – things of very different character, and the most desired by all the princes of Negroland. One of these was a 'mágani-n-algúwa' (a medicine to increase his conjugal vigour); the other, some rockets, as a 'mágani-ni-yáki' (a medicine of war), in order to frighten his enemies. Not being able to comply with these two modest wishes of his, I had great difficulty in convincing him of my good will.[110]

A Hausa folktale tells of a king who, needing help of this kind, mentioned to his court that he already had a marvellous concoction. Before long all his chief ministers had severally and in private visited the chief, hoping to get some for themselves. Though the king thus failed to find a remedy, he took much consolation in the discovery that he and his courtiers were all in the same boat.[111] Nor were the problems of love confined to the great, if we may quote Barth again:

. . . a young man took me aside and entreated me earnestly to give him a remedy against the dislike of people. I, however, soon succeeded in making him confess that he meant only the dislike of one girl, who, he said, did not relish his haughty demeanour, and that he was reduced to a state of desperation, and wished for nothing but to die in battle.[112]

The search for a cure for barrenness may be illustrated by an animal fable of the Hausa, about Malam Cat, who went upon his travels offering such a cure, and was able to trick the chicken into roasting itself in the hope of conceiving[113] – or should this be an illustration rather of a doctor's payment? Too much conjugal vigour might lead to complications with venereal disease, which was a widespread danger. In Indonesia, it was popularly believed that to sleep with a healthy woman would effect a cure, and one ruler, it is said, accomplished this, employing a black slave.[114] I have not found the same belief explicitly mentioned in black Africa, but if it is there, it might be yet another contributory factor to the buoyant internal market for slaves.

We have come thus far without directly confronting our final main question, what is the role of healing in the process of Islamization? Before discussing this, I should like briefly to summarize the threefold pattern of Islamic development which, in a very broad sense, undergirds the history of Muslim black Africa. In the first stage, Islam exists in quarantine, observed only by outsiders, visitors, such as was the case, I think, in ancient Ghana as al Bakrī described it in the eleventh century. To this succeeds a stage of mixing, in which local people begin to adopt Islam, often quite seriously but usually without regarding it as an exclusive loyalty, so that Pagan beliefs and practices survive and mingle with their Muslim counterparts. This is admirably exemplified in Mali as ibn Baṭṭūṭa described it in the fourteenth century. Thirdly and finally comes a stage of reform, in which the local Muslims themselves react against mixing, and attempt to purify the observance of Islam in their own countries; the nineteenth-century jihād of Usuman dan Fodio is an excellent instance. The process has not begun everywhere at the same time, nor advanced everywhere at the same rate, so that at any given time, including today, examples of all three stages may be found side by side. Nor has progress been everywhere maintained, and it is possible to slip back from one stage to the preceding, though I am persuaded that the fundamental tendency has been towards a purer understanding of the faith by black Muslims, towards the third or reform stage.[115]

If we set our sketch of Muslim faith healing against this backdrop, it is clear that those characteristics of the healer which we singled out – his status as a welcomed immigrant, the fear which he inspired, and his ability to earn his living – greatly strengthen him as a pioneer representative of Islam whilst that religion is still, in the particular village or chieftaincy concerned, in the quarantine stage. And, as healing often reaches across denominational divisions, it is an activity which fits easily into the mixing stage. Individuals in health difficulties turn equally to Pagan and to Muslim practitioners, hoping for help from either, or from both. A fable from French West Africa tells of a pretty young wife, dying of an unknown illness, who turned in vain to charms, to the advice of the old women of the village, to the prayers of the Muslim clerics, until at last a Pagan priest was able to throw light upon her predicament.[116] From Liberia comes an account of Muslim clerics, and others, alike trying to cure a woman of barrenness.[117] For an African example of quite another kind, Sufi Sahib, the South African saint already mentioned was visited during his lifetime by South African Hindus as well as Muslims, and these continue now to visit his tomb.[118]

In this situation, in which Islamic procedures are often regarded as utilitarian measures which, though on the whole they are better performed by good Muslims, may be performed on behalf of anyone, Muslim, mixed Muslim, or Pagan, it is not surprising that there is little direct connection between conversion and cure. Where such a connection does exist, it seems often to be a case of curing, followed by conversion as an act of gratitude. For example, Sule-Dyay the elder is said to have been the only Muslim among the Tengella princes of Futa Toro, on the Senegal. He had sent his son, as was the custom of the Tengella, to study with Muslims to the north. When the son and his teacher returned, they found the father ill; the teacher, a sharīf, healed him, and sharīf and son then persuaded the father to adopt Islam.[119] In Mossi country, the modern Upper Volta, the Pagan Nobéré chief converted when a Hausa Muslim cured him.[120] In southern Ghana, one of the first two Fante Muslims, both converts from Christianity, came over when the prayers of a Hausa cleric were efficacious in bringing him a child.[121]

If we set this beside the usual sequence in those Christian churches in black Africa which stress faith healing, we may more easily see the contrast, for here acceptance of Christ is part, indeed the central part, of the healing process. This emphasis has led, in areas where Muslims and Christians are both active, to a competitive spirit quite unlike the live-and-let-live style of mixed Islam. Here is an account of a Christ Apostolic Church revival meeting in Ibadan. A woman

> has had continual aches, and has been to University College Hospital, and also 'prayed to Mohammed', but in vain; now she has acknowledged Christ as Lord. She goes down to general applause . . . a boy Sanusi, son of what is described as 'a worshipper of Mohammed', cured of deafness. . . . People who are Muslims have their names taken down by one of the pastors, who will seek to make them full members of their congregations.
>
> About half of those whom I saw testify were Muslims, and this is fully publicized. Much rhetorical point is made of the fact that Christ is the Son of God, not merely a Prophet; so Mohammed can be unfavourably compared to him. It is assumed, also for the sake of argument, that Muslims pray *to* Mohammed (and do not get replies from him); can Mohammed cure, like Christ can, it is asked?[122]

Among people who are already committed to Islam, albeit often of a mixed kind, healing may be associated with a striving towards reform. This occurs in two general ways. First, illness may be regarded as God's vengeance upon wrongdoers; this is one aspect of the punitive illness of which we have already spoken, but it appears more clearly when epidemics strike a whole people. The *kafi* epidemic which smote Songhay in the 1530s was interpreted as a judgement upon Bengan Koreï, who had exiled his own father – a pilgrim, to compound the offence – and who went in for various innovations of pomp, music, new instruments, and so forth.[123] It has recently been suggested that Shaybānī, chiefly familiar to Africanists (through Jackson's writings) for his account of 'Hausa' and Timbuktu, later became a saint after inward conversion brought about by the plague.[124] Jackson said of this plague, in 1799, that Moroccans thought it

> a judgement of the Omnipotent on the disobedience of man, and that it behoved every individual to amend his conduct, as a preparation to his departure for paradise.[125]

In the Christian context, all the Aladura churches in West Africa, as already suggested, probably derive from the influenza epidemic of 1918. There are Pagan parallels also, as among the Gurage of Ethiopia, who may suffer from ritual illnesses if they have committed offences against the Gurage social code,[126] but the situation in Paganism is a subject lying somewhat beside our Islamic theme.

The second connection between healing and reform is more individual, when some pious action is regarded as a necessary prerequisite for, or a suitable acknowledgement of, healing. Freeing a slave is mentioned several times as such an act. When the Ottoman official in charge of Egypt in 1521 fell ill, he set free many slaves, and gave alms of wheat and 1000 silver coins to the students of al Azhar and of other schools.[127] Usuman dan Fodio wrote:

> I have heard that the people of Gobir or some of them – when a man is sick – sacrifice a male or female slave and believe that thus they will be saved from death. . . . Let such an one know that God and His Prophet are far from him, nor will God accomplish for him his desires and requests. Were he to free the slave, it were more likely to effect a ransom. Such an action would be far removed from sin.[128]

Such emancipation by slave owners was evidently quite common in East Africa.[129] An act of more lasting commitment was performed, for example, by those who, perhaps chronically ill, entered the Murīd *daras* in Senegal, hoping to be cured by their marabout or cleric masters.[130] Garrick Braide, whom we have cited already more than once, provides a Christian parallel: 'People who had been healed stopped drinking and whoever ignored the warning died immediately'.[131]

Fully fledged reform movements, however, may act to curb some of the marginal accretions and excesses of faith healing. In Morocco in the eleventh century, one of the heresies of the Barghawāṭa, against whom the Almoravids warred, was that their leader spat in the hands of his followers, and they carried this carefully to their sick, to assure healing.[132] Usuman dan Fodio condemned various practices of this kind, such as the employment of earth from shrines.[133] His son, Muḥammad Bello, wrote a number of treatises, and his interest here, as in divination and other such subjects, may have stemmed from his reformist conviction that non-Islamic, or mixed Islamic, elements – though not orthodox amulets and the like – should be excised.[134] A Vai manuscript from Liberia reveals the reformer's zeal against accretions, but the words I have italicized suggest that just a trace of mixer's nostalgia for the old ways remains:

> I wish that ye would always pray to me when ye lie down. If ye pray to me when ye are sick, I shall restore you to health; for I am stronger

than all Greegrees. Do ye not see that there is too much Greegree palaver? One says, this Greegree can cure you; and another says, this Greegree can cure you; but I say, that I speak only one word and not more. If somebody tells you to pray, and ye say, 'I will not pray, prayer-palaver is a lie', ye cannot see heaven, but will go to hell. . . . *I like every man's ways*; but those of Momodulamini (Muḥammad al Amīn) surpass all others.[135]

Doughty noted a similar transition in Arabia. At Teyma, especially among the beduin, exorcism and the control of jinn were the great skills in medicine,

yet afterward at Hayil, I found exorcists only living under tolerance, – such kind of ungodly superstition, and pretended dealings of brain-sick men with the nether world, is not, perchance, to the reformed stomach of the Wahaby religion.[136]

With this reforming reaction, admittedly of limited scope, against some aspects of that same medical practice which has so substantially contributed to the initial establishment and maintenance of Islam in black Africa, our wheel has come full circle, and our study may be concluded.

NOTES

1 Time and Tune: BBC Radio for Schools: 'Hassebu'. I am indebted to Crispin Fisher, aged 8, for having brought this passage to my attention, inadvertently, while playing the part of Hassebu.
2 J. C. Froelich in I. M. Lewis, ed., 1966, 169.
3 L. C. Briggs, 1960, 42.
4 H. S. Lewis, 1965, 42.
5 For further discussion of the relationship between cleric and merchant, see Benjamin Anderson, 1971, Introduction.
6 See below, 59.
7 Ibid., 53.
8 See above, 13–22.
9 Ibid., 1–12.
10 For a similar attempt, with another theme, see H. J. Fisher, 1971.
11 J. D. Y. Peel, 1968, 127–8; see also H. W. Turner, 1967, II, 141.
12 Cf. H. J. Fisher, 1970, 273–4.
13 I have borrowed the term from C. Elgood, 1970, 181 ff., who gives a fairly long and rather ghastly account.
14 It is clear that a number of African peoples did practise this in some form. W. C. Harris described it in Ethiopia, though he was unable to persuade anyone, Muslim, Christian or Pagan, to try the lymph which he had himself brought: Harris, 1844, II, 158, 160–1. A specifically Muslim attitude does not emerge clearly from my information. Vaccination was common in North Africa: see E. Daumas and A. de Chancel, 1856, 395–6. Inoculation has been described in Ghadames, on a major route across the desert; see A. de Motylinski, 1904, 167. Most authorities regard vaccination as having been introduced into the Sudan by Muslims. In northern Liberia, for

example, some Mandingoes inoculated, and this was occasionally copied: G. Schwab, 1947, 388. In East Africa, Burton spoke of the vain attempts of the Arabs to teach the Wajiji, an inland people, inoculation: R. Burton, 1860, II, 63. Nachtigal said that vaccination was known in Bornu, through the Arabs, though it was not widely applied: G. Nachtigal, 1967, II, 468. Barth, on the contrary, said that although smallpox was a very fatal disease in the Central Sudan, Muslims there were prevented by religious prejudice from indulging in inoculation: H. Barth, 1857–8, I, 425, and II, 536. Tully, in Tripoli in the late eighteenth century, similarly remarked, concerning plague, that 'it is contrary to the Mahometan religion to endeavour to avoid contagion': R. Tully (or more exactly, his sister), 1816, 79, cf. 83. The question is evidently still a live one: see Ḥamdān ibn 'Uthmān Kojah, 1968. Barth thought that it was several Pagan tribes who observed the sensible precaution of vaccination to the best of their abilities: II, 536. For Yoruba practices, connected with the Shopanna cult, see U. Maclean, 1971, 39. For an account of smallpox allegedly induced and inflicted on another person by magic, see N. Owen, 1930, 89–90.

15 J. Graham Forbes, 1904, gives a somewhat hair-raising description, including one Muslim remedy (entirely natural, without any religious element). Richardson, in Ghadames in the mid-nineteenth century, describes an illness called 'arak al 'abīd, the slaves' disease, which is apparently guinea-worm; people believed that it was caught by merchants visiting the Sudan, and carried back by them: J. Richardson, 1848, I, 196. But Graham Greene was told in Liberia that it had been introduced southwards, carried down from the Sahara by Mandingo traders: G. Greene, 1963, 190.

16 Elgood, 1970, 158, discusses this specifically for sixteenth-century Persia. He deals only with bullet wounds, but damage resulted also from bursting guns, gunpowder burns, and so forth. El-Tounsy burnt himself thus in Wadai, and was healed with olive oil over sixty years old, given him by the Sulṭan: Sheykh Mohammed ibn-Omar el-Tounsy, 1851, 65–6. For other such accidents, see H. J. Fisher and V. Rowland, 1971, 228. Bowen reported that in nineteenth century Yorubaland gunpowder was thought good for asthma, of which he had seen several cases, 'though I believe it never cures them': J. Bowen, 1968, 232. Nachtigal mentions gunpowder in the treatment of whooping cough in Fezzan: G. Nachtigal, 1967, I, 148. See also Note 60 below.

17 For incidental notes, see B. Alexander, 1908, II, 122, and D. Denham and H. Clapperton, 1826,11.

18 Bivar and Hiskett, 1962, 138.

19 Abdullahi dan Fodio, 1963, 7. See also M. Last, 1967[1], 209, 1967[2], 7–8.

20 I. M. Lewis, 1961, 258; he mentions an edition published in Cairo in 1938.

21 This is confirmed by Peel, 1968, 296: 'Yoruba Muslims view their religion in a similar way to how Yoruba Christians view theirs, but never come to assert that one must forsake all material means and rely solely on God for healing, supporting themselves by scriptural argument and religious emotion'.

22 Daumas and de Chancel, 1856, 2.

23 A. J. Arkell, 1955, 217–20.

24 Barth, 1857–8, II, 495.

25 Ibid., II, 517.

26 W. B. Harris, 1895, 5.

27 Ch. de la Roncière, 1919, 73–4.

28 C. Fyfe, 1962, 192.

29 T. Lewicki, 1960, 10–12; or see idem, 1969, 67.

30 Aḥmad ibn al Amīn al Shinqīṭī, 1911, 506; 1953, 133.
31 Briggs, 1960, 209.
32 Richardson, 1848, I, 361.
33 J. F. Schön, 1885, 92.
34 Cf. A. G. B. and H. J. Fisher, 1970, 56–7, and the references there; J. B. Andrews, *Les Fontaines des Génies* (*Seba Aioun*), Algiers, 1903. For an Indonesian parallel of medical craft diffused through slaves, see C. S. Hurgronje, 1906, I, 20n.
35 Elgood, 1970, 148–9, citing the *Qarabadin* of ʻAlī Afzal Qatiᶜ.
36 Briggs, 1960, 43, repeats the story, but R. Mauny, 1961, 463, rejects it.
37 J. B. Black, 1952, 280.
38 Al Shinqīṭī, 1911, 506; 1953, 132–3.
39 ʻKano Chronicle' in H. R. Palmer, 1967, III, 105.
40 See below, 53.
41 Cf. e.g. H. T. Norris, 1968, 144–5, 148–51.
42 C. Monteil, 1924, 96.
43 S. Hillelson, 1937, 670–1.
44 W. C. Harris, 1844, III, 50.
45 J. Hunwick in C. Allen and R. W. Johnson, eds., 1970, 14.
46 Al Shinqīṭī, 1911, 509–101; 1953, 137–8; the above version is taken from Fisher and Fisher, 1970, 57.
47 Maclean, 1971, 99; cf. 86, 140, 142 for other cursing mentions.
48 R. Marty, 1926, 255–6.
49 P. A. Benton, 1912, 30.
50 El-Tounsy, 1851, 619–21.
51 E. D. Earthy, 1955, 212.
52 Ibn Abī Zayd al Qayrawānī, 1945, 215.
53 F. M. Brodie, 1967, 93–4.
54 Quoted in Elgood, 1970, 141.
55 E. A. Ayandele, 1970, 356.
56 D. B. Cruise O'Brien, 1971, 105.
57 Ibid., 232, citing Amadou Diouf; it is proper to add that the Mourides have been the subject of controversy, and have in some cases at least been unjustly accused of obscurantism, etc.
58 C. M. Doughty, 1923, I, 438.
59 Peel, 1968, 117–18.
60 F. A. de Chateaubriand, 1811, I, 189–90. In Tripoli, in the late eighteenth century, European consular houses fearing the plague fumigated with a mixture of bran, camphor, myrrh, aloes and gunpowder: Tully, 1816, 84.
61 Nachtigal, 1967, II, 298.
62 28 June and 6 July, 1971; it was apparently used to good effect in London during the cholera outbreak of 1854.
63 Jean-Léon l'Africain, 1956, I, 139.
64 J. Ogilby, 1670, 384.
65 H. Clapperton, 1829, 59; natron was also used for horses, see above, 42, n. 17.
66 Daumas and de Chancel, 1856, 245, 396.
67 Elgood, 1970, 253.
68 Ibn Abī Zayd, 1945, 149.
69 Schwab, 1947, 385–6.
70 C. H. Robinson, 1896, 108. For a modern healer, fourteen times a pilgrim, see M. Chailley *et al.*, 1962, 14–16.
71 J. Chapelle, 1957, 260–1.
72 Doughty, 1923, I, 257.

73 C. A. Willis, 1926, 9.
74 J. R. Willis, 1970, 61–2.
75 G. Buselli, 1924, 286. This was at Igennawen, meaning Blacks, Sudan.
76 P. Marty, 1920, II, 55, 59.
77 Mahmoud el-Ka'ti, 1964, 170–91; the author likens this to the mosque of el-Kerkhi in Baghdad.
78 J.-C. Froelich, 1962, 164–7.
79 F. Alvares, 1961, I, 166; cf. I, 262.
80 W. A. Shack, 1966, 193.
81 W. C. Harris, 1844, II, 152–3.
82 M.-J. Tubiana, 1964, 176–7.
83 El-Tounsy, 1851, 214–15.
84 W. B. Harris, 1895, 19–21.
85 Marty, 1920, II, 122 ff.
86 R. Jobson, 1932, 69.
87 Mohamed Abdelkafi, 1968, 1.
88 Daumas and de Chancel, 1856, 84–5.
89 Doughty, 1923, II, 257–8.
90 Al Shinqīṭī, 1911, 506; 1953, 133; cf. Doughty, 1923, I, 438.
91 A. J. N. Tremearne, 1913, 169–70.
92 From R. Lander's journal, in Clapperton, 1829, 280.
93 Denham and Clapperton, 1826, 203–4.
94 El-Tounsy, 1851, 356–7. In a treatment resembling the use of perfume, the smoke of the same burning is used against fever.
95 Tully, 1816, 80.
96 G. R. Smith, 1969, 274.
97 Cf. e.g. Maclean, 1971, 67–8.
98 Schwab, 1947, 387. He described slate-water administered by a Mandingo Muslim to a baby suffering from malaria; a sneezing powder was also used. To those interested in curious, but sometimes illuminating, aspects of the African past, I recommend the sneeze.
99 Turner, 1967, I, 9.
100 Schwab, 1947, 387.
101 Turner, 1967, II, 154.
102 H. J. Fisher, 1972.
103 Earthy, 1954–5, 212.
104 Clapperton, 1829, 273.
105 Ayandele, 1970, 357, 359.
106 Doughty, 1923, I, 572.
107 R. Basset, 1899, 451, citing the *Kitāb al Siyar* of al Shammākhī.
108 Al Bakri, 1965, 326–7/184.
109 Chapelle, 1956, 264, refers to this.
110 Barth, 1857–8, II, 66–7; see also Clapperton, 1829, 160–1.
111 E. P. Skinner, 1969, I, 272–3.
112 Barth, 1857–8, II, 536; see also II, 525.
113 Skinner, 1969, I, 97–8.
114 Hurgronje, 1906, I, 133; the son born of the union subsequently proved an embarrassment.
115 This outline is discussed in more detail in H. J. Fisher, 1973, 31ff.
116 A. Arcin, 1907, 471.
117 E. Dammann, 1932–3, 262.
118 G. R. Smith, 1969, 276.
119 Siré-Abbâs Soh, 1913, 36. The same account, 85–6, mentions that later, after the Muslim revolution in Futa Toro, it was customary to go north in

search of healing, as did the almami, Abdoul-Bubakar, in the mid-nineteenth century. See also 33–4 for another example of clerical healing.
120 N. Skinner, in I. M. Lewis, ed., 1966, 359.
121 H. J. Fisher, 1963, 117.
122 Peel, 1968, 176–7. Muslim/Christian medieval rivalry of a different kind is reported from Buganda, where in 1881 an Anglican commented on his Muslim and Roman Catholic colleagues: 'The Arab, Kambi Mbaya, is now attempting to cure the king of his long-standing stricture. Wheaten flour, with almonds, seems to be the remedy! M. Lourdel, who has no idea of medicine, is also continuing to supply his Majesty every day with some bottles of drug. He goes to court every day'. A. M. Mackay, 1890, 188.
123 J. Rouch, 1953, 202.
124 Allen and Johnson, 1970, 41.
125 Cited in ibid., 41.
126 Shack, 1966, 167.
127 B. Dodge, 1961, 77–8, apparently citing ibn 'Iyās.
128 H. R. Palmer, 1914, 59.
129 M. W. H. Beech, 1916, 148.
130 O'Brien, 1971, 173.
131 Ayandele, 1970, 356.
132 Ibn Abī Zar', 1860, 181.
133 M. Hiskett, 1962, 594.
134 M. Last, 1967, 209 and note; see also idem, 1967², 6–7
135 S. W. Koelle, 1849, appendix, 19.
136 Doughty, 1923, I, 548.

REFERENCES

Abdallahi dan Fodio, *Tazyīn al waraqāt*, ed. Hiskett, Ibadan, 1963.
B. Alexander, *From Niger to Nile*, 2 vols., London, 1908.
C. Allen and R. W. Johnson, eds., *African Perspectives*, Cambridge, 1970.
F. Alvares, *The Prester John of the Indies,* 2 vols., Cambridge, 1961.
B. Anderson, *Journeys to Musadu*, London, 1971.
A. Arcin, *La Guinée française*, Paris, 1907.
A. J. Arkell, *A History of the Sudan to 1821*, London, 1955.
E. A. Ayandele, *Holy Johnson*, London, 1970.
Al Bakrī, *Description de l'Afrique septentrionale*, trans. and ed. de Slane, Paris, 1965.
H. Barth, *Travels and Discoveries . . .*, 5 vols., London, 1857–8.
R. Basset, 'Les Sanctuaires du Djebel Nefousa', *Journal Asiatique,* XIII, 1899.
M. W. H. Beech, 'Slavery on the East Coast of Africa', *Journal of the Africa Society*, XV, 1916.
P. A. Benton, *Notes on some languages of the Western Sudan*, London, 1912.
A. D. H. Bivar and M. Hiskett, 'The Arabic Literature of Nigeria to 1804', *Bulletin of the School of Oriental and African Studies*, XXV, 1962.
J. B. Black, *The Reign of Elizabeth*, Oxford, 1952.
T. J. Bowen, *Adventures and Missionary Labours . . .*, London, 1968.
L. C. Briggs, *Tribes of the Sahara*, Cambridge, Mass., 1960.
F. M. Brodie, *The Devil Drives*, London, 1967.
R. F. Burton, *The Lake Regions of Equatorial Africa*, 2 vols., London, 1860.
G. Buselli, 'Berber texts from Jebel Nefûsi', *Journal of the Africa Society*, XXIII, 1924.

M. Chailley *et al.*, *Notes et études sur l'Islam en Afrique noire,* Paris, 1962.
J. Chapelle, *Nomads noirs du Sahara*, Paris, 1957.
F. A. de Chateaubriand, *Travels in Greece, Palestine, Egypt and Barbary . . .*, 2 vols., London, 1811.
H. Clapperton, *Journal of a Second Expedition . . .*, London, 1829.
E. Dammann, 'Vai-Erzählungen,' *Zeitschrift für Eingeborenen Sprachen*, XXIII, 1932–3.
E. Daumas and A. de Chancel, *Le grand désert: itinéraire d'une caravane du Sahara au pays des Nègres*, Paris, 1856.
D. Denham and H. Clapperton, *Narrative of Travels and Discoveries . . .*, London, 1826.
B. Dodge, *Al-Azhar: a millennium of Muslim learning*, Washington, D.C., 1961.
C. M. Doughty, *Travels in Arabia Deserta*, 2 vols., London, 1923.
E. D. Earthy, 'The impact of Mohammedanism on Paganism in the Liberian hinterland', *Numen*, II, 1955.
C. Elgood, *Safavid Medical Practice: or, The Practice of Medicine, Surgery and Gynaecology in Persia between 1500 AD and* 1500 *AD,* London, 1970.
A. G. B. Fisher and H. J. Fisher, *Slavery and Muslim Society in Africa*, London, 1970.
H. J. Fisher, *Ahmadiyyah*, London, 1963; 'Independency and Islam: the Nigerian Aladuras and some Muslim comparisons', *Journal of African History*, XI, 1970; 'Muslim prayer and military activity in the history of Africa south of the Sahara', *Journal of African History*, XII, 1971; 'Dreams out of the Ivory Gate', *African History Seminar*, S.O.A.S., 2 February 1972; 'Conversion reconsidered . . .', *Africa*, 1973.
H. J. Fisher and V. Rowland, 'Firearms in the Central Sudan', *Journal of African History*, XII, 1973.
J. G. Forbes, 'Native methods of treatment in West Africa', *Journal of the Africa Society*, III, 1904.
J.-C. Froelich, *Les musulmans d'Afrique noire*, Paris, 1962.
C. Fyfe, *A History of Sierra Leone*, London, 1962.
G. Greene, *Journey without Maps*, London, 1963.
Ḥamdān ibn 'Uthmān Kojah, *Jazā'irli; itḥāf al munṣifīn wa 'l udabā' fī'l iḥtirās 'an al wabā* (A treatise on quarantine, showing that the use of preventive measures against plagues is not forbidden by Islam), Algiers, 1968.
W. B. Harris, *Tafilet: The Narrative of a Journey . . .*, Edinburgh and London, 1895.
W. C. Harris, *The Highlands of Aethiopia*, 3 vols., London, 1844.
S. Hillelson, 'Aspects of Muhammadanism in the eastern Sudan', *Journal of the Royal Asiatic Society*, 1937.
M. Hiskett, 'An Islamic Tradition of Reform in the western Sudan', *Bulletin o, the School of Oriental and African Studies*, XXV, 1962.
C. S. Hurgronje, *The Achehnese*, 2 vols., Leyden, 1906.
Ibn Abī Zar', *Roudh el-Kartas*, ed. Beaumier, Paris, 1860.
Ibn Abī Zayd al Qayrawānī, *La Risala . . .*, ed. and trans. Bercher, Algiers, 1945.
Jean-Léon l'Africain (Leo Africanus), *Description de l'Afrique*, trans. Epaulard, 2 vols., Paris, 1956.
R. Jobson, *The Golden Trade*, London, 1932.
S. W. Koelle, *Narrative of an Expedition into the Vy Country . . .*, London, 1849.
M. Last, *The Sokoto Caliphate*, London, 1967; 'A note on the attitudes to the supernatural in the Sokoto jihād', *Journal of the Historical Society of Nigeria*, IV, 1967.

T. Lewicki, 'Quelques extraits inédits relatifs aux voyages des commerçants et des missionaires Ibādites nord-africaines au pays du Soudan occidental et central au moyen âge', *Folia Orientalia,* Krakow, II, 1960; *Arabic external sources for the history of Africa to the south of Sahara*, Wroclaw, 1969.
H. S. Lewis, *A Galla Monarchy*, Madison, Wisc., 1965.
I. M. Lewis, *A Pastoral Democracy*, London, 1961; *Islam in Tropical Africa*, ed., London, 1966.
(Mackay) *A. M. Mackay*, by his sister, London, 1890.
U. Maclean, *Magical Medicine: a Nigerian case study*, London, 1971.
Mahmoud Ka'ti, *Tarikh el-fettach*, ed. Houdas and Delafosse, Paris, 1964.
P. Marty, *Etudes sur l'Islam au Dahomey*, Paris, 1926; *Etudes sur l'Islam et les Tribus du Sudan*, 3 Vols., Paris, 1920.
R. Mauny, *Tableau géographique de l'ouest africain*, Dakar, 1961.
Mohamed Abdelkafi, *One Hundred Arabic Proverbs from Libya*, London, 1968.
C. Monteil, *Les Bambara du Ségou et du Kaarta*, Paris, 1924.
A. de C. Matylinski, *Le dialecte berbère de R'edamès*, Paris, 1904.
G. Nachtigal, *Sahara and Sudan*, 3 vols., Graz, 1967.
H. T. Norris, *Shinqīṭī Folk Literature and Song*, Oxford, 1968.
D. B. Cruise O'Brien, *The Mourides of Senegal* . . ., Oxford, 1971.
J. Ogilby, *Africa: being an accurate Description* . . ., London, 1670.
N. Owen, *Journal of a Slave-Dealer*, London, 1930.
H. R. Palmer, *Sudanese Memoirs*, 3 vols., London, 1963; 'An Early Fulani conception of Islam', *Journal of the African Society*, 1914.
J. D. Y. Peel, *Aladura: a religious movement among the Yoruba,* London, 1968.
J. Richardson, *Travels in the Great Desert of Sahara in the years 1845 and 1846*, 2 vols., London, 1848.
C. H. Robinson, *Specimens of Hausa Literature*, Cambridge, 1896.
Ch. de la Roncière, 'Une histoire du Bornou au XVIIe siècle . . .', *Revue de l'histoire des colonies françaises*, VII, 2, 1919.
J. Rouch, *Contribution à l'histoire des Songhay,* Dakar, 1953.
J. F. Schön, *Magana Hausa: native literature*, London, 1885.
G. Schwab, *Tribes of the Liberian Hinterland*, Cambridge, Mass., 1947.
W. A. Shack, *The Gurage: a people of the Ensete Culture*, London, 1966.
Al Shinqīṭī, *Al Wasīṭ fī tarājim udabā' Shinqīṭ*, Cairo, 1911; trans. Teffahi, Saint Louis, Senegal, 1953.
Siré-Abbâs Soh, *Chroniques du Foûta sénégalais*, ed. Delafosse and Gaden, Paris, 1913.
N. Skinner, *Hausa Tales and Traditions*, originally compiled by Frank Edgar, Vol. I, London, 1969.
G. R. Smith, 'A Muslim Saint in South Africa', *African Studies*, XXVIII, 1969.
El-Tounsy (al Tūnisī), *Voyage au Ouaday*, trans. Perron, Paris, 1851.
A. J. N. Tremearne, *Hausa Superstitions and Customs* . . ., London, 1913.
M.-J. Tubiana, *Survivances préislamiques en pays Zaghawa,* Paris, 1964.
R. Tully, *Narrative of a ten years' residence at Tripoli*, London, 1816.
H. W. Turner, *History of an African Independent Church*, 2 vols., Oxford, 1967.
C. A. Willis, *Report on Slavery and the Pilgrimage*, 1926, unpublished typescript at the School of Oriental Studies, University of Durham.
J. R. Willis, *Al-Ḥājj 'Umar . . . and the doctrinal basis of his . . . movement*, Ph.D. Thesis, University of London, 1970, unpublished.

IV

Saints and Sulṭāns: The Role of Muslim Holy Men in the Keira Sultanate of Dār Fūr[1]

R. S. O'Fahey

Socialantropologisk Institut, University of Bergen

Dār Fūr and the Keira State

The Keira Sultanate was one of a series of states in the belt of savannah land below the Sahara, known to the Arab writers as the bilād al Sūdān, 'Land of the Blacks', which occupied what is now the westernmost province of the Republic of the Sudan, Dār Fūr, 'The Home of the Fur'. To the west of the Keira state lay Wadai and to the east, separated by Kordofan and the White Nile, lay the Funj Sultanate of Sinnār. Very little is known of the history of Dār Fūr before the Keira, but we can distinguish two dynasties or states before the Keira, the Daju and Tunjur, although we know nothing of the nature or extent of their rule.[2]

The Fur, the largest non-Arab tribe in Dār Fūr (1956 Sudan Census, 303,000), today live mainly to the west and south of Jabal Marra, the central mountain massif in the province. Linguistically they are very isolated; Greenberg places their language in a separate sub-group of his main Nilo–Saharan group, but it does not appear to be related to any other language spoken in Dār Fūr.[3] The Keira lineage probably began to unite the Fur clans of Jabal Marra in the sixteenth century, but did not emerge as a Muslim dynasty until the middle of the seventeenth century under Sulaymān Solongdungo. Solongdungo (Fur, 'Arab') appears in the various traditional accounts as the son or descendant of a Keira mother and an Arab father, who drove out the Tunjur and whose rule is associated with the establishment of Islam as the court religion. He is described as uniting the Fur and non-Fur peoples of the Jabal Marra region and as conquering the area around the mountain range. The impetus for imperial expansion probably came from long distance caravan trade since the genealogical date for Solongdungo coincides with the earliest references to Dār Fūr trading with Egypt.

The Keira dynasty ruled in Dār Fūr until 1874 and was restored in

1899 by 'Alī Dīnār, who succeeded in preserving his kingdom's independence until 1916, when Dār Fūr was conquered by the British and he himself killed. After Solongdungo, the next wave of Keira expansion, north and west, and the early organization of the state is associated with Sultan Aḥmad Bukr 1128/1715–6—1141/1728–9. In the mid-eighteenth century the Keira were engaged in a series of wars with Wadai, in which the latter seems to have had the advantage, since two Keira Sultans lost their lives in the wars. Indeed with the power of Wadai growing in the west, Dār Fūr seems to have turned eastwards into the orbit of the Nilotic Sudan, with important religious and cultural consequences. Sultan Muḥammad Tayrāb, 1176/1762–3—1200/1785–6, was responsible for extending Keira rule eastwards into Kordofan at the expense both of the Musabba'āt, a group related to the Keira who lived in western Kordofan and the now declining Sinnār Sultanate.

Tayrāb's successor, 'Abd al Raḥmān al Rashīd, 1201/1786–7—1215/1800–1, both re-organized the administration of the empire, which now stretched from the borders of Wadai (roughly the present Chad/Sudan frontier) to the White Nile, to conform more closely to Islamic practice, and encouraged the settlement in the Sultanate of merchants and holy men. His reign marked the apogee of Keira power. In 1821, the armies of Muḥammad 'Alī Pasha, the ruler of Egypt, entered Sinnār without resistance, while an army under the daftardār Muḥammad Bey Khusraw invaded Kordofan; the Keira cavalry, in chain mail and armed with lances, went down before firearms at a battle fought just north of Bāra and the province was irretrievably lost to the Sultanate. However, the comparatively stiff resistance of the Fur and difficulties elsewhere in the Sudan, combined to postpone the projected Turco-Egyptian invasion of the Sultanate itself. Dār Fūr was allowed a period of grace, aided by the circumspect policy pursued towards their powerful neighbour by Sultan Muḥammadal Faḍl 1215/1800–1—1254/1838, and his son and successor, Muḥammad al Husayn al Mahdī, 1254/1838—1290/1874. The end of the old Keira state came when the slave-trading potentate of the Baḥr al Ghazāl, al Zubayr Raḥma Manṣūr, invaded the Sultanate from the south in 1290/1874 and defeated Sultan Ibrāhīm's army at Manawāshī. The Fur, at least, never really accepted either the Turco–Egyptian regime or the Mahdiya and a series of shadow Sultans appeared in Jabal Marra from the Keira family, to whom the Fur showed impressive loyalty, until the restoration of the Sultanate by 'Alī Dīnār.

The Coming of the Holy Men

The process of Islamization within the Keira Sultanate is difficult to document; we do not, for instance, possess any record comparable to the collection of biographies of holy men from the Nilotic Sudan, the Ṭabaqāt of Wad Ḍayfallāh.[4] Although Trimingham places Dār Fūr within his Eastern or Nilotic cycle of Islamic penetration, which is distinguished by profound Arabization and the widespread influence of the Ṣūfī ṭarīqas, religious influences emanating from West Africa were as important.[5] Dār Fūr became the meeting ground of several different African Islamic traditions, from Egypt, from the Nilotic Sudan and from North Africa via West Africa.

The holy men (Sudanese Arabic, fakī, plural fuqarā') who came to Dār Fūr were of diverse origin and varied attainments. They included Arabs from the Ḥijāz, such as Muḥammad ibn Ṣāliḥ al Kinānī, who became Imam to Sultan Muḥammad Dawra, 1154/1741–2—1159/1746–7, who built a mosque for him at Terjil in south-western Dār Fūr.[6] Among the Ja'alīyūn immigrants from the Nilotic Sudan was Idrīs, who settled in the Sultanate in the reign of Sultan Mūsā in the late seventeenth century. The descendants of Idrīs became the Imams of Turra, on the western side of Jabal Marra, where they looked after the tombs of the Sultans and the royal archives and regalia.[7] A later Ja'alī immigrant was Ḥasan al Aḥmar, an ancestor of the famous Kordofan shaykh of Mahdist times, al Manna Ismā'īl; Ḥasan went to southern Dār Fūr in the eighteenth century and settled at Ḥufrat al Naḥās and who was, 'famed for his knowledge of Muḥammadan law'.[8] Thirty years later, Ḥasan's clan was forced to leave Dār Fūr and settle in Kordofan. It is probable that most immigrants from the east came from families already settled in Kordofan, since there are few references in the Ṭabaqāt to fuqarā' going directly to Dār Fūr from the Nile region. Thus the father of 'Izz al Dīn, qāḍī to Sultan 'Abd al Raḥmān, came originally from Bāra, a Ja'alī trading settlement established in Kordofan some time in the mid-eighteenth century.[9]

In the case of immigrants from the west, the holy men were usually passing through Dār Fūr on pilgrimage (ḥajj). When the trans-Sudanic route was first used by pilgrims is unknown, but the establishment of Muslim dynasties in Wadai and Dār Fūr in the sixteenth/seventeenth centuries no doubt served to make it safer and more popular. From the west came many Fulani; a Fulani fakī, 'Ali al Fūtūwī, from Baqirmi, met Sultan Aḥmad Bukr on his way to Mecca. The Sultan invited him to settle and this the fakī agreed to do upon his return from the Ḥijāz. When he came back to Dār Fūr, the Sultan gave him an estate at Majalla in western Jabal Marra. The family of 'Alī were to prosper and become politically influential.[10] Another but later immigrant from Baqirmi was less fortunate; Muḥammad al Bulālāwī settled at the court of Sultan Muḥammad al Ḥusayn, who showed him much favour. Unfortunately he fell foul of the powerful Dār Fūr notable, the wazīr Aḥmad Shaṭṭa, who made his life so unbearable that he fled to Khartoum. There he persuaded the Turco–Egyptian Governor that, because of his royal birth, he had claims to parts of Dār Fūr and lands farther west. He was sent with a small force to the Baḥr al Ghazāl to try and oust al Zubayr, but was himself killed.[11]

As an inducement to settle in the Sultanate, the holy men were often granted estates (Arabic, ḥākūra, plural ḥawākīr; Fur, *ro*, plural *rota*), usually consisting of a group of villages, which were exempt from all taxes save the customary Islamic ones, zakāt and fiṭr. Often the Sultan would build a mosque, create an ḥākūra to support it, which would then be granted, usually on an hereditary basis, to a fakī and his descendants. Thus Mālik, a son of 'Alī al Fūtūwī, grew up with the future Sultan, 'Abd al Raḥmān, and when the latter became ruler, received extensive estates around Kerio, near the capital al Fāshir, and a mosque was built there; the family still own the estates.[12] 'Umar al Tūnisī, the father of the writer, made a favourable impression on the same Sultan and the latter granted him an ḥākūra at Gerli, on the western slopes of Jabal Marra, but the fakī was not happy with the area, since the Fur on the estate could not speak Arabic and he could not speak Fur, so he was given another estate.[13]

In these dealings between Sultan and holy men, the motives of both parties seem fairly clear. The holy man would be attracted by the material rewards and prestige that he could find on the Islamic frontier. The peregrinations of Muslim scholars in search of judicial or political employment is a common theme in Islamic history as the career, for example, of ibn Khaldūn illustrates. 'Umar al Tūnisī moved from Tunis to Cairo, then to Sinnār, from Sinnār to Dār Fūr and then to Wadai and then home; in all his moves, he was able to capitalize on his scholarly reputation – he had been at al Azhar University – and his experience of the wider Islamic world.[14]

Such expertise was of immense value to a Sudanic sulṭān. Undoubtedly religion was not the only motive for granting ḥawākīr to holy men; such people newly established by the sultan's favour, could provide a new local focus of loyalty, breaking down the old clan and tribal particularisms. Such a process kept repeating itself, since the immigrants would either assimilate their newly-acquired followers or identify with them.

The Political Role of Holy Men

The fuqarā', whether recent immigrants or long settled, were but one group within the complex political structure of the Dār Fūr state.

But they had several assets; their prestige as holy men and occasionally miracle workers was considerable. Mālik al Fūtūwī is said to have struck blind those Keira princes who opposed the accession of the young Muḥammad al Faḍl.[15] Generally their lack of tribal links within the state made them useful and reliable servants to the Sultans. Sometimes the reverse was true; Mālik was described as the guardian at court of the Fulani – presumably the nomad Fulani (Bororoje) who were and are to be found scattered throughout Dār Fūr.[16]

In the view of Muslims from the Islamic heartlands, the Keira Sultans were parvenus; a view probably shared by those Arabs nominally subject to the Sultanate.[17] To counteract this, the fuqarā' were able to provide the Sultans with fake genealogies, giving them an impeccable Arab ancestry. Both the Dār Fūr and the Wadai dynasties claimed 'Abbāsid origin.[18] The fuqarā' could also write their letters in the appropriate rhetoric of Islamic chancery practice. They could even take their place in the military campaigns of the Sultans; 'Umar al Tūnisī led a contingent of North African musketeers in one of the campaigns of the Wadai Sultan Ṣābūn.[19]

The combination of religious prestige and a position of relative neutrality in local politics led some of the holy men into a mediatory role. In positions of real or apparent stalemate, intervention by the fuqarā' could be a useful way out. This was not always successful; 'Alī al Fūtūwī and a qāḍī from Katsina in Northern Nigeria tried to intervene in a civil war between Sultan Muḥammad Dawra and his son, Mūsā 'Anqarīb. They arranged a meeting between father and son, making the former swear on the Quran that he would not harm the latter. The meeting took place, but the father promptly murdered his son.[20] In a later civil war between Sultan 'Abd al Raḥmān and his nephew, Isḥāq, several fuqarā', including Mālik b. 'Ali al Futūwī, tried to intervene. They were not only unsuccessful, but actually incurred the Sultan's hostility.[21]

A more successful example of intervention by the fuqarā' occurred at Bāra in 1200/1785–6. The great Sultan, Tayrāb, died on campaign at Bāra, leaving the Dār Fūr army far from home and without a Sultan. Despite protracted intrigues, none of the Keira contenders for the supreme position could seize power. With the power struggle deadlocked, the notables invited the fuqarā' to mediate. The fuqarā' went to the Keira princes and asked them to choose one of their number as Sultan. After further negotiation, the Keira princes chose 'Abd al Raḥmān and the holy men then made the princes swear on the Quran to accept the choice.[22]

By the nineteenth century, with the increasing centralization of power in the hands of the Sultan and his officials at the capital, al Fāshir, the old style of succession disputes, which were decided on the battle field, gave way to palace intrigues. The holy men appear to have lost something of their religious prestige and were now to be found as officials of the state and as individuals were often involved in palace coups. In part this was a reflection of their increasing integration into the Dār Fūr ruling class. Some fuqarā' acquired land and power because of their position as tutors to the Sultan's children; a fakī Muḥammad, a cripple and a noted scholar, was appointed by 'Abd al Raḥmān as tutor to his children and rewarded with estates.[23] 'Abd al Raḥmān himself grew up with Mālik al Fūtūwī at Kerio and seems to have been regarded as a fakī before he became Sultan.[24] Some holy men began to marry into the royal family; Shaykh Jāmūs of the Bornu community of Manawāshī in south-eastern Dār Fūr married a daughter of Tayrāb and was later suspected by 'Abd al Raḥmān of intriguing on behalf of Tayrāb's surviving sons. It is said that the Sultan tried to have Jāmūs murdered, but the plot misfired.[25]

As the holy men and their families proliferated in the later Sultanate, they began to acquire secular positions of power. Thus two brothers from Baqirmi, Muḥammad Tamr and Ḥammād, settled among the Berti tribe in northern Dār Fūr on their way back from pilgrimage. A son of Ḥammād, Mūsā Warāk, was appointed qāḍī by Sultan Tayrāb and today three of the leading Berti chiefly families trace their descent from the brothers.[26] Mālik had many sons; one became *shartai* or chief of the Kerio region, while another, Muḥammad Salāma, with the court title of wazīr became secretary to Sultan Muḥammad al Ḥusayn, who gave him an estate in Dār Mīma in eastern Dār Fūr. This was probably a reward for the crucial part Salāma had played in ensuring the succession of Muḥammad al Ḥusayn.[27] The Sultan was himself perhaps the most pious of the Keira rulers and invited many holy men to his court, like the unfortunate Muḥammad al Bulālāwī.

The Judicial Role of the Holy Men

In the states of the eastern Sudanic region, Wadai, Dār Fūr and the Sinnār Sultanate, little attempt was made by the rulers to create a Muslim judicial hierarchy. Holy men were occasionally appointed as judges, but there appears to have been no continuity in the appointments. The influence, political or judicial, of a fakī derived from his personal prestige and not from any position in a formal hierarchy. In a multi-tribal state like Dār Fūr, which contained both Arabs and non-Arabs, nomads and cultivators, sophisticated traders from North Africa and Egypt and semi-pagan Fur, the needs of the Sultan were best served by a flexible system, which recognized both local custom and the central authority.

The English traveller, W. G. Browne, who visited Dār Fūr in the reign of ‘Abd al Raḥmān, commented on the dominating position of the Sultan in judicial matters,

> The monarch indeed can do nothing contrary to the Koran, but he may do more than the laws established therein will authorize, and as there is no council to control or even to assist him, his power may well be termed despotic. He speaks in public of the soil as his personal property, and of the people as little else than his slaves.

and,

> When manifest injustice appears in his [i.e. the Sultan's] decisions, the Fukkara or ecclesiastics express their sentiments with some boldness, but their opposition is without any appropriate object and consequently its effects are inconsiderable.[28]

Thus although both Tayrāb and ‘Abd al Raḥmān appointed qāḍīs, their judicial function seem to have been limited to advising the Sultan on the Islamic law. In fact throughout the history of the Sultanate, judicial authority was kept firmly in the hands of the Sultan and the senior tribal and court chiefs. Serious cases such as homicide, whether deliberate or accidental, large-scale theft, inter-tribal disputes and occasionally adultery were tried before the Sultan or the senior chiefs. The death penalty was confined to the Sultans, although it appears that in the nineteenth century provincial commissioners, called maqdūms, were also able to impose the death sentence.

It seems, however, that at least ‘Abd al Raḥmān had some sort of panel of judicial assessors recruited from the fuqarā’ to advise him, although it is not clear whether all the members of the panel had the title qāḍī. The names of the leading members of the panel or committee are already familiar; they included Mālik al Fūtūwī, Shaykh Jāmūs and ‘Izz al Dīn, whom Muḥammad al Tūnisī described as the head qāḍī in Dār Fūr.[29] But it seems that the final decision always rested with the Sultan although he would generally follow their rulings on points of Islamic law.

NOTES

1 This paper is based upon research for my Ph.D., ‘The Growth and Development of the Keira Sultanate of Dār Fūr’, for the University of London, 1971. I must gratefully acknowledge grants from the Central Research Fund, University of London, and from the Research Committee, University of Khartoum, towards the cost of two trips in Dār Fūr, April to July 1969 and 1970.

2 See H. G. Balfour Paul, 1956, 8–14.

3 J. Greenberg, 1961.

4 Wad Dayfallāh, 1930.

5 J. S. Trimingham, 1959, 46, and I. M. Lewis, ed., 1966, 4–6.

6 A. J. Arkell, Papers.
7 M. A. MacMichael, 1926, 75–7.
8 A. R. C. Bolton, 1934, 229–41.
9 Interview, Taqī al Dīn, al Fāshir, 14.6.1970; al Tūnisī (el-Tounsy), 1965, 117; 1845, 108.
10 Interview, Taqī al Dīn, al Fāshir, 9.5.1970.
11 G. Nachtigal, 1971.
12 Na'ūm Shuqayr, 1903; and interview, Ādam, Kerio, 18.6.1970.
13 Al Tūnisī, 1965, 67–9; 1845, 48–9.
14 R. S. O'Fahey, 1969, 66–74.
15 Al Tūnisī, 1965, 130, 324; 1845, 124, 350.
16 Al Tūnisī, 1965, 126–7; 1845, 118–19; this link between the family of 'Alī al Fūtūwī and the Fulani nomads still exists today.
17 A rather patronizing tone runs through al Tūnisī's works.
18 Shuqayr, 1903, 446, and al Tūnisī (el-Tounsy), 1850, 70–1.
19 Al Tūnisī, 1850, 199–206.
20 Nachtigal, 1971, 282–3.
21 Nachtigal, 1971, 291–3.
22 Al Tūnisī, 1965, 98; 1845, 84; and Shuqayr, 1903, 452–3.
23 Interview, Muḥammadayn, al Fāshir, 9.6.1970.
24 Al Tūnisī, 1965, 99–100; 1845, 88–9; and Shuqayr, 1903, 452.
25 Nachtigal, 1971, 293.
26 Arkell, Papers.
27 Nachtigal, 1971, 306, and interview, 'Abd al Ḥamīd, al Fāshir, 9.5.1970.
28 W. G. Browne, 1799; 1806, 276.
29 Al Tūnisī, 1965, 117; 1845, 108.

REFERENCES

A. J. Arkell. *Papers*, Library of the School of Oriental and African Studies, London.

A. R. C. Bolton, El-Menna Ismail: Fiki, *Sudan Notes and Records*, XVII, 1934, 229–41.

W. G. Browne, *Travels in Egypt, Syria and Africa*, London, 1799; 2nd ed., containing further material, London, 1806.

J. Greenberg, *The Languages of Africa*, The Hague, 1961.

I. M. Lewis, ed., *Islam in Tropical Africa*, London, 1966.

H. A. MacMichael, 'A note on the burial place of the Fur Sultans at Tura in Jebel Marra', *Sudan Notes and Records*, IX, 2, 1926.

G. Nachtigal, *Sahara and Sudan*, trans. A. G. B. and H. J. Fisher with R. S. O'Fahey, London, 1971.

R. S. O'Fahey, 'Al-Tūnisī's travels in Dār Fūr', *Bulletin of the Centre of Arabic Documentation*, Ibadan, V, 1 and 2, 1969, Interviews, 1970: Ādam Muḥam-Madmuḥam madayn, al Fāshir; Aḥmad Abbo Ādam, Kerio; Amīn 'Abd al Ḥamīd, al Fāshir; Muḥammad Layīn Taqī al Dīn, al Fāshir.

H. G. Balfour Paul, *History and Antiquities of Darfur,* Khartoum, 1956.

Na'ūm Shuqayr, *Ta'rīkh al Sūdān al qadīm*, Cairo, 1903, 3 vols. in 1, reprinted Beirut, 1967.

J. S. Trimingham, *Islam in West Africa*, Oxford, 1959.

Al Tūnisī (el-Tounsy), *Tashḥīdh al adhhān bi sīrat bilād al 'Arab wa 'l Sūdān*, ed. Mus'ad, 'Asākir and Ziyāda, Cairo, 1965; trans. Perron, *Voyage au Darfour*, Paris, 1845; *Voyage au Ouaday*, Paris, 1950.

Wad Dayfallāh, *Kitāb al Ṭabaqāt*, ed. Ṣuddayq, Cairo, 1930.

V

The Development of Islam In Hausaland

Mervyn Hiskett

School of Oriental and African Studies
University of London

At the turn of the eighteenth and nineteenth centuries a revolutionary movement arose in Hausaland (now known as Northern Nigeria) that was to have a profound influence on the subsequent history of the area. At its centre was a man who bore the Hausa name Shehu Usuman dan Fodio – the Shaykh 'Uthmān, son of Fodio. The movement that he led, and the successful jihād or holy war that he fought to reform Islam in Hausaland, brought about important changes in this part of Africa. This paper is about the history that led up to his movement; and the effects that it had on the subsequent development of Hausa society.

1. *The Early History of Hausaland*

The Hausas are not a tribal group, but a community of people of various ethnic origins who speak a common language – Hausa. They emerged as a result of immigration from the North into the western Sudan, probably in the tenth century A.D., although the sources, of which the most important is the 'Kano Chronicle' (H. R. Palmer, *Sudanese Memoirs*, Vol. III, Lagos, 1928), may be chronologically unreliable. These immigrants mixed with the indigenous inhabitants and, after the lapse of several generations, established mastery over them. The society at the time the immigrants arrived was organized, as far as we know, in scattered village groups, on a clan basis, and not subject to any central authority. But the immigrants built walled towns and set up city states that controlled the surrounding countryside and thus acquired territorial boundaries.

By the fifteenth century, Hausaland was under Bornu, allegedly an Islamic state since A.D. 1085. By the sixteenth century a homogeneous people was in being, with a common language; and it is probably early in this century that they acquired the ethnic label 'Hausa'. By now the seven original states of Hausa legend – Daura, Kano, Rano

Katsina, Zazzau, Gobir and Garun Gabas – were associated with seven others – Kebbi, Zamfara, Nupe, Gwari, Yauri, Yoruba and Kwararafa; and the Saharan empire of Songhay dominated the area. Later, in the seventeenth century, Bornu again became overlord of most of the Hausa or Habe states (the term Habe is Fulani and means 'non-Fulani', it is used conveniently to describe the dynasties ruling Hausaland before the Fulani conquest); but by the eighteenth century a number of independent kingdoms had emerged, each under the discrete and arbitrary rule of Habe chiefs, some of whom were nominally Muslims, but who did little more than extend patronage to Muslim scholars and traders in and around their courts. By the middle of the eighteenth century the extent of the Habe Kingdoms was broadly from the River Niger eastward to the River Jamaari; and from a point just south of the Saharan town of Agades southwards, down to the River Benue.

2. *The Establishment of Islam in Hausaland*

Islam may have penetrated into Hausaland as early as the fourteenth century, for there is some evidence of Islamic names in the king-lists of that time. But it was not until the end of the fifteenth century that an Islamic presence was firmly (and unmistakably) established. Traditionally, Islam is said to have been brought by a North African cleric, Muḥammad al Maghīlī (d. 1504). In fact, it is likely that it was the result of a more complex pattern of events made up of influences from Islamic Bornu, and the impact of North African, and later Egyptian, Islamic culture, brought in across the Sahara desert by the extending of the medieval desert trade routes down into sub-Saharan Africa.

But although Islam was unmistakably established by 1500, it was certainly not generally accepted. What seems to have happened is that individual Muslims from the peripheral areas of North Africa and Egypt – traders seeking gold and slaves, and scholars after the lucrative patronage of the courts – came into the Habe kingdoms and settled. They formed the nuclei of small Islamic communities that gradually began to affect the surrounding animist culture of the native people. The first stage was the nominal acceptance of Islam by some of the chiefs and courtiers; but this amounted to little more than the adoption of Islamic names in addition to indigenous titles, and participation in certain Islamic rites, for instance the annual sacrifices, and perhaps attendance at Friday mosque. This much identification with Islam was accepted as prestigious by the chiefs' still pagan subjects. But they were certainly not prepared to see their traditional cults wholly abandoned; and the chiefs were probably unable to accept Islam wholeheartedly, even if they had wished to do so. The result was that the two cultures existed side by side, and sometimes merged to produce what has been termed 'mixed' Islam – that is some Islamic practices carried on together with animist customs and rites.

As for the representatives of Islam, they began to widen their circles to draw in indigenous converts; and in this way coteries of native scholars grew up in certain urban centres of Hausaland – particularly Kano and Katsina. These scholars were, of course, literates in an otherwise preliterate society; and this gave them the status and the power of an élite. They functioned in such roles as court astrologers, religious teachers, scribes, Islamic rain-makers, military advisers, physicians, and so on; and, of course, their literacy was seen as evidence of superior magical powers, and the local leaders valued their presence at court for the prestige it brought. They themselves seem to have acquiesced quite readily in this comfortable situation. Only occasionally did one of them have enough courage to protest at the mixing of Islam with paganism; and while the careers of such activists were sometimes spectacular, their tangible achievements were few, although occasionally, as in the case of al Maghīlī, their writings became important sources of ideas for future generations. But usually they were content to follow a life of scholarship. They studied the books brought in across the Sahara, that their literacy made available to them; and then they began to write themselves. Soon they produced a corpus of local Islamic literature written in classical Arabic, from which it is clear that by the first half of the seventeenth century, the small Islamic communities were fully at home in the intellectual world of Islam; and therefore not so far removed from the ideas and attitudes of late medieval and renaissance Christendom, upon which so much of our own civilization is built. But, of course, in Hausaland, as in Europe at an equivalent stage of intellectual development, such scholarship was the preserve of a tiny minority, and its impact on the lives of ordinary people was slight. It did, nevertheless, have some significant consequences. The existence of literacy in Arabic in the Hausa-speaking areas meant that the themes of early Islamic history, the tales of the Prophet Muḥammad, and much of Middle Eastern folklore as it was recorded in Arabic sources, must have begun to circulate in oral form, far beyond the circle of those who were able to read Arabic books; and the results of this can be seen in the strong Islamic colouring in Hausa folktales. Also, it is likely that Islamic astrology and various forms of Islamic divination and fortune-telling were also sifted down to a popular level and began to influence the lives of the animist population as early as the seventeenth century, although the sources are insufficiently informative to prove this conclusively.

3. *The Beginnings of an Islamic Reform Movement*

The generally passive attitude of the Muslim literati changed slowly, but nevertheless perceptibly. For there began to emerge from among them individuals, by now deeply influenced by Islamic ideology and conditioned by Islam's literate culture and scholarly disciplines, for whom the surrounding pagan way of life became increasingly offensive. One of the earliest manifestations of their pious discontent occurred in Kano during the early seventeenth century, when two native Islamic theologians energetically disputed with each other as to whether the customs and behaviour of the nomadic Fulani were compatible with Islam. By the end of the eighteenth century the increasingly urgent tone of Islamic disapproval became apparent in a number of works in which scholars pointed accusing fingers at local un-Islamic customs and behaviour, and urged the adoption of Islamic alternatives. The kind of things they objected to were the idolatrous rites of animism – sacrifices and libations to various objects of worship, – failure to observe the Islamic food prohibitions, and the prohibited degree of marriage, and the survival of inheritance through the female line, in defiance of Islamic law, which prescribes inheritance through the male line. They also frequently expressed puritanical disgust at the bawdy popular song of the Hausas, and their addiction to dance and traditional music; while the bombastic formal praise-singing of the Habe courts struck these ardent monotheists as both idolatrous (because according to the strict teaching of Islam, only God and the Prophet Muḥammad are worthy of praise) and vainglorious. By the late eighteenth century a certain Shaykh Jibrīl ibn 'Umar, a scholar noted for his zeal and the rigour of his doctrines, had this to say:

> As for what comes after, know that one who considers the people in the Sudan, nay, one who takes note,
> Will see nothing from them except him who claims Islam with an ample mouth,
> Covering himself by fasting and prayers against his being accused of most foul sins,
>
> One who is pleased with the judgments of paganism which God has removed by imposing the Sharīa,
>
> Thus abandoning the Sharī'a, and nakedness with women, and mingling with them is the same,
> And depriving the orphan, and having more than four wives is similar to it,
>
> And also altering the laws without an interpretation from the chief men,

Thus also following [the opinions of] the ancestors in paganism, without concealment,

And thus adultery and drinking wine, and manslaughter, and the selling of freemen . . .

Such mounting dissatisfaction with life as it was in the Habe kingdoms, as contrasted with the Islamic ideal, can be seen, in retrospect, to have ushered in the movement of the Fulani reformer, Shehu Usuman dan Fodio and his associates, who were among the most able and articulate of the dissenting intellectuals.

To sum up so far: the indigenous way of life of the pre-Islamic Hausas continued for several centuries, side by side with the exotic culture of Islam and often mixing with it; but gradually the Muslims, who were an *élite* in a preliterate society, became dissatisfied; and by the eighteenth century this began to show itself in the gathering volume of their protest.

4. *The Fulani Holy War*

The Shehu Usuman dan Fodio, a member of the Fulani clan of the Toronkawa that had been domiciled in Hausaland since the fifteenth century, was born in 1754; and he spent his youth and early manhood in the kingdom of Gobir, acquiring the education traditionally given to the young in any scholarly Muslim household. He studied Islamic law, theology and mysticism, as well as Arabic grammar and literature; and it is clear from his own writings that his studies left him with a strong commitment to the Islamic ideal of an ordered and hierarchical society, regulated according to the written legal code of of the Sharī'a (Islamic code of law) and conforming in its government and administration to the constitutional theories evolved by the medieval Islamic jurists. This ideal he contrasted with the daily life around him; and from his conclusions his reforming attitudes arose.

He spent many years as an itinerant missionary and teacher in the Habe kingdoms of Gobir, Zamfara and Kebbi. And his powers of persuasion, combined with certain political and economic factors favourable to change (important among them probably, an increase in slave-raiding and slave-dealing in the recent past) won him widely-based support. In addition to his powers as a preacher, he had considerable skill as a political manipulator; and his missionary activities were combined with the cultivating of alliances that later proved useful to him.

It seems that he did not deliberately seek armed revolt against the Habe. He made several attempts to win successive sultans of Gobir to his side, and they responded to some extent. But in the end it became clear that the new expansionist power of Islam could not go on accepting the parallel existence of the indigenous animist cult; while from the Habe point of view it became obvious that to go on tolerating the reformers' activities was too damaging to traditional authority. War finally broke out in 1804, as a result of a train of events that neither side intended; but, given the irreconcilable nature of the conflicting interests, it was well-nigh inevitable.

The Muslims, naturally, saw the war as a jihād, or Holy War, against infidels. To the Habe it started as a punitive expedition against rebels. At first the Muslims were on the defensive, but several spectacular victories enabled them to go over to the attack. The early battles were fought in the cockpit of Kebbi and Zamfara; and the campaign hinged on the Muslims' attempts to take the walled towns, particularly the capital city of Alkalawa, the heart of the Gobir enemy. Although probably superior to the Gobir forces, and their Berber allies, in morale and possible also in military techniques, the Muslims had no decisive edge; and the outcome remained open until *c.* 1808, when Alkalawa eventually fell. The Muslims then launched a series of offensives that were obviously expansionist, and that led to the subjugation of almost all the former Habe states, which were then formed into the new Fulani empire, with its centre at Sokoto. From Sokoto the descendants of the Shehu ruled what had been the kingdoms of Gobir and Zamfara, while the other Habe kingdoms were given to subordinate commanders, or emirs, who had a loose feudal relationship with Sokoto. In so far as it was practicable to do so, the Fulani reformers created a political structure that conformed to the classical Islamic pattern of an 'imamate', or 'caliphate', a theocratic feudal structure that rested on the central authority of a caliph governing according to the Sharī'a, and was believed to conform to the precepts of divine revelation.

5. *The Result of the Fulani Conquest*

The question whether and to what extent the Fulani reformers succeeded in realizing their aims has been the subject of some scholarly argument (for instance, M. G. Smith and J. Spencer Trimingham have argued against their success). It probably defies a clear-cut answer, since the criteria and values differ, even among contemporary historians. But it seems most useful to attempt an assessment according to the framework of reference that the reformers set up for themselves, not according to extraneous standards.

It was clearly the Shehu's view that an orthodox and politically unified Islamic society was more pleasing to God than the religiously ambivalent and politically fragmented one that had existed under the Habe. There is no doubt that the Fulani jihād created the central caliphate described above; and that it did away with the old particularist structures of the Habe. Although the Sokoto caliphate subsequently declined in power and authority, it was still substantially intact a century later, when it was finally submerged in the colonial occupation. Thus one major aim of the reformers had certainly been realized.

As far as is known, the Habe ruled by local custom and their own whims; and not by any universal and generally recognized legal code. The reformers imposed the Islamic Sharī'a throughout the whole of the conquered territories. Of course it did not work perfectly. But at the time of the British occupation, the Sharī'a was the form of 'native law and custom' operating in the Fulani domains; and was accepted and retained as such by the British administration. Indeed, it is still the basis of the Northern Nigerian legal system today. Once again, this was a tangible achievement.

One characteristic of the reform movement was the way the leaders used vernacular poetry as religious propaganda, circulating it in manuscripts among their supporters in the surrounding Habe kingdoms; and later throughout their empire. They thus created a written vernacular literature where, as far as is known, none had previously existed. The result was that Islamic teachings and ways of life became more widely disseminated among the Hausa-speaking people than was possible before the jihād, when literacy was confined to Arabic; and as the vernacular literature spread, so did the awareness of an Islamic identity.

6. *The Colonial Occupation*

The results of the British occupation were complex. Initially, of course, such actions as the curtailment of slavery and the introduction of new ideas and material goods, were a set-back to the traditional Islamic way of life. But in the long run the more stable conditions created by the colonial administration, the improvement in communications, the growth of urbanization and so on, assisted the spread of Islam; while the colonial administration also protected and preserved the Islamic hierarchy through its policy of 'Indirect Rule' when that hierarchy might otherwise have collapsed under the pressures of social and political change. Whereas the result of European occupation elsewhere in West Africa was usually to stimulate African nationalism, in Northern Nigeria the more common reaction was to turn to Pan-Islamism; and where Southern, Christian, Nigerians tended to look for inspiration to personalities such as Kwame Nkrumah, Northern Nigerian Muslims were fascinated by the examples of the Republic of the Sudan, Saudi Arabia, Pakistan and, to a lesser extent, Egypt. Certainly the less than half-hearted commitment of a conservative Muslim population in Northern Nigeria, and of their traditional rulers, to the nationalist ideals and aspirations of Southern Nigerians, was one important factor in the complex pattern of causes that led to the recent civil war.

To sum up: Islam in Northern Nigeria can be seen to have brought both advantages and disadvantages for the society that adopted it. For instance, it created cultural homogeneity that, to a large extent, overcame the fissiparous forces of tribalism; and it left a political, legal and intellectual heritage that was valuable. It also created literacy; although the advantages of this were largely destroyed by the imposition of a different form of literacy during the colonial period.

On the other hand, Islamic conservatism was sometimes an obstacle to what is conventionally called 'progress' in such matters as education, health, legal reform; while a strong sense of Islamic identity now makes it difficult for the Muslim North to live in harmonious relationship with other, powerful, non-Muslim groups in the Federation.

VI

Some Aspects of Islam in the Southern Sudan during the Turkiya

Richard Gray

School of Oriental and African Studies
University of London

One of the major consequences of Muḥammad 'Al'īs conquest of the Funj kingdom in 1820 was to open the White Nile to sailing craft. By 1841 his expeditions had penetrated a thousand miles south of Khartoum, and a vast area, hitherto almost completely isolated, was suddenly exposed to the forces of the outside world. There are at least three ways of examining the subsequent contact with the peoples of the south. From a liberal, humanitarian, imperialist, western viewpoint one can attempt to analyse the causes of a failure: repeatedly the hopes of harnessing the south to commercial profits, Christian evangelism or a harmonious and peaceful 'development' have ended in apparent disaster. Alternatively one can focus attention on southern reactions, and discern, from the very earliest period of Shilluk confrontation with their northern Funj and Baggara neighbours until the present mass involvement of the last few years with the Anyanya, a theme of stubborn, proud resistance to alien rule and influences.[1] Or thirdly one can view Muḥammad 'Alī's initiative as inaugurating a dramatic expansion of an Arabic–Islamic frontier which in the northern Sudan extended back to the arrival of Arab nomads from the seventh century onwards, and had been reinforced by the Pilgrimage to Mecca and the settlement of holy men from Egypt and the rest of the Muslim world. Historians of the southern Sudan have on the whole concentrated on the first of these major themes – the present writer being no exception – and their principal sources have been the records and observations of European – and to a much lesser extent 'Turkish' and Egyptian travellers and participants. These sources are patently insufficient if one wishes to study southern reactions or the theme of assimilation into the Islamic culture of the north; and adequate investigation of these themes demands the preservation and scrutiny of indigenous sources, particularly of the fast-fading memories and oral traditions in both north and south. This paper merely attempts to bring together some of the scattered references in European sources to the expansion of Islam in the south during the Turkiya.

Initial contact with the south was concentrated on two tribal areas, those of the Shilluk and the Bari. Previously Shilluk raiding parties with their canoes had been the most powerful riverain force on the White Nile.[2] At the end of the eighteenth century the Shilluk controlled the important river-crossing at Alays on the caravan route from Darfur to Sennar, and reports in Darfur indicated their attitude to Islam:

> When transporting Mohammedans across the ferry, they occasionally exhibit the importance which their situation gives them. After the Muslim has placed himself in the boat they will ask him: 'Who is the master of the river, Ullah or rubbani. . . ?' 'God is the master of it' (is the reply). 'No', answers the Shilluk, 'you must say that such a one (naming his chief) is the master of it, or you shall not pass'.[3]

Even after Muḥammad 'Alī's conquest, traders were massacred at this ferry, and Shilluk raids to the north of Alays continued as late as 1853, but already a more peaceful contact with Muslim traders was being established in the Shilluk heartland. The initiative came from Jellaba (petty traders) operating not from the river route but overland from Kordofan and Tegali, the small Muslim sultanate in the Nuba mountains. With the permission of the Shilluk *reth* (king) they came to trade in ivory and settled at Kaka, the northernmost Shilluk settlement. They were joined by Selim Baggara and by malcontents fleeing from Turco–Egyptian rule. Gradually their numbers increased until by 1860 seventeen of the twenty-one large groups of homesteads were inhabited exclusively by Arabs. Many of the Shilluk at Kaka began to wear cotton clothing, and a visiting boat in 1858 was met by Shilluk women bringing 'eggs and beautifully branded gourds for sale' and Arab women with 'merissa, cotton-cloth, harnesses, etc.,'[4] Yet the influence of this and other Arab settlements on the mass of the Shilluk seems to have been of minimal significance. The reth refused all contact with Turkish officials and traders from Khartoum, and an attentive Austrian observer thought that despite its many contacts with the Shilluk Islam was 'still unable to strike one root here'.[5] The old pattern of canoe raids to the north was, however, being reversed by the late 1850s: increasingly the Shilluk from around Kaka accompanied Baggara horsemen on raids against their Dinka neighbours. Some of these northern Shilluk openly expressed their desire to be 'emancipated from the tyranny of the *reth* and his counsellors' while by the rest of the Shilluk they were regarded as the slaves of the Arabs.[6] In September 1860 the *reth* reacted violently against this disruptive influence and expelled many northerners from Kaka, one of whom, Muḥammad Kahir, a Dongolawi trader, collected a flotilla of thirteen boats and sacked the *reth*'s capital in 1861.[7] The subsequent reaction of the Shilluk to Islam may well have been governed by their largely hostile contacts with the north during the rest of the century, but acculturation among the northernmost Shilluk and Dinka is a theme which might well repay careful investigation.[8]

Early contact with the Bari at the head of the navigable stretch of the White Nile was largely dominated by European merchants and missionaries. Here it was Christianity rather than Islam which failed to make an impression on the Southerners, and here the European traders pioneered the way for subsequent disaster. Islam, with its sanction of the slave trade, has often been blamed for the spread of hostility between north and south. This interpretation is due partly to the British humanitarians' preoccupation with the slave trade, and is based almost entirely upon the observations of three British explorers, Speke, Grant and Baker, who, arriving on the scene relatively late, witnessed scenes of large-scale violence and concluded that they were the result of slave trading. The evidence of earlier observers, however, reveals that the slave trade was not initially responsible. Instead the main factors producing a deadlock were the complete unpreparedness of the tribes to meet the demands of the ivory trade and the ruthless determination of the European traders to wrest a quick and easy profit. In the creation of this deadlock and hostility the attitude of the 'Turkish' officials and the Arab boat-crews was of secondary importance. Certainly it seems to have been one of rapacity and unmitigated contempt for the naked, savage 'abids' ('abīd), and the sharp division between Islam and the pagan world doubtless contributed to this attitude. The soldiers and boats' crews, who under the early Government expeditions were accustomed to capture or purchase the occasional woman or child, continued to do so under the European traders. By 1855 many of the boats which arrived in Khartoum carried from ten to thirty slaves who would fetch about £7 each. But this was a very slight number, for the Sudan counted its slaves in thousands, and the profits gained by the sale of these few slaves were completely dwarfed by those of the ivory trade at this period. During this first phase the demand for slaves was almost entirely confined within the traditional pattern of tribal life, the slaves often being purchased from a friendly tribe by whom they had been captured. The market for slaves was not, as yet, an exacerbating factor. It is also important to realize that not only Muslims held this attitude of ruthless contempt. A remark such as that of one of the 'Turkish' officials on the first exploratory expedition – 'it is necessary to sow terror; the route we follow will then be easier' – is closely paralleled by that of a Christian trader: 'beyond el-Eis (Alays) it is necessary to distrust all those who do not fear us'.[9]

The European traders attempted to break the deadlock with the Bari and other riverain tribes by establishing in the interior permanent trading settlements (*zeribas*) staffed with armed northern servants and soldiers. Henceforth the White Nile ivory trade became dependent on violence and brought the slave trade in its train. Yet in much of the area it was the European traders who were primarily responsible for this development. It was they who exploited tribal rivalry in order to capture cattle and slaves: cattle to reward friendly tribes for ivory and services received, slaves to repay their Arab soldiers and so to offset their heavily increased overhead expenses. The devastation produced by this system of divide and plunder was the dominant factor in subsequent relations with the peoples of the interior, leaving a legacy of suspicion and hatred towards any alien intruder. But around the settlements a new plural society also began to develop and from 1869 onwards these scattered, fragile nuclei of acculturation were taken over by the Khedive Ismā'īl and his administrators in Equatoria.

There was however one area where Muslim northerners were the sole pioneers, an area which later became of very great importance. To the south of Darfur in the midst of a sparsely populated wilderness a mixed Muslim population of 'Furanjs, Jallabas, Bornouse, Dajo, Nuba, etc.', worked the celebrated copper mines of Hofrat en Nahas. Most of the copper passed via Darfur into the network of Muslim trade (Barth found that a 'considerable supply' was imported annually into Kano), but some of it was traded to the pagan peoples to the south. Contact with these people was slight, but at the end of the eighteenth century the first European to reach Darfur learnt that small expeditions were penetrating into these lands via Hofrat en Nahas. Sometimes these expeditions were full-scale military raids whose profits in slaves were dependent on large-scale plunder, but usually they consisted of Jellaba who brought on donkeys a small supply of beads, copper, and blue Egyptian cottons, and traded them for ivory and slaves with the Kreish and northernmost Azande. Markets became established and their fame spread so that the first Egyptian expeditions up the White Nile and the Bahr el Jebel heard rumours of Muslim traders to the west, while a few years later a riverain Dinka told a European trader how he had travelled twenty days to the 'Korek' (Kreish) where he sold slaves and ivory to 'black and red' merchants who rode donkeys and camels. By 1853 some

Jellaba from Kordofan had pioneered a fresh overland route skirting the south-east boundary of Darfur and were reported to be carrying on 'a very good business through the import of cowries, cotton and beads'.[10] The activities of these Jellaba involved no direct large-scale subjugation of peoples, but, as in the Banū Shanqul, the Galla country and much of East Africa, the Arab trader was forced to pay the local chief a toll for every load of goods which he wished to pass through the territory. On this frontier Islam also advanced, and occasionally Muslim immigrants gained political advantages. One example is provided by the traditions of the ruling family of the Feroge, recorded by Father Santandrea in 1946. They claim to be descended from Feroge, a Bornu pilgrim returning from Mecca, who settled 'to preach Islam' at the court of Chief Akpi, ruler of the small Kaligi tribal settlements at Jebel Ere and Jebel Tambili, about eighty-five miles east of Hofrat en Nahas. 'Surrounded by a halo of holiness and learning, (Feroge) soon gained great ascendancy over commoners and favour with their ruler, who gave him his daughter Zahra in marriage', and on Akpi's death, Feroge succeeded him with the support and protection of the Sultan of Darfur'.[11] Later this group moved southwards conquering other minor units, but political victories of this sort were rare and on a very small scale, for on the whole power remained firmly in the hands of local rulers in this early period of Muslim penetration.

This equilibrium was rudely disturbed when the Khartoum traders discovered a passage up the Bahr el Ghazal and established *zeribas* near its headwaters. By 1862 their expeditions had reached what was probably the Mbomu river, and with the force which was at their disposal these traders rapidly subdued the chiefs who had been previously able to tax the Jellaba. In 1870, for instance, Schweinfurth found the Gudyoo previously a Kreish chief 'and a great patron of the slave traders had now settled down as an ordinary sheik' under the sovereignty of one of the traders. Under the security of the *zeriba* system itinerant Jellaba were able to travel freely throughout the area of the Bahr el Ghazal. 2,700 arrived in 1870 and it was estimated that a further 2,000 were permanent residents in the *zeribas*. Schweinfurth's encounter in a *zeriba* with 'a speculative slave trader from Tunis who was now making a second journey over Darfoor' was but a striking example of the extent of the network of overland Muslim trade. Most of these men invested their puny capital in a bullock or donkey purchased in Kordofan or Darfur which they loaded with cotton-cloth, cheap Belgian firearms and other goods needed by the Arabs in the *zeribas*. When they arrived in the Bahr el Ghazal they sold the animal and their goods for four or five slaves, whom they marched north across the deserts, making a comfortable profit provided that the slaves survived the horrors of this march. Others acting as the agents of wealthy Kordofan and Darfur slave-traders, settled in the *zeribas* where they acted as Fakirs and collected hundreds of slaves for their employers, so that this overland route exported about 12–15,000 slaves per annum and completely dwarfed the slave trade on the White Nile with its total of 2,000 in the peak years.[12]

The history of the violence of chaos connected with the ivory and slave trades is the principal explanation of the insignificant religious impact of Islam. The area of peaceful contact with the peoples of the Southern Sudan was pitifully minute. Within the immediate circle of the traders' *zeribas* and the Government's stations, however, a slow yet steady process of acculturation seems to have taken place. Unfortunately, in the Dar Fertit area of the Bahr el Ghazal, where this process seems to have been most advanced, documentary records are almost non-existent. In 1879–1881 Gessi, under the command of Gordon, attempted to establish an ordered rule in this area. He found the smaller tribes, including the Kreish, who originally had been on terms of equality with the Jellaba, gathered in broken groups around the *zeribas*. They were adaptable agriculturists and he found that they were willing, unlike most unbroken tribes, to collect rubber and cultivate cotton. Together with numerous slaves abandoned by the Arabs these people had developed a keen desire for cotton clothing, and most of them appear to have become permanent adherents to Islam.

In the riverain arca of the Bahr el Jabal, around the government stations, there developed, as Gordon put it, 'a semi-native semi-arab by contact population of lads and women' who came to work for the soldiers, and who, finding the station 'much more amusing than their native houses', refused to be repatriated. He encountered an example of a whole village, many of whose inhabitants were Arabic-speaking, moving into the neighbourhood of a station, and as he watched the inevitable string of Acholi, Bari or Madi wives who everywhere accompanied the soldiers, he became convinced that 'no nation could uproot Egypt from these lands even if they possessed them. Arabic must be the language of these countries'.[13] Emin also found many strong links between the stations and the neighbouring African village or tribal section, and on his tours of inspection he met several semi-Arabicized chiefs. One of them, an Acholi, seemed to Emin to be 'a thorough Dongolaui in appearance and manners, dresses exactly as they do, sits on an Anqareb and regales his guests with coffee', and in another district Emin reported that 'at every hamlet we passed the chief came to greet us generally dressed in a long coloured shirt and a tarbush'.[14] Since the Acholi shared the common Nilotic scorn for clothing of any kind, this was impressive evidence of the assimilation of Islamic material culture. It is much harder to assess the extent to which the Islamic religious belief and practice was gaining ground amongst southerners. Emin Pasha once remarked that 'during more than twenty years' rule, Islam has scarcely made ten proselytes in the whole of our provinces'.[15] Emin himself followed the practice of Islam while he was in Equatoria, and was a scrupulously careful recorder of conditions and events, so on the face of it this might seem to be a fairly conclusive piece of evidence. Certainly it demonstrates the narrow limits of Islamic impact, yet this comment was written after a disheartening tour of the Rohl district which might well have led him to underestimate the spread of Islam in the south, and it is of course difficult to know exactly what he meant by 'proselytes'. The only concrete piece of evidence that his diary provides is the fact that at the feast of 'Id al Ṣaghīr in 1881 'all the chiefs of the neighbourhood' were present at the government station at Lado,[16] though whether their motive for attending was religious, political or merely hedonistic is of course difficult to say.

I doubt whether much progress could be made in studying this Islamic frontier until detailed research is carried out, especially for the Dar Fertit area, using two other kinds of evidence. The first would be the reports of British administrators and Christian missionaries in the first years of the twentieth century, though just how much of the detailed local reports survive I do not know, and the other, and more important, would be indigenous oral traditions which are of course rapidly disappearing, especially under present conditions.

NOTES

1 I have elaborated this point in the *Journal of Contemporary History*, I, 1971, 108–20.
2 For a re-assessment of early Shilluk history, see P. Mercer, 1971.
3 W. G. Browne, 1799, 560, quoted in Mercer, *loc. cit.*
4 Fr. Kirchner, 30.1.1858–25.4.1858.
5 M. Th. von Heuglin, 1869, 94.
6 G. Beltrame, 1881, 86.
7 R. Gray, 1961, 76–7.
8 Mr. J. W. Frost of the University of California, Santa Barbara, is currently engaged on a study of the Shilluk.
9 Quoted in Gray, 1961, 17.
10 Ibid., 65–6.
11 S. Santandrea, 1964, 146.
12 Gray, 1961, 67–8.
13 Ibid., 113.
14 Ibid., 142–3.
15 G. Schweinfurth, ed., 1888, 414.
16 F. Stuhlmann, ed., II, 1919, 229.

REFERENCES

G. Beltrame, *Il fiume bianco e i Denka*, Verona, 1881.
W. G. Browne, *Travels in Egypt, Syria and Africa*, London, 1799.
R. Gray, *A History of the Southern Sudan*, London, 1961.
M. Th. von Heuglin, *Reise in das Gebiet des Weissen Nil*, Leipzig, 1869.
Fr. Kirchner, *Diary*, 1858, Verona Fathers archives.
P. Mercer, 'Shilluk Trade and Politics from the Mid-Seventeenth Century to 1861,' *Journal of African History*, XII, 3, 1971.
S. Santandrea, *A Tribal History of the Western Bahr el Ghazal*, Bologna, 1964.
G. Schweinfurth, ed., *Emin Pasha in Central Africa*, London, 1888.
F. Stuhlmann, ed., *Die Tagebücher von Dr. Emin Pascha*, II, Hamburg, 1919.

VII

Modernization: Islamic Law

J. N. D. Anderson

Institute of Advanced Legal Studios, London

in consultation with N. J. Coulson

School of Oriental and African Studies
University of London

However strong an impetus for change in the traditional family law of Islam may derive from the circumstances of modern life, in the contemplation of Islamic jurisprudence social need or desirability does not *per se* provide any adequate justification for legal reform. In so far as Sharī'a law is regarded as the expression of divinely ordained, and therefore eternally valid and immutable, standards of conduct, it is for the law to prescribe and determine social progress and not for social progress to mould and fashion the law. The Sharī'a, according to Islamic philosophy, does not grow out of society but is imposed upon society from above. Where, therefore, there arises in fact in modern times a social situation which makes a change in the law desirable, such a change will represent a legitimate expression of Sharī'a law only if it can be shown to be in conformity with the accepted dictates of the revealed will of Allāh; in other words if it rests upon a juristic basis which does not contradict the fundamental Islamic ideology of the divine law.

It is clear, therefore, that the scope for legal reform, however great the social impetus for such action, depends basically upon the extent to which the terms of the traditional law are deemed to constitute binding and irrevocable expressions of the divine will. From medieval times until the middle of the present century, the general view was that the legal manuals authoritative in each school, and dating from the medieval period, constituted a final and perfect expression of Sharī'a law; in sum, that each and every rule of law recorded therein must be treated as a divine ordinance. This view went under the name of the doctrine of taqlīd (lit. 'imitation'), by which judges and jurists alike were bound to adhere to the law as expounded in the medieval manuals. Any deviation from this was regarded, in strict theory, as taking impermissible liberties with the divine law and therefore inadmissible.

It was the apparently insuperable restrictions of the doctrine of taqlīd which caused the Turkish government of the 1920s to abandon the Sharī'a entirely and adopt in its place Western codes as the only practicable means of achieving reform in the family law. But such a total break with Islamic tradition, at least in the sphere of family relationships – to which area, in fact, Sharī'a law had been more and more confined during the course of several decades – proved unacceptable to the other Muslim countries of the Middle East and North Africa. Here ways and means were found to mould and adapt the Sharī'a law, as applied through the courts, to the changing circumstances of society.

As long as jurisprudential thought was dominated by the doctrine of taqlīd, the only acceptable juristic basis for reform lay in the principle of siyāsa (lit. 'governmental administration'). According to the traditionally authoritative treatises on Islamic public law, this meant that the political executive, while it certainly had no legislative power as such, nevertheless had the power to make administrative regulations to effect the proper application of Sharī'a law through the courts. As interpreted by the modern reformers, this doctrine of siyāsa enabled the political sovereign to issue directives to his courts designed to achieve one of two principal purposes. First, he might restrict the jurisdiction of his courts by denying them the competence to entertain cases which did not meet prescribed evidential – or other – requirements. The courts might thus, for example, be precluded from hearing claims which were not supported by documentary evidence. Secondly, the sovereign could define the jurisdiction of his courts in the sense that he could direct them to apply one particular doctrine, in any case of divergence among the traditional authorities, to the exclusion of every variant.

Naturally enough, the view which would be chosen from among the traditional authorities for application by the courts would be that variant deemed best suited to contemporary social needs. This principle of selection can, no doubt, be justified on the ground that the various doctrines of the different Sunnī schools are regarded as equally authoritative expressions of Sharī'a law, but it was developed by the modern reformers to an extent which was certainly never visualized by traditional jurisprudence. For the reformers very soon ceased to limit their choice to authoritative variants within the school traditionally applicable in the area concerned or to the dominant doctrine of another Sunnī school. Instead, they sometimes selected opinions which could claim only the tenuous authority of some individual jurist of bygone days and which had traditionally been regarded as invalidated by the general consensus of opinion. In a few cases, moreover, the only authority which could be adduced for the view selected lay outside the corpus of Sunnī doctrine altogether, and had to be sought in the law of one of the sectarian schools, particularly the Shī'a. Finally, by a process termed talfīq, or 'patching', elements from the views of different schools and jurists were combined to form a composite legal rule which was, in fact, wholly new, although its component parts could each claim the most respectable lineage. It should, moreover, be noted that the various opinions thus combined not infrequently rested on diametrically contrary legal arguments!

But even when pursued to these extremes, the doctrine of siyāsa provided only a limited potential for reform, and over the last two decades the doctrine of taqlīd itself has been ever more openly challenged. Support has grown for the view that the authority of the doctrine expounded in the medieval legal manuals is not absolute and infallible. Jurists of today, of course, commonly admit to being bound by the dictates of the Quran and the sunna just as their predecessors were; but they claim not to be bound by the interpretations which their predecessors placed upon those dictates. On the contrary, they assert the right of ijtihād, or 'independent interpretation' of the ancient texts in the light of contemporary social circumstances. It is on this basis that the most striking reforms of the traditional law have been effected. In practice, moreover, this modern ijtihād means not only that a proposed reform may be justified by a fresh interpretation of a specific text of the Quran or the sunna, but also that a novel rule may be considered a legitimate expression of Allāh's law because it is not *contrary* to any specific text – on the grounds that the authoritative texts themselves adjure Muslims to obey those who have been set in authority over them. It may be that this modern ijtihād is a highly subjective process, inasmuch as it is frequently used to justify a legal rule first conceived by the reformers on straightforward grounds of social need; but this is in fact to say little more than that the jurists of today are proceeding in the same way as did their predecessors in the early centuries of Islam.

We turn now to concrete examples of reforms in the law of family relations and succession which have been effected through these various juristic media in the Muslim countries of North Africa. Perhaps those which best illustrate the principles outlined above (and which will, at the same time, prove of most interest to non-lawyers) are the reforms which have been introduced in the field of divorce and polygamy. These two subjects are much less technical than the intricacies of the law of testate and intestate succession; but the reforms effected in this sphere also, in parts of North Africa, are of such intrinsic interest that they, too, demand at least a cursory treatment.

First, then, the law of divorce, for there can be little doubt that it is the traditional law on this subject which has proved the major bane, all down the centuries, of the structure, security and happiness of Muslim family life. Polygamy – in the accepted sense of a man being married to a plurality of wives at one and the same time – has grown increasingly rare, in recent years, in most parts of the Muslim world; but what might well be regarded as successive polygamy – i.e. the practice of marrying one wife, divorcing her, marrying another, and then repeating the whole process – has been distressingly common. The discarded wife not only suffers the emotional shock of rejection, but often considerable financial loss; she is deprived of the custody of her children, just when the bonds of affection between them may have become very strong; and she is apt to go steadily down in the social scale. The fear of this fate – which is, in most cases, an ever present possibility – not only undermines a wife's sense of security but may well serve to deepen her attachment to the family of her birth at the expense of the husband who may so easily discard her.

In those parts of North Africa in which the Ḥanafī law until recently prevailed, the wife was also faced with the fact that she could not herself obtain even a judicial dissolution of her marriage, however badly her husband treated her, unless she had been given in marriage before reaching the age of puberty – and then only if the marriage guardian concerned was other than her father or paternal grandfather – or if her husband proved entirely unable to consummate the marriage. But in Libya, Algeria, Morocco and (for the most part) in Tunisia, it has been the Mālikī law which has traditionally been applied, and this is much more liberal in this respect. Legislation enacted in Egypt in 1920 and 1929, moreover, has largely adopted Mālikī law in these matters; so the position today is that an ill-used wife can obtain a judicial divorce throughout a large part of the Muslim world if her husband fails to provide her with proper maintenance, treats her with cruelty, goes away and leaves her for an inordinate time, or proves on marriage to be afflicted, without her knowledge (or consent to the marriage notwithstanding), with some disease of body or mind which makes married life dangerous – or, indeed, if, in some cases, he develops such a disease subsequent to the marriage.

But a right to demand a judicial dissolution of marriage has also been given, in Morocco, to a wife whose husband marries another wife contrary to a stipulation to the contrary which she has had inserted in her marriage contract – or, even where no such stipulation has been inserted, if she can show that the second marriage has caused her injury. In the case of a stipulation, this reform represents the adoption of the Ḥanbalī doctrine, as against that of the other three Sunnī schools – which all regard the legal effects of marriage (including a husband's right to be married to as many as four women at the same time) as laid down by the divine Lawgiver, and not capable of limitation or adaptation at the whim of the parties. Here the Ḥanbalīs sensibly pointed out that, while the divine law might permit a man to indulge in polygamy, it certainly did not require him to do so; so in this matter, as in others, Muslims must be bound by their stipulations. But the second part of the provision (namely, that a woman who has not made any such stipulation can demand a judicial divorce if her husband's second marriage has caused her injury), this must be regarded as an enlargement or expansion of the normal scope of the Mālikī doctrine of divorce for cruelty.

In Tunisia, however, the reformers have gone much further than this, and have provided that a woman can obtain a judicial divorce, if she so insists, whatever the circumstances may be – with the solitary proviso that, if she so insists without such justification as the Code of Personal Status provides (which in practice simply means that her husband has failed to support her), then she must pay him such financial compensation as the court may decree. The only justification which can be found in Islamic law for this provision is a tradition that on one occasion Muḥammad, when confronted with a woman who demanded divorce on the grounds that she had conceived an aversion to her husband (but who admitted that he had not committed any 'matrimonial offence'), told her to refund her dower and then ordered her husband to give her what must be regarded as a compulsory khul' (i.e. divorce for a financial payment provided by the wife). In Algeria, again, a wife can now obtain a judicial divorce on the grounds of her husband's adultery.[1] This can, presumably, find its juristic justification either as an expansion of the scope of 'cruelty', or on the basis that, under the classical law, the husband would have been liable to execution.

But it has always been somewhat easier, in Islamic law, to grant rights of divorce to an ill-used wife than it has been to limit the traditional right of a Muslim husband to submit her to unilateral repudiation. In the dominant view of the Ḥanafī school even repudiations pronounced under compulsion, as a jest, in a state of intoxication, or as an oath or threat were alike regarded as effective. In recent years, legislation in all the countries concerned has greatly mitigated this extreme doctrine. But it is only in Tunisia and Algeria that a divorce pronounced outside a court of law has been deprived of any legal effect. In Tunisia a judicial divorce may, indeed, be demanded by the husband as of right, provided only that he is prepared to pay his wife the financial compensation which the court may decree; and the same seems to be true in Algeria if attempts to conciliate the parties have failed.[2] In Morocco, on the other hand, there is no legislation which decrees that the repudiation of a wife outside a court of law is devoid of legal effect, but there is a provision which makes it incumbent on a husband to give his divorced wife some financial compensation. This gives legislative effect to the Mālikī doctrine of what is termed mut'at al ṭalāq. Several provisions along these lines have also been proposed in Egypt, but none of these have yet been promulgated as law.

When we turn to the question of polygamy, we find that this has been restricted in Morocco and completely prohibited in Tunisia. In Morocco it is expressly provided that 'If any injustice is to be feared between co-wives, polygamy is not permitted' (which represents no no more than a statutory enactment of the explicit teaching of the Quran); that even a wife who has not insisted on any suitable stipulation in her contract of marriage may (as has already been noted), 'refer her case to the court', should her husband have married another wife, 'to consider any injury which may have been caused to her'; and that 'the contract of marriage with the second wife must not be concluded until she has been informed of the fact that her suitor is already married to another woman'.[3] But the Tunisian Code of 1957 went much further and explicitly forbade polygamy, in any circumstances whatever, under legal sanction. It is interesting in this context, moreover, to note that President Bourguiba, in commenting on this point, did not content himself with the usual reference to the 'Verse of Polygamy' in the Quran, with its explicit prohibition of polygamy if the husband has any fear that he may not treat a plurality of wives with equal justice (coupled, as is common today among reformers, with the assertion that such impartiality of treatment is beyond the capacity of any man other than a Prophet, so it is within the competence of the State to forbid a union which must inevitably prove sinful!). Instead, he also went so far as to say that there were certain human institutions, such as slavery and polygamy, which made sense at a certain stage in the development of society, but which were repugnant to the civilized conscience today. This is certainly a revolutionary doctrine; but the fact remains that this attitude has been adopted by one after another of the countries of the Muslim world in regard to slavery.

It is also noteworthy that the Code of 1957, while it explicitly forbade polygamy under penal sanctions, did not include any provision which stated that a marriage contracted in defiance of the law would be regarded as null and void. Indeed, the Code of Personal

Status, considered by itself, might well have been construed in the opposite sense; and this view was in fact put forward, when I first visited Tunisia a year or two later, by some of the leading Muslim jurists of the old school. Government officials, on the other hand, took the view that such a marriage would have no legal significance, on the grounds that the Civil Code expressly provides that any contract contrary to public policy is void; that marriage is always regarded in Islamic law as a contract; and that the explicit prohibition of a polygamous union provides clear proof that such a contract is contrary to public policy. This, too, was the unequivocal view of the President himself, as he told me personally. But, however this may be, the question has now been decisively solved by Decree of 24 February 1964, which explicitly states that a polygamous marriage is void of legal effect.

In the law of testate and intestate succession we must be still more selective and concentrate on two or three examples out of a comparatively wide field of choice. Thus one of the gravest weaknesses in the Islamic law of intestate succession has always been the fact that orphaned grandchildren are totally excluded from any share in a grandparent's estate if a son of the grandparent concerned also survives – on the basis of the traditional principle that 'the nearer in degree excludes the more remote'. But while this may have worked reasonably satisfactorily when the solidarity of the family was a basic feature of society (and an uncle could, perhaps, be trusted to take adequate care of his nephews or nieces), it is obvious that it may cause a lot of quite unnecessary hardship today. So first the Egyptian and then the Tunisian and Moroccan reformers (to confine our attention to North Africa) devised the ingenious expedient of what are called 'obligatory bequests', according to which it is incumbent on a grandparent, in such circumstances, to make a bequest in favour of such orphaned grandchildren as would otherwise be excluded from any share in his or her estate. This bequest (or these bequests) must represent what the deceased parent of these grandchildren would have received had he or she survived the grandparent, provided this does not exceed the 'bequeathable third'; it is to be suitably reduced if the grandparent had made a gift *inter vivos* to the grandchild or grandchildren concerned; it is to take priority over any voluntary bequests; and it is to be decreed by the courts even where the grandparent has in fact failed to make any such provision. In Egypt and Tunisia, moreover, these bequests are applicable in regard to the offspring of a predeceased son or daughter (indeed, in Egypt even in the case of a predeceased son's daughter), whereas in Morocco they are granted only to the children of a predeceased son. In the first case the argument is that the daughter (or son's daughter) concerned would herself have been entitled to inherit, had she survived, and that her estate would in due course have passed to her children; whereas, in the second, the argument prevails that the children of a daughter are normally on an entirely different footing, in the Sunnī law of succession, from that of the children of a son.

Another weakness in the ancient system, in terms of urban life today, is the prominence traditionally given in Sunnī law to the agnatic members of an 'extended family' (or 'tribal heirs') even at the expense of the much more immediate family of the deceased. Thus a daughter would, indeed, receive half her parent's estate, but the residue of the estate might well go to a distant agnatic cousin; and a daughter's children would be completely excluded by an agnate, however distant he might be. Where no agnate survived, moreover, even a Quranic sharer (such as a daughter) was never entitled, under the Mālikī doctrine, to take the rest of the estate under the doctrine of the radd or return, and the residue went, instead, to the Public Treasury. But an addition made in 1959 to the Tunisian Law of Personal Status not only gave Quranic sharers the right to the return in the absence of any agnatic heir, but provided that a daughter or son's daughter would exclude from this return even the closest agnatic collateral (such as a brother or, of course, a sister). This reform, for which there was no precedent whatever in Sunnī law (and only a very loose precedent in that of the Shī'īs) has effectively limited succession, in Tunisia, to the 'nuclear family' – in all cases in which any child or grandchild is a claimant.

It is also noteworthy that the Egyptian Law of Testamentary Bequests, 1946, has provided that the rule, previously applicable to all the Sunnī schools, that no bequest may be made in favour of one who is, in the circumstances, also entitled as an heir (unless, in the Ḥanafī and dominant Shāfi'ī doctrine, the other heirs consent to such bequest after the death of the testator), has been changed, and a testator may now make a bequest (without any such consent) to anyone, heir or non-heir, provided this does not exceed the bequeathable third. This represents an unacknowledged adoption of the doctrine of the Ithnā 'Asharī branch of the Shī'a. Exactly the same principle has also been given legislative effect in the Sudan. It can be used in favour of any heir (e.g. to make special provision for a son or daughter who is in particular need); but it is particularly noteworthy that it provides a ready means by which a man can make more suitable provision for his widow (whose share of one-eighth of his estate, in any case in which the deceased is survived by a child, is woefully inadequate – an eighth which must, moreover, be shared with any other surviving wife or wives). It is also noteworthy that the Tunisian provision which decrees that any Quranic sharer shall be entitled, in suitable circumstances, to the radd (or return) makes no exception – contrary to normal Sunnī practice – in the case of the spouse relict; so this, again, distinctly improves the position of a widowed wife.

Hitherto, in this paper, attention has been confined to matters of family law, in its widest connotation, since this is the only part of Islamic law which has been in force, as such, in most of these countries in recent years – although it is true that some of the provisions in the Civil Codes in Egypt and Libya, and many provisions in those which prevail in the Maghrib, are in fact of Islamic origin. Our attention has also been restricted almost completely to the countries of the extreme north of Africa – except, that is, for a very occasional reference to the Sudan (a country in which, it may be remarked, many of the reforms subsequently promulgated in Egypt were first put on trial, under the influence of a succession of Egyptian occupants of the office of Qāḍī 'l Quḍāt, and in which certain other Egyptian reforms have been adopted, almost *in toto*, subsequently to their promulgation in Egypt). But it may be of interest, in conclusion, to make a few remarks about an area just south of the Sahara where Islamic law was, until recently, of much more extensive application.

In those states which formerly constituted the Northern Region of Nigeria, some two-thirds of the population would claim to be Muslims. In what was often termed the 'Holy North' of that Region, moreover, Islamic law was for many years extensively enforced under Emirs who owed their position – and their orthodoxy – to the Hausa-Fulani Jihād, or Holy War. Over 90 per cent of all criminal cases were, in fact, handled in the 'native' courts, and this meant that, in the staunchly Muslim areas, both the substantive and the procedural law was almost entirely derived from the Mālikī books. Some fifteen of the leading Emirs, moreover, had the right to try even capital cases in their courts. As in other colonial territories, however, a considerable amount of English law, modified or expanded by local legislation, was also introduced. The result was that two quite separate systems of criminal law prevailed: the Nigerian Criminal Code (the provisions of which were derived from English law) in the High Court and the magistrates' courts; and the Islamic law, as locally interpreted, in the native courts (to say nothing of pagan customary law in areas where Islam had not penetrated).[4] This anomaly, naturally, led to many problems. But it was homicide cases which gave rise to the most acute of these, since there were wide differences between the circumstances in which a homicide constituted a capital offence under the two systems. Not only so, but even a deliberate homicide, according to the Mālikī system, gave the 'heirs of blood' the right (but never the duty) to claim talion only if the blood of the victim was equal in value to that of the killer – with the result that execution could never be claimed if the accused was a Muslim and his victim a non-Muslim (and only one-third of the blood money payable for a Muslim victim if the deceased was a Christian, and one-fifteenth – in many Provinces – if he was a pagan!). There was also a statutory penalty of one year's imprisonment. It should, however, be added that there were certain circumstances in which the death penalty was always applicable, whether or not the heirs of blood so desired; that some Emirs imposed heavier penalties in the interest of public order, as a matter of siyāsa (see above); and that the most serious abuses to which this system would otherwise have given rise were avoided, in Colonial days, by the right of British administrative officers to transfer cases from the native courts to the High Court – a right which they exercised fairly freely in suitable circumstances.

All the same, it was not surprising that the non-Muslims of the Region felt distinctly apprehensive on the threshold of independence, when British officers would be withdrawn and the Islamic law might, they feared, be even more extensively applied. It was in these circumstances that the Northern Nigerian Government was persuaded to send three Missions to Pakistan, the Sudan and Libya (three Muslim countries which had recently attained independence) to find out how they conducted their legal and judicial affairs; and then, subsequently, to appoint a Panel of Jurists (on which I was myself privileged to serve as the only European) to consider how conflicts between the 'received' English law, on the one hand, and the indigenous or Māliki law, on the other, could be avoided.

In the result the Panel recommended that the only practicable solution was for the Islamic criminal law, both substantive and procedural, to be abandoned in favour of a new Penal Code and Code of Criminal Procedure (which, we suggested, should be modelled on those of the Sudan, which had themselves followed the pattern previously set in India). To the great credit of the Northern Nigerian Government this recommendation (together with all but one of over thirty other recommendations) was promptly accepted in principle and subsequently promulgated. As a result the only relic of the Islamic criminal law in Northern Nigeria today may be found in provisions – which, it was insisted, must be inserted in the Penal Code – which make illicit sex relations a criminal offence if committed by those whose religious or customary law so regard them, and which also penalize the consumption of alcohol even in the most moderate quantity, by Muslims only, except for medical purposes. It is, perhaps, of some significance in this context that this last point has, it seems, given rise to the phenomenon that today young Muslims not infrequently, I am told, go into a bar and demand a 'Kola Penal Code' –

which, by interpretation, means a Coca-Cola laced with gin or some other hard drink the presence of which cannot easily be detected because of the colour of the Coca-Cola!

NOTES

1 Decree of 1959 issued under the *Personal Status Ordinance*, 1959, article 11.
2 Ibid., Article 21.
3 *Code of Personal Status and Inheritance*, 1958, article 30.
4 In point of fact indigenous customary law had interpenetrated the pure Islamic law, to some extent, even in the most rigidly Muslim areas.

VIII

North West Africa: Independence and Nationalism

Nevill Barbour

Before approaching the specific subject of this article, namely Independence and Nationalism in North West Africa, it is essential to form a clear picture of the precise area which we are discussing, and of its past history. For our purpose, North West Africa means the area lying west of the Egyptian frontier and that of the Sudan as far as the 20th parallel and in which the language of the majority of the people, and (with the exception of the Spanish Sahara, Ceuta and Melilla) of the government, is Arabic. For this reason it is also known by the Arabic name of 'the Maghrib', meaning 'the west'; this has the same implications as the English 'West Country', used to describe Devon and Cornwall, indicating not only their geographical position but also the different racial origin of the early inhabitants; these in the case of the Maghrib were Berbers. On the north, the area is limited for 1500 miles by the coast of the Mediterranean and on the south-west by 1200 miles of the Atlantic. The southern limit is harder to define, but roughly it coincides with the 20th parallel, north of which however the States of Chad, Niger and Mali extend somewhat, while Mauritania projects a whole 300 miles to the south of it. The latter thus includes in its inhabitants who total one million 200,000 persons whose mother tongues are specifically West African. On the west, moreover, an enclave is formed by the Spanish Sahara which adjoins the Atlantic Coast south-west of the Canary Islands. This desert area covers 100,000 square miles but contains only some 60,000 inhabitants, of whom half are nomads, present only in the rainy season. On the Mediterranean coast Spain possesses also the ports of Ceuta and Melilla which have for centuries been Spanish, and are inhabited overwhelmingly by Spaniards. Apart from these enclaves, the Maghrib is today divided into four independent states with Mediterranean coasts and one, Mauritania, which borders only on the Atlantic. On the west Morocco has an Atlantic as well as a

Mediterranean coast; its area is 166,000 square miles and its population something over 14 million. South of Morocco but now separated from it by the Spanish Sahara and western Algeria lies Mauritania, which stretches south to the Senegal river, covering 419,000 square miles with a population of about a million. Algeria lies to the east of Morocco, with a territory of 850,000 square miles, of which 7/8ths are desert, rich in oil and natural gas; its population is over 12 million. Tunisia follows with 48,000 square miles and a population of over 4,500,000. Finally to the east Libya has an area of 810,000 square miles, also mostly desert and even richer than Algeria in oil with a population of 1,500,000. The total area of the Maghrib is therefore 2,393,000 square miles with a population of 33,000,000, increasing annually by 3 per cent to 4½ per cent. In the four principal states the population is concentrated in the 100 miles adjoining the sea, while in Mauritania it is densest in the far south. In general the Maghrib is cut off from the rest of Africa by the Sahara more completely than it is from Europe by the sea, or from the Middle East by land; at one point Morocco is only eight miles from Spain, while Tunisia is only 90 miles from Sicily. Thus though belonging to the African continent the Maghrib can also be regarded as an extension of Europe to the south, or of the Middle East to the west. Thus, while it has never been occupied by the inhabitants of Western or Central Africa during historical times, it has on the contrary been dominated on a number of occasions by peoples from the Middle East or from Europe, while in the tenth century Egypt was occupied from Tunisia. The oldest identifiable inhabitants of North Africa in historical times appear to have been the Berbers. Their language, Tamazight, is classed as Hamitic and thought to be related to those spoken, or formerly spoken, in the Nile Valley, though we have no indication when or how they arrived from the Middle East. Early in the first millennium B.C. they were followed by Phoenicians from Tyre, speaking a language related to Canaanitish and Arabic. These established a state whose capital was Carthage and which exercised a cultural and political influence along the coasts of North West Africa as far as Mogador, and on the islands of the Mediterranean from Sicily to Cartagena and Cadiz, both of which are names of Phoenician origin. In 146 B.C. the Romans put an end to their political power, but their cultural influence persisted much longer. Roman and Byzantine rule, briefly interrupted by the Vandals in Tunisia, continued for some seven centuries till it was finally ended by the Arab conquest in the seventh century A.D. These new arrivals – the Arabs – unlike the Phoenicians and the Romans arrived by land, not by sea. They spread, therefore, along the principal lines of communication and made their capitals inland as at Qayrawān and

Fes or in sites protected from direct naval attack like Tunis behind its lagoon. Meanwhile, with each fresh conquest the definitely Berber population tended to be reduced to the mountains or further to the west. Thus today we find the Berber-speaking people occupying principally the Middle and High Atlas ranges in Morocco and the anti-Atlas farther south, as well as the Moroccan Rif, and the Algerian Kabyle mountains and the Aurès. Farther east there are a number of Berbers in Tunisia and Tripolitania while one group has actually survived within Egypt, at the oasis of Siwa. By 1086 nomad Berbers known as the Almoravids, who came from Mauritania, not only made themselves rulers of Morocco and the rest of North West Africa as far as Algiers, but also crossed the Straits of Gibraltar and with the Andalusian Muslims as their allies defeated the Castilian Christians in a decisive battle near Badajoz. Soon they replaced the Andalusian princes and ruled Muslim Spain themselves. Their power was however soon weakened by the attacks of another group of Berbers, not nomads, who came from the Atlas south of Marrakesh, the Almoravid capital; by 1150 they were replacing them as rulers of Muslim Spain as well as of North Africa, including Tunisia whose ports they freed from occupation, or at least from a protectorate, by the Sicilian Normans (1148–60) who were themselves largely Arabized in their way of life and their science. The Almohads as the Almoravids before them, though Berbers, were soon very strongly Arabized and though by 1248 they lost all power in al Andalus, where only Granada remained an independent Muslim state until 1492, their period of rule in North West Africa resulted in the widespread development of Arab culture, both by the employment of officials from al Andalus and by the vast numbers of refugees who left Spain before the advancing Christians of Castile and Aragon. In North West Africa itself Arabo-Berber domination remained fairly complete until the latter part of the fifteenth century, when Portugal occupied many Moroccan ports and Spain a little later most of the North African ports from the Moroccan frontier to Tripoli. The Moroccans however by 1541 succeeded by their own efforts in ending any significant Portuguese influence. In the eastern Maghrib Spanish influence was challenged and, after a struggle lasting until 1574, was more or less completely ended by the intervention of an eastern Muslim power, the Ottoman Turks. In this way the central and eastern portions of the Maghrib were converted into three Ottoman military dominions which came to be known as Regencies or the Barbary states. These were governed by Turkish-speaking people, soldiers or sailors, who were however very largely of European origin, coming from the Balkans, Hungary or even Venice, who were in general converts or the children of converts. It was thus that Algiers, being the first place which the Ottomans directly controlled in North West Africa, became a separate unit and the centre of Turkish power. It was formed by the absorption in the west of territory which was in general of Moroccan character and in the east by territory previously subject to the influence of Tunis, notably the Constantine, Bône, Bougie areas, while Tripolitania on the east was taken to form the Regency of Tripoli. The three Regencies derived their wealth largely from privateering (which was not the same as piracy),[1] as did Malta of the Knights which was founded by Charles V expressly as a counter to Algiers. With various modifications, such as increasing independence of Istanbul, this system lasted for three centuries, during which Europe grew steadily richer and more developed while North Africa stagnated and became weaker. By 1800 the practice of privateering and of enslaving Europeans began to seem intolerable to the European powers. The Barbary states themselves modified their practice, but deprived of their main source of revenue they were forced to impose heavier taxes on their Arab subjects which resulted in their steadily losing popularity. Tunis and Tripoli meanwhile acquired hereditary dynasties of Turkish origin, which faced similar difficulties. In 1830 the French government, which had long had designs on Algeria, invaded the Regency and expelled the Turkish rulers. After much hesitation she embarked also on the conquest of the Arab interior in a cruel war. This was made the pretext for wholesale confiscation of tribal lands and large scale European colonization, with the result that the coastal cities acquired Europcan majorities while the Algerians were driven inland. The process finally resulted in the creation of what was known as Algérie française, though the settlers were in fact by origin as much Spanish, Italian and Maltese as they were French. In 1834 the Ottomans, fearing the seizure of Tripoli also, resumed direct rule there; and only the threat of French naval measures prevented them from doing the same in Tunis. In 1878 French agreement to the British occupation of Cyprus was followed by the withdrawal of British support of Tunisian independence; and in 1881 France, anticipating Italian aims, imposed a Protectorate on a bankrupt Tunis. The European occupation of North West Africa was later completed when Italy in 1911 drove the Turks from Libya, and in 1912 when the French imposed their Protectorate on Morocco, with the recognition of the Spanish right to control the northern tenth of the country. It is to be noted that the Protectorates imposed on Tunisia and Morocco were very different from the conquest of Algeria or the final Italian conquest of Libya. At least in outward form the local governments were preserved, the ruling families being guaranteed the maintenance of their position and the inhabitants remaining officially their subjects.

With regard to Mauritania its southern portion had been incorporated in French West Africa in 1904; the northern portion was occupied in 1934 when the 'pacification' of South Morocco had been completed.

Having thus I hope given a fairly clear idea of the area which we are discussing, of its long history, of the mixed origins of its population and of the various invasions of which two (as well probably as the original Berber inhabitants) came from the Middle East and two from Europe, but none from central or west Africa, we can now turn to our specific subjects of 'nationalism and independence'. Two of the present states, Tunisia and Morocco, had a distinguished past as independent units – Morocco for something like 1,000 years; while Tunis, at first the centre of Arab power in North West Africa, later became virtually independent under a succession of Arab and Berber dynasties until the coming of the Turks and Spanish about A.D. 1500. It then became an Ottoman Regency in 1574. In 1705, when a leader of Turkish origin was recognized as hereditary ruler, Tunis recovered a semi-independent status which lasted until the French occupation in 1881. The restored Tunis however was a much diminished state since its western portions had been taken by the Ottomans to enlarge the Regency of Algiers while the eastern portion, Tripolitania, had been taken to form the Regency of Tripoli. It would, however, not be correct to speak of nationalism in the modern sense with regard to these regimes. They were peoples held together by a common religion and a common dynasty rather than by the sense of forming a nation as we know it today. The Ottoman assumption of power had in effect been welcomed by the masses in the first place because it was less weak and compromising with the Christians than their own rulers. The conception of a joint devotion of all the inhabitants of a given area to something called a nation would only come with the conquering Europeans when they arrived in the nineteenth and twentieth centuries and then it would be adopted by their new subjects, in spite of their rulers' efforts to treat them as if their previous conceptions were something which never would, should, or could change. In the beginning opposition to the growing Ottoman influence had been noticeable principally in the reigning dynasties, and the officials who feared that they might be displaced. The people on the contrary welcomed the prospect of more determined and successful resistance to the Christian invaders. In Morocco, in fact, where the local people were able to expel the Christians themselves, the Ottomans were never able to impose their rule. Nationalism in the modern sense of the word was a European importation which the European rulers, however hard they tried, could not avoid spreading among the peoples whom they conquered.

After saying this, it remains to consider what precise religious, racial, linguistic or other elements came together to form the types of nationalism which came into existence in North West Africa, where we have to draw a distinction between the Protectorates and the conquered states, and consider also the special cases of Mauritania and the Spanish Sahara. Of the elements which we have mentioned in the history of the Maghrib, neither the Carthaginians nor the Normans appear to have left behind them elements capable of revival in some nationalist form.[2] The case of the Romans, however, was quite different. They left behind them such magnificent relics of their civilization in the form of ruined cities and artistic remains that they served, over a thousand years later, as a stimulus to French and Italian nationalism, since both peoples pictured themselves as the heirs of Rome. On the other hand having already independent national centres of their own the French and Italians did not, like the Zionists, feel impelled from the beginning to stake a national claim to land long since occupied by others. The Italian settlement in Libya was in any case much too short-lived to permit the growth of such feelings. It was, however, a different matter in Algeria. Here the settlers of various European origins soon began to develop Algerian nationalist sentiments. Whenever France itself was in difficulties they seized the occasion, as in 1848 and 1871, to reject the governors sent from France and – in the second case particularly, set about establishing some sort of improvised governmental system of their own. Unlike the Dutch settlers in South Africa, however, they were too near the seat of the colonizing power and too aware of the potential strength of the Arabo-Berbers to maintain an attitude of self-reliance *vis-à-vis* their metropolis. The Muslims of Algeria having no glorious independent Muslim past to dream of restoring at first turned to the idea of 'assimilation', by which they hoped to become citizens of equal status with the Europeans, in a country where they formed the majority. Oddly enough, assimilation later became the last despairing aim of the European Algerians also, though in their eyes it signified the submergence of the Muslim majority among the French by the complete and total union of Algeria with France. This was their hope when they brought General de Gaulle to power in 1958, and it was a bitter blow to them when they finally realized that he did not himself believe in the practicability of such a solution. In Tunisia and Morocco, though protectorates, the French government also envisaged a perpetual link, with France as the dominant element; but this was to be brought about little by little without the harsh means of conquest or the complete destruction as in Algeria of the existing traditional society. As the eastern Arab world was by degrees liberated, however, the French realized that they could not hope to hold all North Africa, and in 1954 Mendès-France negotiated laboriously a measure giving Tunisia a large degree of internal autonomy while still retaining certain important controls. The position was, however, radically changed by the outbreak of the Algerian rising in November of the same year and the increasing evidence that Moroccan nationalism had only been increased by the deposition of the Sultan in 1953. It was decided, therefore, to abandon the two Protectorates and concentrate all available forces on preserving what was still thought of as Algérie française. Thus early in 1956 Morocco was granted independence (with the meaningless provision that it was 'independence within interdependence'), after which it could no longer be denied to the more advanced Tunisia in an equally generous form. All efforts were now concentrated on Algeria to which an army of 500,000 men was sent while the frontiers were cut off by fortified fences. It was not till 1962, after 10,000 French soldiers and an unknown number of Algerians, probably over 250,000, had been killed and 2,000,000 peasants 'resettled', at the best in well-built new villages, at the worst in what were really concentration camps, that independence was negotiated with provisions for the continued existence of the settlers. The latter however realizing that their dominance was ended fled to the number of 800,000 after an outburst of terrorism, leaving the Algerians to manage as best they could. Here we must turn for a while to consider the position of Spanish Morocco. The long and distinguished past of Muslim Spain had left memorials in Andalusia – such as the Mezquita or former Mosque, now the Cathedral at Cordoba, and the Alhambra at Granada, of which the Andalusians were intensely proud. Their long Muslim past had moreover given them the idea that in spite of the differences between Christians and Muslims there was a certain geographical unity between the two shores of the Straits of Gibraltar and also a tradition of *convivencia* or living together. Thus a prominent member of the Spanish administration wrote in 1954 that the speed and certainty with which Morocco recovered her personality and historic greatness would be the measure of the value and efficacy of their work. These are words which would be inconceivable even from the lips of such an admirer of things Moroccan as General Lyautey was. 'Spain envisages tomorrow,' he continued, a 'free and great Moroccan people who will be united with Spain in the closest brotherhood . . . a people who will cooperate with her in a magnificent renaissance of Hispano-Arabic culture'. The insuperable difficulty here of course was the Spanish devotion to Christianity and the Moroccan devotion to Islam. Certain important differences however did result from the French and Spanish outlooks. Unlike the French who gave all government education in French, the Spanish encouraged education in Arabic, and for a time dispatched Moroccans at government expense to study in the Arab east, and always left them free to do so at their own expense. Nor did the Spanish ever attempt to build up Berber opposition to the Arabs as the French at one time did – though this may have been in part due to the fact that Abdelkrim, the hero of the Rif War, typical Berber that he was, had emulated the Berber empires of the past by welcoming Arab influences and encouraging the adoption of Muslim Sharī'a law.

At this point we must consider the attitude, as regards nationalism, of the Berbers. These, as we have noted already, are today, as Berber-speaking units, concentrated chiefly in the Moroccan Atlas and the Rif, and in Algeria in the mountains of Kabylie and the Aurès. They are today primarily a settled agricultural people, highly virile, making excellent soldiers, ready to travel in order to make a livelihood but returning to their families in the homeland when they have saved sufficient money. They have a fine tradition of folk dancing and singing. The bond uniting them, so far as they are united, is the fact that they speak one of a number of dialects of a language which is said to be Hamitic, that is related, if distantly, to the languages of the Nile Valley and to Semitic. They appear in fact to have come from the Middle East, though precisely when and by what route remains unknown. They resisted the imposition of Arab rule in North West Africa far more determinedly than did the majority of the Christians in Spain, but having adopted Islam became its stoutest defenders against the Christians. One of the most striking features about them is that in spite of their fierce spirit of personal and group independence they appear never to have developed nationalist feeling, in the sense of wishing to compose a distinct nation distinguished by the use of a national language. On the contrary, the great Berber empires used Arabic and adopted Arab customs. A story, told of the Moroccan Sultan Mawlāy Sulaymān (1792–1822), is characteristic. When campaigning near Tadla in the Middle Atlas in the effort to suppress a Berber rising, he was defeated and taken prisoner by them. They thereupon treated him with the greatest respect as their Imam, the women crowding round to kiss the hem of his garments while the men begged his pardon and escorted him back to his capital. In the following year they were again in rebellion. I myself, when visiting the Kabyle country two years before the outbreak of the independence struggle, was driving down to the plain in a hired car with a local chauffeur. As we began to descend, he remarked to me 'They're all Arabs living here'. Uncertain of his meaning, I asked whether he meant that they were not Berbers. 'Oh no', he said, 'Arabs and Berbers, you know, are all the same; they eat alike and they pray alike. I mean that they're not Europeans'. The French in Morocco, thinking to attract Berbers to themselves established a school at Azrou where the Berbers were to be taught in French and not learn Arabic. When the nationalist struggle began, however, its former pupils proved to be amongst the most ardent Arab nationalists. Since independence a Berber party has been founded by a Berber Minister. Its object, however, seemed to be to resist efforts of the Istiqlāl Party to set up their authority as supreme; it would probably react in the same manner towards any other party, be it the King's own men if they should attempt to set up an interfering authoritarian regime. Resistant always to central regimes, Berbers do not appear easily to develop nationalist sentiments. The first Premier of independent Morocco was in fact a Berber.

We are thus left only with Arab nationalism to consider as a vital force in North West Africa. This, however, has itself to be considered in two aspects. The first is the individual nationalism of a particular state, Morocco, Algeria, Tunisia, Libya or Mauritania. The other is the pan-Arab nationalism which imposes a certain uniformity of sentiment not only on the Maghribī but on all Arab states, and a readiness to assist one another against any foreign, i.e. non-Arab, attack. The former nationalism is akin to that which existed in the various Italian or German states before they were unified under one government; here too the disagreements arise from the past history of each unit. Tunisia cannot altogether forget that it was for centuries the centre of Arab power in North West Africa as it had been once of Carthaginian and then of Roman power. Nor can Morocco altogether forget that there was a period when two great dynasties made it, after the fall of the Caliphate of Cordoba, into the principal power in North West Africa. Nor can either country easily forget that it was the Ottoman establishment in Algeria that rivalled Morocco's influence and reduced Tunisia by lopping off its western portion to enlarge the Algiers Regency and its eastern portions to create the Regency of Tripoli. This process was carried on by the French who succeeded the Turks in Algeria, for they took a little more from Tunisia and removed from Moroccan influence and vague supremacy not only the central Saharan area of Tuat in 1902 but also transferred to Algeria the former Moroccan sphere of influence around Tindouf, with its mountain of iron ore, and created a separate state out of the Arabic-speaking portions constituting northern and central Mauritania. The French recognition of Mauritania as an independent state in 1961 and its introduction into the United Nations was in consequence met by an Arab refusal inspired by Morocco to admit it to the Arab League.[3] The subsequent quarrel with Algeria then led the impulsive Ben Bella to engage in frontier fighting against Morocco in 1963 which was ended by the mediation of the Organization of African Unity but not settled definitely until 1970. At that date the Algerian government of Colonel Boumedienne came to agreements with both its Arab neighbours, Morocco and Tunisia. Agreement was reached with the former that Tindouf would remain under Algerian sovereignty but be jointly exploited by both countries and the ore exported through a Moroccan port. At the same time Morocco recognized the Mauritanian government, while rejecting a Spanish suggestion for joint exploitation of the very rich phosphate deposits in the Spanish Sahara which area the Spanish would have recognized as an independent state, in spite of the minuteness of its population in comparison with its extent. Algeria also settled various problems with Tunisia with which her relations had more than once been extremely strained during the Ben Bella regime. The pan-Maghribī or more properly pan-Arab feeling comes into play however at moments when a foreign danger threatens an Arab country. One such case is of course the dispossession of the Palestinians. On the occasion of the 1967 war for example there was general Maghribī willingness to supply military aid. As however the war ended in six days, the only troops who actually arrived in Egypt were the Algerians, who remained for several years. The high point of pan-Maghribī cooperation however was reached much earlier, in 1958, when Moroccan and Tunisian independence was not yet fully secured and the French effort was directed in full force against Algeria. In April 1958 a Maghrib Unity Conference met in Tangier, organized by the dominant political parties of Morocco, (Muslim) Algeria and Tunisia, and attended by the Moroccan Foreign Minister and the Vice-Premier of Tunisia in their Party capacities and by leaders of the Algerian Front of National Liberation. It was presided over by Allal el Fasi, President of the Istiqlāl and leading protagonist of Maghrib unity. This recommended the formation of a Provisional Algerian Government and of a Maghrib Assembly of 60 members, with a permanent secretariat of six. The Committee of Six actually met, but with the split in the Istiqlāl Party and the coming into power in France of General de Gaulle, which raised new hopes, the project collapsed except for the formation of the Algerian Provisional Government; this four years later succeeded in negotiating the independence of Algeria. So far the chief results of pan-Arab nationalism are the cultural and economic cooperation organized by the Arab League and individual arrangements between the various Maghribī states. Cooperation in general is however greatly hindered by the division of the Arab world into monarchical or western-oriented states on the one hand and strongly socialistic states, inclined to alliances with the communists, on the other. In the Maghrib this renders difficult close cooperation between Morocco and Tunisia on one side and the new revolutionary and strongly Arab and Islamic Libya on the other. Algeria for the moment seems to occupy an intermediate position.

Before closing, a word should be said concerning the Jewish nationalism, known as Zionism. This has greatly prejudiced the relations of Arabs with Jews, many of whom had originally come to North West Africa as refugees from Spain. As a result of Zionism, the greater part of the Jewish population has, for Zionist motives or for security, now left the area. Those from Tunisia, Libya and Morocco mostly availed themselves of Zionist offers to settle in Palestine, where they have not all found life very easy. Algerian Jews, on the contrary, who had nearly all received French citizenship under the Crémieux Decree of 1870, mostly preferred to settle in France.

NOTES

1 Privateering had to be preceded by a declaration of war and captured privateers enjoyed the rights of prisoners of war.

2 The Phoenicians did however serve as a claim for a distinctive Maltese nationality after the departure of the Knights, on the grounds that the Maltese language was basically Phoenician. It is probable that the Maltese spoke Phoenician in antiquity, but it is now admitted that the present speech is based on North African Arabic.

3 Arab nationalism is nevertheless strong enough to have caused on occasion serious disturbances between Arabophones and the speakers of African languages in south Mauritania, whom they insisted must learn Arabic as a condition of public employment.

IX

Sudanese Nationalism and the Independence of the Sudan

G. N. Sanderson

Royal Holloway College
University of London

The over-simple model by which independence is achieved through the ultimately irresistible pressure of a 'mass' nationalist movement is more than usually inappropriate in the Sudan. Had such pressure existed, the British would have been very vulnerable to it at any time after about 1945. From the early 1940s the Sudan government, not without some misgivings among its more authoritarian elements, had begun to seek active Sudanese political support. To this end it mobilized its oldest friends, the rural chiefs and well-to-do urban notables who dominated the Advisory Council set up in 1943; but it also contracted an alliance with Sayyid 'Abd al Raḥmān al Mahdī, the leader of the neo-Mahdist Anṣār 'sect' and an avowed though apparently moderate nationalist. The worthies of the Advisory Council were undoubtedly 'sound' and conservatively-minded; the Sayyid certainly needed the British if he was ever to fulfil his scarcely veiled ambition to become their political heir. But neither the Council nor the Sayyid could have countenanced the forcible repression of a vigorous nationalist movement, had such a movement existed.

The support of 'Abd al Raḥmān and of the traditional leaders of Sudanese society, at first merely convenient, became crucially important with the coming of peace, which more than ever precluded the British from seeking a merely repressive solution to their political difficulties in the Sudan. In 1947, after the hearing of the Anglo-Egyptian dispute on the Sudan before the UN Security Council, Sudanese support became absolutely indispensable. Britain had justified her presence in the Sudan by the contention that she was preparing the Sudanese for the independence that Egypt's claims denied them. For this claim to be credible, the British had to demonstrate the existence of significant Sudanese support for their policy of gradual 'constitutional advance'. Indeed, when such support was no longer forthcoming at the end of 1952, Britain almost immediately lost control of the course of political events in the Sudan.

Yet throughout this period the administration had been able, with only a minimal use of force, to contain nationalist agitation at a level which offered no real threat to public security or even to administrative routine. As late as 1950 the Sudan government, in spite of its apparently vulnerable position, seems to have been confident of its ability to play for time and to regulate very closely the pace of 'constitutional advance'. Nor, down to the middle of 1952, had the government normally experienced much difficulty in obtaining adequate Sudanese support. Indeed, during 1951, by a fairly non-commital tactical retreat from its rather negative position of the previous year, the government was temporarily able to secure a broader range of collaboration than at any time since 1945.

One way of explaining this rather odd situation is to point out that the nationalist movement was 'weakened' by sectarian divisions, and especially by the rivalry between Sayyid 'Abd al Raḥmān al Mahdī and Sayyid 'Alī al Mīrghani, the hereditary head of the powerful Khatmīya ṭarīqa. This sectarian schism among the nationalists was then exacerbated by the use which the co-domini made of it. Egypt supported, if not the Khatmīya itself, at any rate the Khatmīya's political allies. Britain, more discreetly but very effectively, backed Sayyid 'Abd al Raḥmān and the Umma party which was little more than 'Abd al Raḥmān's political 'front' organization.

This explanation is sound as far as it goes; but it does not explain nearly enough. It does not explain why, from 1936 to 1940, the administration was prepared not merely to tolerate but actively to foster 'secular' nationalism. It does not explain the rapprochement, from 1941 onwards, between the government and 'Abd al Raḥmān, whose political behaviour had previously been often regarded as very suspect – and never more so than in the period 1935–40. It does not explain why Sayyid 'Ali al Mīrghani, between the wars a totally reliable supporter of the administration, became in 1944 the patron of the more radical nationalists and the ally of Egypt. The 'nationalist weakness' thesis positively increases the difficulty of explaining why, even before 1945, the Sudan government had been forced to abandon its position as arbiter and manipulator of Sudanese politics, and to descend into the arena as an ill-concealed partisan of 'Abd al Raḥmān – a posture which led, in October 1946, to the Sayyid and the Sudan government tacitly combining to oppose and even defy HMG, and forcing the redoubtable Ernest Bevin abruptly to reverse his Sudan policy.

The crisis of October 1946 was one of the two occasions during the 'national struggle' when public order was, or seemed to be, seriously threatened. The other was that of the Anṣār demonstrations of 1 March 1954. In October 1946, self-conscious nationalism was still no more than the cult of a small *élite*; by March 1954, the 'struggle' against the British had been decisively won. 'Nationalism', as such, had little to do with either of these crises; but 'Abd al Raḥmān had a great deal to do with both of them. They were both demonstrations, and very effective ones, that the 'Sudan Question' could not be peacefully settled without regard for the Sayyid's wishes and aspirations.

It is time to change the focus. Perhaps the growth of nationalism is not after all the central theme in the progress of the Sudan towards independence. It may be more enlightening to consider nationalism as simply a new input (and down to about 1951 an input of comparatively minor importance) into an already well-developed struggle for political influence in the Sudan. The closer the Sudan seemed to self-determination, the higher grew the stakes in this internal conflict. Not surprisingly, the struggle for the power-legacy of the British soon tended to take precedence over the 'national struggle' proper. It was this powerful negative feed-back which kept the Sudan Government firmly in the saddle until, late in 1952, the Sudanese competitors succeeded in temporarily reversing their priorities and so cornering the British.

It was not merely that the nationalists were 'divided' and 'weakened' by this power-struggle; they were almost completely absorbed into it. In the early 1940s secular nationalism had no resonance, and indeed no meaning, outside a comparatively small circle of white-collar intelligentsia. The nationalist leaders, seeking an *ersatz* popular following through a link with the Anṣār or the Khatmīya, inevitably became bound to sectarian chariot wheels. This subordination was never indeed quite total. Ismā'īl al Azharī, combining militant secular nationalism with 'anti-British' stridency and great tactical skill, became an important political force in his own right. But even al Azharī lost much of his influence when the Khatmīya withdrew its support from him between 1949 and 1952. The fate of the nationalists is indeed hardly surprising, for it was shared by the co-domini themselves. Britain and Egypt began as powerful patrons of the opposing factions; but they too found themselves subordinated to the Anṣār-Khatmīya conflict. They ended as expendable auxiliaries who were duly discarded when they had outlived their usefulness – the British by 'Abd al Raḥmān in October 1952, the Egyptians by the Khatmīya at the end of 1954.

At the heart of the internal contest in the Sudan lay the ambitions of 'Abd al Raḥmān al Mahdī. His rise from obscurity dated from the First World War, when he had offered, and delivered, the loyalty of his rural Anṣār to a government at war with the Turks. Rewarded by grants of land and lucrative government contracts, 'Abd al Raḥmān became a rich man. To the dismay of the Sudan administration, he used his wealth to extend his political and religious influence, and his 'baraka' further to increase his wealth. Building up a clandestine network of agents, exacting tribute in the form of zakā and of unpaid labour on his plantations, holding court in quasi-regal style at Aba and later at Khartoum, the Sayyid began to emerge as a centre of power and authority rivalling that of the government. From the early 1920s onward, the Sudan government was from time to time quite seriously disquieted by his political behaviour. When in 1926 an inexperienced Governor-General (Archer) made advances to the Sayyid which the Political Service deemed inopportune, a group of senior officials did not hesitate to engineer Archer's dismissal.

Yet 'Abd al Raḥmān carefully avoided any direct conflict with government. Indeed, he almost invariably demonstrated an almost embarrassing willingness to cooperate with it. When the government attempted to cut him down to size, he assumed an air of injured innocence. With every outward mark of deference and respect, he invariably obeyed – for a while – any specific orders given to him. Overt opposition was not the Sayyid's tactic; his behaviour suggests rather that he was determined to build himself up to be 'l'homme inévitable' on the day when, sooner or later, the British handed over at least some of their power. It was only after the British became clearly unable to make – or underwrite – a transfer of power in his favour that 'Abd al Raḥmān came out decisively against them.

In the later 1930s the Sayyid's behaviour had been more than usually disconcerting. He now seemed to be attempting to add another string to his political bow by courting the younger generation of western-educated intelligentsia, a group not much loved by most traditional leaders and for a decade intensely disliked and distrusted by the administration as carriers of the 'septic germs' of democracy and nationalism. Unloved and distrusted the intelligentsia might be, but as junior officials they were indispensable to the functioning of the régime, and their political capture by 'Abd al Raḥmān was a very disturbing prospect.

The leaders of this intelligentsia were at that time very moderate nationalists, asking no more than the opportunity of being trained to succeed the British in the rather remote future. They had little or nothing in common with the revolutionary nationalists of 1924 – even where individuals active in 1924 had remained in political life, they were by now either the soundest of 'sound elements' (like 'Abdallāh Khalīl) or at most very moderate gradualists (like 'Arafāt Muḥammad 'Abdallāh). In reaction against the petty sectarian quarrels which had sterilized 'educated' politics in the Sudan since 1931, these leaders had so far rejected 'Abd al Raḥmān's overtures: they had even maintained their 'little magazines' out of their own pockets rather than accept the Sayyid's proffered subsidy.

Sir Stewart Symes, Governor-General since 1934, was already anxious to encourage 'moderate' secular nationalism as a safeguard against the revival of Egyptian influence among educated Sudanese. 'Abd al Raḥmān's manoeuvres gave an added urgency to this policy; and in spite of the predictable misgivings of his provincial governors, Symes insisted on forestalling the Sayyid by giving active encouragement to these admirably moderate, admirably non-sectarian young nationalists. In 1938 the government recognized, though explicitly not as a politically representative body, the Graduates' General Congress whose foundation it had encouraged. The details were worked out, in friendly collaboration, between the future scourge of the 'imperialist oppressors', Ismā'īl al Azharī, and J. C. Penney, who as Controller of Public Security was immediately responsible for the detection and surveillance of 'subversive' political activity.

The experiment was not a success. Government was reluctant to consult Congress on any matters of real importance; Congress was soon ill at ease in the strait-jacket of the Azharī-Penney arrangements, and found specific matter for complaint in the slow pace of 'Sudanization' and of educational development. To the government, the political behaviour of Congress was totally unsatisfactory. It attempted to insist upon its representative quality; it flirted with Egypt; worst of all, in its disenchantment with the government, it showed every sign of yielding after all to the blandishments of 'Abd al Raḥmān. In the course of 1940 the Sayyid's press began to urge that Congress should be 'broadened' by the inclusion of 'merchants and others'; he seemed well on the way to capturing the very organization which official strategy had planned as a counterpoise to him. In October 1940 the Civil Secretary (Newbold) upbraided the Congress leaders for their political pretensions in language of apparently calculated rudeness; he may already have written off Congress as a usable political instrument.

But snubs to Congress, however severe, did not solve the problem of 'Abd al Raḥmān, who demonstrated his influence when the Congress elections at the end of 1940, conducted on sectarian lines, were easily won by the Anṣār. In the course of 1941 the government attempted a solution by deciding to treat the Sayyid as an ally rather than as a potential enemy. This course had many obvious attractions. 'Abd al Raḥmān might succeed in moderating an increasingly radical Congress; he also seemed quite reliably anti-Egyptian, a consideration of mounting importance as Egyptian influence in the

Sudan steadily increased. But the very fact that the Sayyid had been able to *compel* the government to accept his alliance meant that he was gaining the initiative in political strategy. Five or six years later, when the political respectability of British rule had become almost entirely dependent on 'Abd al Raḥmān's cooperation, the 1941 decision must have looked disconcertingly like an application of the maxim: 'If you can't beat him, join him!'.

In 1941 the government called off the campaign of administrative and fiscal harassment of the Sayyid which it had begun in 1936; and Congress was duly quiescent under studiously moderate Anṣār committees. But the government soon ceased to draw this political dividend from its new alliance, for the Sayyid's control of Congress did not last. In 1942 a group of young, secular-minded militants, linked by close ties of personal friendship and nicknamed the Ashiqqā' (full brothers), was able to manoeuvre the moderate Anṣār executive into presenting and re-iterating the famous 'twelve demands' – for self-determination immediately after the war and greater Sudanese participation meanwhile. Newbold rejected the demands without ceremony, and broke off all official relations with Congress. Under further Ashiqqā' pressure, Congress amended its constitution to admit elementary school 'graduates' 'and their equivalent'. In the elections at the end of 1942, the Ashiqqā' captured control of the enlarged Congress under the leadership of Ismā'īl al Azharī, who was already something of a Congress elder statesman, and at the same time at least a 'fringe member' of Sayyid 'Abd al Raḥmān's entourage. It is reliably reported that Azharī sought the patronage of 'Abd al Raḥmān for this militant group. Such patronage was obviously incompatible with the Sayyid's new relationship to government, and it was refused. Significantly, in the course of 1943 the moderate Anṣār members – 'Abd al Raḥmān's political 'connection' – began to secede from Congress.

The Ashiqqā' now formally organized themselves as a political party, the first to emerge in the Sudan; but the party had no future as a mass organization unless it could attract some sectarian support. In 1944 Azharī sought and obtained this support from Sayyid 'Alī al Mīrghanī. Sayyid 'Alī had been curiously neglected by the British since the later 1930s. His record as a prop of the régime was so long and so unblemished that they seem to have taken his 'reliability' for granted; but his 'reliability' was not, and could not have been, proof against the government's new course of alignment with 'Abd al Raḥmān. Sayyid 'Alī had every reason, both personal and historical, to look upon the possible domination of the Sudan by 'Abd al Raḥmān as the ultimate disaster. Moreover, the Khatmīya had traditions of cooperation with the secular power going back to the

Turco-Egyptian conquest. He had therefore been happy to support a theoretically half-Muslim administration which in practice showed great deference to 'orthodox' Islam, and which often tended to treat 'Abd al Raḥmān as a political suspect.

'Ali al Mīrghanī was a man of intensely conservative outlook, who was quite out of sympathy with radical secular nationalism. His patronage of the Ashiqqā' and its successors was always to be cautious and conditional, and was indeed sometimes withheld for quite lengthy periods. But in 1944 he could not stand idly by while 'Abd al Raḥmān monopolized British political support – perhaps ultimately to emerge as 'Sultan of the Sudan' under some form of British protection or over-rule. He needed a weapon against his rival; and he may well have decided, since 'reliability' was apparently no longer rewarded, to imitate 'Abd al Raḥmān's tactics and demonstrate his nuisance-value in opposition.

On the principle that 'the enemy of my enemy is my friend', the Ashiqqā'-Khatmīya alliance sought Egyptian support, and (largely though not entirely for that reason) perforce campaigned on a platform of 'unity with Egypt'. Hence the double paradox of Sudanese nationalism: the 'progressive', politically ambitious 'Abd al Raḥmān demanding 'the Sudan for the Sudanese', but denounced by the militants as 'the tail of the imperialists'; while those very militants, with the support of the conservative and reluctantly 'political' 'Alī al Mīrghanī, are apparently committed to a programme short of full independence. In 1945 the Umma party emerged as 'Abd al Raḥmān's formal political organization. A belated attempt by 'independent' members of Congress to re-unite the national movement predictably failed early in 1946.

There was indeed another political force in the field; but it was a weak and fluctuating force, which the British to their cost persistently overrated. This was what the administration liked to call the 'country party' – the rural chiefs and notables (and some of their urban equivalents), who were jealous of 'Abd al Raḥmān, especially as a potential Sultan, but were no less distrustful of militant radicals and their Egyptian supporters. This force had in 1944 been mobilized in the Advisory Council; Newbold scarcely troubled to conceal his hopes that this more amenable body would steal some of Congress' political thunder. More discreetly, he may also have hoped that it would be some counterpoise to the increasingly indispensable 'Abd al Raḥmān.

Increasingly indispensable, because the Ashiqqā', followed rather less rigidly by the Khatmīya, had already deployed its strongest weapon – a refusal to engage in any formal political dialogue with the government, and a boycott of any constitutional machinery that the government might set up. But the 'country party', itself by no means free from sectarian rifts, proved a broken reed. Most of its members were privately very satisfied with the *status quo*, but could hardly say so in public. They had little capacity for collective organization, and less for tactics or propaganda. Occasional cautiously-worded public warnings against undue haste, and frequent private lamentations to sympathetic British officials, formed the sum of their political activity until the end of 1951, when with British encouragement they belatedly organized themselves as the grotesquely misnamed Socialist Republican Party.

The Sidqī–Bevin Protocol of October 1946, with its apparent recognition of Egyptian sovereignty over the Sudan, revealed the full extent of the administration's alignment with, and dependence upon, Sayyid 'Abd al Raḥmān. The Umma threatened to boycott the Advisory Council (which the Ashiqqā' was already boycotting); and there were Anṣār riots in Omdurman. Whether or not the latter were in themselves a grave threat to public security, the attitude of the Sudan Political Service certainly made them so. The Governor-General (Huddleston) flew to London, saw the Prime Minister (Attlee), and was prepared to resign unless HMG modified its policy. An unknown but certainly significant number of administrative officials, both senior and junior, seemed prepared to follow suit. Under this pressure, backed by the protests of retired senior officials led by the patriarchal Wingate, Downing Street hastily reversed itself.

The extreme reaction of the Sudan Political Service was perhaps based as much upon its intense – almost pathological – loathing for Egypt and all things Egyptian as upon cool political calculation. However this may be, its tacit but complete alignment with 'Abd al Raḥmān in this crisis carried a serious political penalty. By destroying any real prospect of re-insuring with 'Ali al Mīrghanī and the Khatmīya, it left the administration even more dangerously dependent on 'Abd al Raḥmān's continued cooperation and goodwill. In 1950–51 the government did its utmost to woo the Khatmīya, hoping to profit by the prolonged estrangement between 'Ali al Mīrghanī and Azharī. The effort was not quite fruitless; there was a short period of rather distant and tentative collaboration between the government and the Khatmīya in its political guise as the 'National Front'. But the confidence of 'Ali al Mīrghanī was never regained.

Indeed, from 1946 until the latter half of 1952 there was no fundamental change in the Sudanese political situation. 'Abd al Raḥmān became increasingly importunate in his demands for early independence; but he was restrained from extreme measures by his continuing need for British support, not least because the intransigent Egyptian claim to sovereignty precluded any possibility of his coming to terms with Cairo. Meanwhile, the Ashiqqā' always, and the Khatmīya usually, persisted in their strategy of boycott. In 1951 the rift between Azharī and the Khatmīya led to a slight thaw in the relations between the two Sayyids; but their mutual suspicions always frustrated any effective understanding or collaboration. Hence the continued confidence of the Sudan government in its ability to play for time.

Late in 1951 this deadlock began to loosen up a little; but not primarily because of internal Sudanese developments nor even because of the increasingly aggressive tactics of Egypt, which culminated (October 1951) in the unilateral abrogation of the Condominium Agreement and the proclamation of Farouk as King of the Sudan. What gave teeth to the Egyptian attitude was the very heavy pressure upon the Foreign Office from the US State Department to buy Egyptian support for American cold war strategy by recognizing the claims of Egypt. The Americans became the more importunate as their conviction grew that only a resounding success in the Sudan could save the monarchy from a revolution which would almost certainly increase Russian influence in Egypt.

It was largely as a counter-move to this American pressure that HMG now began to press the Sudan government to introduce, considerably sooner than either would really have wished, a constitution providing for representative government and some semblance of internal autonomy during an indeterminate 'transitional period'. As the Civil Secretary pointed out confidentially to provincial governors in February 1952, it was necessary to hasten plans for self-government 'because of events outside British control'. This was a move to which the United States could hardly object in public – although in private, and to the intense irritation of the British, their embassy in Cairo continued to give aid and comfort to Ismā'īl al Azharī.

In October 1952 the stalemate was finally broken. The military government in Egypt, which had seized power in July under the half-Sudanese Muḥammad Najīb (Neguib), at last abandoned, in its negotiations with the Umma, the Egyptian claim to sovereignty and admitted the right of the Sudanese to self-determination. On this basis the Sudanese competitors for power were able to conclude a temporary truce, during which, with Egyptian assistance, they set a time-limit for the progress of the Sudan to full independence (or union with Egypt); and drew up a set of constitutional rules to regulate the power-struggle within the Sudan (January 1953). The British successively deserted by 'Abd al Raḥmān and then by the 'Socialist Republicans', their last and least effective supporters, had no alternative but to concur. These arrangements, which were in form mere amendments to the constitution that the British themselves had introduced, were duly embodied in the Anglo-Egyptian Agreement of

12 February 1953. This sudden and complete collapse of effective British control was followed, at the end of 1953, by the decisive electoral victory of a Khatmīya-Ashiqqā' coalition over 'Abd al Raḥmān and the Umma. Thereafter, under the vigilant eyes of Ismā'īl al Azharī as Prime Minister, and of two international commissions which included Egyptian and Sudanese members, the sole political function of the British was to ensure the smooth running of the arrangements for bringing their own rule to an end.

It was fitting that the crucial events in the overthrow of British power should have taken place in the field of diplomacy. The 'national struggle' within the Sudan had itself been conducted throughout as a diplomatic 'game', if only because the British were, almost from the outset, precluded from more than a minimal use of force. But the Sudanese participants were well content to have it so. The two Sayyids were anything but revolutionaries. Nor, when it came to the point, were even the more militant secular politicians. All concerned aspired to take over the existing system in working order – a goal unlikely to be achieved by the politics of popular insurrection. Indeed, the secular nationalists, most of whom had been career officials, at times tended to identify independence rather narrowly with the Sudanization of the key administrative posts.

Moreover, the Sayyids and the politicians alike were old hands at the diplomatic game. They had learned to play it between the wars, when the Sudan government had skilfully deployed the carrot and the stick in order to 'gain friends and influence people'; and had developed very sophisticated techniques of exploiting internal Sudanese tensions and rivalries to prevent influential collaborators from growing into over-mighty subjects, or combining amongst themselves to oppose the administration. The diplomacy of tactical collaboration, in which even Azharī had participated, was no bad school in which to train for the diplomacy of tactical harassment. The most effective weapon in the 'national struggle' was not 'the masses in the streets'. It was the denial or threatened denial of all political cooperation, as a means of progressively restricting the room for manoeuvre of a government debarred from appealing to the *ultima ratio* of forcible repression. When at the end of 1952 the government's room for manoeuvre finally contracted to zero, the Sudanese had won the game.

It was not only the 'national struggle' which was conducted as a diplomatic game. So too, with infrequent exceptions, was the struggle between the prospective heirs of British power. True, in October 1946 and again in March 1954 'Abd al Raḥmān demonstrated his strength by a show of physical force; the Ashiqqā' did likewise, with less success, when in November 1948 it attempted to disrupt the elections that it was boycotting. But even on these exceptional occasions, the use of physical force was kept under remarkably strict control. The Sayyids, in particular, probably recognized that the one contingency which would have permitted the British to use massive repressive force was frank civil war or a credible threat of it; and the internal conflict was never permitted to develop into anything remotely approaching an 'Ulster situation'.

On this reading of the 'national struggle', the contribution of self-conscious secular nationalism to the independence of the Sudan does not seem very impressive. True, it enabled Azharī to become a major political figure in his own right, and it at least opened the way to an escape from purely sectarian politics. But it was quite powerless to break the deadlock which kept the British so firmly in the saddle between 1946 and 1952; and almost to the end of this period the activities of popular nationalism evidently gave the administration little cause for concern. But then, until about 1951 secular nationalism hardly deserves to be called 'popular'; it was still the cult of the white-collar *élite* rather than a genuine mass movement. In 1951–52, however, the Sudanese trade unions, and especially the politically militant Sudan Workers' Trade Union Federation, converted many artisans and manual workers, above all in the metropolitan 'Three Towns', to left-wing politics and active nationalism. This development, which was greeted with very mixed feelings by the established politicians, was doubtless another nail in the coffin of 'Abd al Raḥmān's monarchical aspirations. But it was surely a superfluous nail. By the end of 1951, at the very latest, Britain was no longer able to deliver the political support without which a neo-Mahdist Sultanate would not have been viable.

It was the fate of secular nationalism to emerge as a mass movement only to find itself, almost immediately, without any serious political battle to fight. After February 1953, the British administration very quickly lost all effective control over the course of political events in the Sudan; and by April 1955 it had been Sudanized out of existence. It soon became obvious that the 'national struggle' had in all essentials been victoriously concluded. The internal power-struggle was of course far from concluded; indeed, it reached its sharpest crisis in 'Abd al Raḥmān's show of force in March 1954. But even in this conflict, popular nationalism had no very satisfying part to play. If not quite a mere spectator, it was at most a kind of Greek chorus, reacting to events rather than initiating them.

In particular, there seems to be little evidence for the widely held view that popular pressure was responsible for the final hasty scramble to immediate independence, which began in August 1955 and short-circuited the very elaborate procedure laid down in the Anglo-Egyptian Agreement. It is however easy to demonstrate the crucial importance of the growing unrest in the Southern Sudan, which had already reached the point of open violence by the end of July. The continued presence of the co-domini and their troops now became intensely embarrassing, and even dangerous, to the Sudanese Government. Both Britain and Egypt were suspected of fomenting, or at least encouraging, the Southern disturbances; and Egypt was known to be anxious to frustrate or delay the declaration of full Sudanese independence by using Southern unrest as a pretext for concerted military action by the co-domini.

Neither the immediate prelude nor the actual transition to independence offered much satisfaction to the frustrated enthusiasm of popular nationalism. In November 1955, by skilful but unedifying manoeuvres in the lobbies, the Parliamentary Opposition all but succeeded in engineering the fall of Azharī in an attempt to deprive him of the honour of leading the Sudan into independence. Azharī's position remained very vulnerable, and a serious political crisis developed. It was resolved, as so many earlier crises and deadlocks had been resolved, by a diplomatic manoeuvre. The rival Sayyids met, with a maximum of publicity, in an atmosphere of ostentatious and unprecedented cordiality. On 3 December they jointly called for national solidarity and the formation of a national (coalition) government immediately after independence. Three days later Azharī complied with this demand. A rather shabby, but nevertheless dangerous, incident had been closed by the intervention, as *dei ex machina*, of the traditional father-figures of Sudanese politics. But the pressure upon Azharī was still considerable; and this pressure doubtless accounts for his remarkable statement on 15 December (a Thursday) that he intended to announce the independence of the Sudan 'next Monday'.

Finally, the actual disappearance of the physical symbols and apparatus of foreign rule was a disappointing anti-climax. The evacuation of the British and Egyptian troops had proceeded without incident and without much publicity, and was complete by mid-November 1955. The officially-sponsored rejoicings which were to have celebrated their departure were however postponed on account of the tense political situation, and never in fact took place. Only the Governor-General now remained. He was by now a mere figurehead, but still an imperial figurehead and the public symbol of the Sudan's dependent status. His final exit was almost farcical. On 15 December he went home on leave, ostensibly to visit his family for Christmas; before his leave had expired, the Sudan was conveniently independent. The hated foreign oppressor finally disappeared, not with a bang or even a whimper, but with the frivolous crepitation of a Christmas cracker.

Perhaps popular nationalism came nearest to its catharsis at the enormous public meetings which assembled in Khartoum and Omdurman to hear the Governor-General formally announce the conclusion of the Anglo-Egyptian Agreement of February 1953. This event, far more than the ceremonial flag-lowering and flag-hoisting of 1 January 1956, seems to have been a genuinely popular occasion. But 'occasions', however exciting or moving, are no substitute for genuine political victories. Since independence, the popular – as opposed to *élitist* – political style in the Sudan has shown a marked leaning towards ostentatiously radical gestures and policies, quite often in matters of apparently very minor importance. 'Radicalism in rather desperate search of something to be radical about' is the impression left with at least one observer. One source of this behaviour may perhaps be an attempt to compensate for the frustrating experiences and undistinguished role of popular politics during the 'national struggle' for independence.

X

Agricultural Development in Libya since Independence

J. A. Allan

School of Oriental and African Studies
University of London

1. *Introduction*

In this paper the physical and historical background to Libyan agriculture will be outlined briefly. Next, the areas of most rapid development will be identified and case studies used to establish the significance of such changes with respect to the resources upon which further long-term development depends, namely underground water.

In 1951 independent Libya inherited an agricultural sector with many problems. Traditional agriculture was much as it had ever been, while twentieth-century developments by Italian colonists were evident in many areas inland from the coastal traditional gardens.

Agriculture was in a poor state. Production was extremely vulnerable to variable rainfall, there had been considerable dislocation with respect to former Italian farms, and there was a serious shortage of capital and skills in terms of modern agricultural development.

1.1 *Physical background to farming in Libya*

Agriculture is concentrated near the coast because it is here that the best underground water and soil resources are found, as well as the most reliable rainfall. Rainfall is nowhere high, however, and one or more years of drought may be followed by years of higher than average precipitation. Even such hardy crops as barley may not receive the 250 mm which they require, in areas which indicate a much higher annual average. Further, the very high average temperatures, even in the winter rainy season, serve to reduce the effectiveness of the meagre rainfall.

Libya's climate restricts the range of crops grown, with barley and the olive normal in the driest margins, and crops with higher water requirements (tomatoes, vegetables, alfalfa, citrus) confined to areas with favourable underground water resources which supplement the overall and periodic deficiencies in rainfall.

1.2 *Historical background*

For three millenias coastal Libya has suffered invasions from the north and east. Relics of urban and agricultural activity associated with the earliest of these occupations in classical times indicate that irrigated agriculture, dry farming and wadi control were carried out more extensively than at present, by Phoenician and Roman farmers.

The Arab advances of the seventh century brought strong nomadic influences and emphasized grazing in the agricultural economy. This pattern was reinforced by the powerful incursion in the eleventh century by nomadic tribes originally from the Arabian Peninsula.

After 1510 some or all of Libya successively came under Spanish, Maltese and Turkish control (1553–1912, including the Karamanli dynasty 1714–1835) and in 1912 Italy took over Western Libya and subsequently the eastern and southern provinces of the country. Any map or air photograph of coastal Libya shows the impact of Italian activity on farming,[1] and during the Italian colonial period the area of irrigated agriculture was doubled in Western Libya.

The period of Italian government and development ended in January 1943 when the British Military Administration (BMA) took over the government of the country.

The British administration was anxious to maintain agricultural production, and its policy was to retain the Italian farmers; the Italian population was still 40,536 in 1946 in Western Libya according to British estimates. The Italian civilian population in Eastern Libya left the country as the result of the advance of British troops into Cyrenaica in 1940–41.

Investment during this period of British administration was not at pre-1939 levels however, and agriculture did not develop at the same pace as in the Italian period. Independence in 1951 introduced uncertainty in the Italian community, and despite reassurances a number left, so that by 1954 there were 37,655 Italians in Western Libya.

2. *Resources allocated to agriculture since independence*

In other respects independence brought improvements in that there was an increase in the foreign assistance extended to Libya. The table (p. 113) shows in some detail the volume and sources of foreign assistance for the post-independence years, and until the time when oil revenues became important.

The early years of independence were years when there was for the first time a surplus of national revenues over national expenditures, as a result of foreign assistance, indeed it was not until 1966 that revenues were brought into surplus again.

The effect of increased foreign assistance between 1951 and 1955

Libya – Foreign Assistance 1950–1965

£ Libyan millions

	1950	1951	1952	1953	1954	1955	1956	1957	1958	1959	1960	1961	1962	1963	1964	1965
UK and French Grants	1·35	1·46	2·23	1·92	2·91	—	—	—	—	—	—	—	—	—	—	—
LPDSA	—	—	0·44	0·72	1·12	1·05	1·02	1·47	0·25	—	—	—	—	—	—	—
UK Grain Grants	—	—	0·25	—	—	—	—	—	—	—	—	—	—	—	—	—
UN Technical Assistance	—	—	—	0·17*	0·19*	0·22	0·26	0·26	0·26	0·26	0·22	0·22	0·22	1·85	1·0	0·82
US Grants	—	—	0·64	0·50	1·52	6·15	4·62	5·89	5·61	11·20	10·85	6·92	6·86	5·44	2·93	0·91
UK Grants	—	—	—	—	—	2·79	2·75	3·00	4·63	3·25	3·25	3·25	3·25	3·25	3·25	—
Totals	1·35	1·46	3·56	3·31	5·75	10·26	8·66	10·63	10·75	14·71	14·30	10·38	10·33	10·54	7·18	1·75

* Underestimates — No information

Source: Bank of Libya 'Statistical Supplement', *Economic Bulletin* Tripoli, July 1967.

is shown in the following table, as is the importance of oil revenue after 1961: (p. 115).

The period 1957 to 1961 was interesting as a time when despite a high level of foreign assistance national revenue at first declined, and then rose more slowly than between 1951 and 1956. It was also the period when oil exploration was getting under way. In 1958 and 1959 national revenue began to rise again, mainly as a result of oil company activity, and partly because of especially high U.S. grants.

The general impact of these economic changes in the agricultural sector were important. During the British Military Administration and in the early years of independence farming was 'running down', and many ex-Italian farms were less productive in relation to activity in the 1930s. Traditional farming continued at a mainly subsistence level.

A number of Italian farms were sold at, or soon after, independence, either to Libyan farmers or in some cases to Palestinian entrepreneurs. The latter developed advanced farms, but in general apart from government-sponsored schemes supported by foreign aid there was little important development in agriculture until after 1961.

In the early 1960s oil revenues were made available by the government to Libyan farmers for the purchases of land, and very important changes date from this period. It will be the purpose of the next section to identify, and where possible quantify, these changes in a number of case study areas, and to show that development has been taking place in the Tripoli triangle,[2] on former Italian farms. Considerable intensification is evident and irrigation has been extended to areas which were under dry farming, or were neglected in the early days of independence.

3. *Agricultural changes since oil*

Oil revenues rose rapidly from £L 14 million in 1962 to over £L 270 million in 1969. Investment in agriculture also increased and over £L 300 million were allocated to this sector in the plan period 1963–68 rather than the £L 169 million originally budgeted.

In addition to benefits from direct government intervention, the agricultural sector also gained advantage from the general improvement in personal incomes. In 1959 GDP per head per annum was amongst the lowest in Africa at £L 15–£L 20 per head. By 1964 it had risen to £L 103 per head and to over £L 200 by 1968, and much of this new wealth was available to farmers as the government provided many new jobs in the ministries, police and armed services after 1962. Also some who had made money out of providing services or labour for the oil companies in their exploration activities, were

Libya – Total Revenues and Expenditures 1944–1967

£ Libyan millions

	1944/45	1945/46	1946	1947	1948	1949	1950	1951	1952	1953	1954	1955
Revenue	1·8	2·0	2·5	2·5	3·1	3·5	3·7	4·2	6·2	9·3	11·2	13·3
Expenditure	2·0	2·2	2·8	3·9	4·6	4·0	5·5	5·9	6·6	8·2	8·8	13·0
Surplus	—	—	—	—	—	—	—	—	—	1·0	2·4	0·3
Deficit	0·2	0·2	0·3	1·3	1·5	0·5	1·8	1·7	0·4	—	—	—

	1956	1957	1958	1959	1960	1961	1962	1963	1964	1965/66	1966/67
Revenue	18·1	20·4	17·0	18·4	22·4	25·7	36·0	63·4	85·8	165·8	187·9
Expenditure	15·4	17·0	20·0	20·6	28·3	34·5	44·4	65·2	100·8	171·8	177·9
Surplus	2·7	3·4	—	—	—	—	—	—	—	—	10.0
Deficit	—	—	3·0	2·2	5·9	8·8	8·4	1·8	15·0	6·0	—

Source: Bank of Libya, 'Statistical Supplement', *Economic Bulletin*, Tripoli, July 1967.

attracted to agriculture, and bought or extended former Italian farms.

These changes have been accompanied by massive increases in food imports, increases variously estimated to have been between 15 per cent and 20 per cent per year in the 1963–68 period. In 1959 Libya produced about 75 per cent of her food requirements, while it is estimated that by 1972 imports will be contributing 75 per cent of food needs. There is therefore a growing market, and a demand which the agricultural sector cannot meet despite significant extensions to and intensification of, irrigated agriculture.

Wages and prices have at the same time risen, although not at the same rates. Price indexes for the food group reveal a doubling of prices between 1955 and 1968. Agricultural wages, however, had moved ahead much more rapidly with a sixfold increase between 1953 and 1968. Such rapid wage inflation militated against the farmer, and foreign labour, especially Tunisian, was becoming a feature of Libyan farming by 1968.

The patterns and volume of investment are reflected in changes in the use of land since oil. Official data are not reliable in this respect, and so comparative air photographs (mid 1950s and late 1960s in date) have been examined, and show, for example at Talbighah, that investment in rural housing has been general on all types of farms, both traditional and ex-colonial, while on the latter there has also been considerable investment in irrigation equipment revealed in large planting of citrus as well as of field crops.

Agricultural output must therefore have risen since oil, although it is unlikely that the increases have amounted to more than 2 per cent per year. This increase should be related to the official estimate of the rate of population increase at 3·7 per cent per year.

5. *Agricultural changes and underground water resources*

Agriculture is dependent on irrigation in most of the Tripoli triangle, and there has been a considerable increase in the use of pumping equipment since oil, and new wells continue to be dug as there is no functioning water law to prevent such development. The increase in pumping has caused the water table to fall, as shown by the yearly deepening of wells at points 20 kilometres from the coast. Observation wells in such areas, e.g. Suwani bin Yadim and Bin Gashir indicate that in the former the fall was at the rate of more than half a metre a year, and in the latter it was approaching one metre per year by 1968. In both cases the rates of decline were increasing, and even at points near the coast, such as Mellahah, there was a small but important decline.

In conclusion it can be said that domestic agricultural production

WATER LEVELS IN WELLS IN THE WESTERN PROVINCE

MELLAHAH, BIN GASHIR, SUWANI BIN YADIM

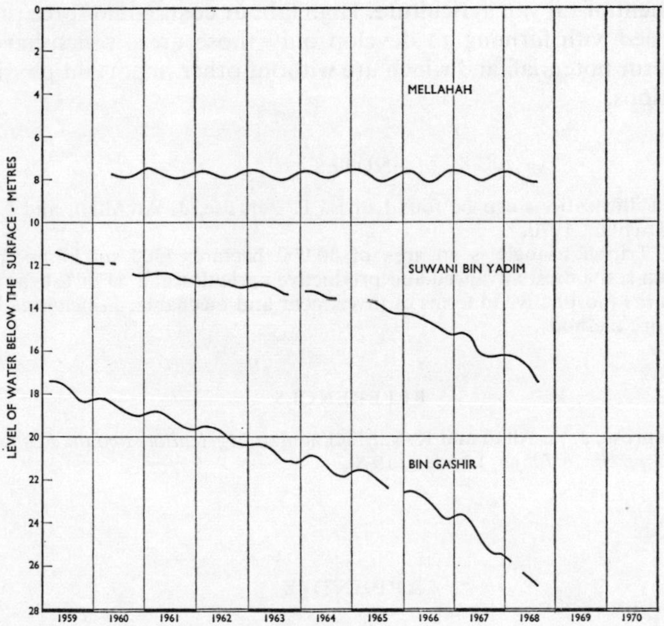

SOURCE :- Ministry of Agriculture, Soil & Water Conservation Department.

Stevens water level recorder in all three wells providing almost continuous records.

in Libya is rising slowly, and that an important part of the increase has come from farms developed by Libyan farmers on areas first developed by Italian colonists. Such rises have come at the same time as a decline in outputs from areas of traditional, irrigated agriculture, concentrated near the coast and the major settlements. Regrettably, underground water, the resource most likely to limit agricultural development, shows signs of serious decline, and it is possible that the rising cost of labour may be in the best interests of the long-term development of Libyan agriculture. High labour costs could force those concerned with farming to develop only those areas which have a long term potential, and which are without other important physical limitations.

NOTES

1 Such illustrations can be found in E. T. Penrose, J. A. Allan, and K. S McLachlan, 1970.

2 The Tripoli triangle is an area of 30,000 hectares (300 sq. kilometres), which is the most advanced and productive agricultural area of Libya. It is also the most active in terms of investment and mechanized (including irrigation) methods.

REFERENCES

E. T. Penrose, J. A. Allan and K. S. MacLachlan, *Agriculture and the Economic Development of Libya*, London, 1970.

APPENDIX

An outline of the research on the agricultural development of Libya since independence

Since independence in 1951 research into the agricultural development of Libya has been sponsored by the Libyan government, by United Nations agencies as well as by foreign and academic bodies. It should be noted that an even greater volume of research material was assembled by the Italian colonial government between 1911 and 1942.[1]

An early United Nations study was that of Higgins in 1953.[2] It was a comprehensive summary of all aspects of economic development giving prominence to agriculture, the agricultural sector being the major contributor to GDP until after oil. A much fuller study was carried out soon after the announcement of the discovery of oil (1958). It was sponsored by the International Bank for Reconstruction and Development and published in 1960.[3] Although a thorough study it underestimated the rate of growth in oil revenues and the distribution of the wealth to the people.

After independence (1951) and before oil (1958) the United States increased her financial assistance to Libya, and some of this aid was directed to USAID missions, which in turn cooperated with United Nations agricultural research teams.[2] Much of this work was hindered by the absence of full and reliable data, and therefore the major long-term contribution of these research teams was in recording some of the physical and institutional criteria relevant to agriculture, for example the work of Cederstrom,[4] Stuart,[5] Ogilbee,[6] Doyel,[7] Maguire,[8] Theodoru[9] etc.

After oil, research concerned with agricultural development was sponsored by the Ministry of Agriculture, by the Census Department (formerly of the Ministry of Economy and Trade and after 1968 within the Ministry of Planning) and by the Libyan University. Population censuses were carried out in 1954 and 1964, and an agricultural census was completed in 1960, the latter being published in 1962.*

In 1965 a comprehensive inventory study including mapping was initiated by the Ministry of Planning. The work was contracted to consultants and air survey companies and completed by 1967; the inventories and reports were accompanied by recommendations for the planned regional development of the country. The air survey and mapping was carried out competently and must prove a valuable record and basis for planning. The inventory reports were, however, less satisfactory, in that they summarized the often inadequate available statistics on a regional basis, and supplemented these with information derived from interviews with local administrators and 'tribal' representatives, who were usually not able to provide accurately the quantitative data being sought.

Studies based on the agricultural census appeared from 1962 onwards, and Attiga[10] the author of one such report was afterwards always uneasy about the accuracy of such records, and revised many, especially those connected with estimates of crop production.

Research by academic institutions and individuals has been continuous since independence. Articles by Fisher appeared in the early 1950s,[11] and he later directed the interests of a number of research students of the geography department of the University of Durham towards Libya. An important item of preparatory work was the bibliography published by Hill in 1959.[12] His own and other unpublished theses[13] were completed at Durham between 1959 and 1961, all of which were studies of aspects of agricultural development in parts of Libya. Some of their findings are summarized in the publication *Field Studies in Libya* edited by Willimott and Clarke (1950).[14] Further work was carried out by Libyan research students in the Department of Geography of the University of Durham during the 1960s.[15]

Contributions by individuals from universities of the United States came in the late 1960s. A study of migration to Tripoli was made by Harrison and published in 1967,[16] and a thesis was completed by Brown treating the impact of oil on agriculture in the cases of Marada and Augila.[17]

The most extensive study of the changes brought about by oil in the agricultural sector was made by a joint project of the Libyan and London Universities. Field work, including detailed land use and crop studies, together with farm inventories were completed between 1966 and 1968 and a report published in four volumes in 1970.[18] The report sets out in Volume I the physical background to Libyan agricultural development since 1911 and comments on recent developments and changes in farming, especially with respect to land use, investment and wages. In Volumes 2 and 3 the results of land use and questionnaire surveys are summarized in maps and tabulations. Volume 4 is a specialised bibliography of maps and air photos. Interesting features of the project were its inter-disciplinary nature in that it involved both economists

* There are reservations concerning the accuracy of these census publications.

and geographers, and also that it was directed jointly by Dr. M. M. Buru, representing the Libyan University, and Dr. K. S. McLachlan acting for the School of Oriental and African Studies, London.

The publications of the above joint research project also treated the water resources of Libya, especially in the western provinces. However, more detailed and lengthy studies were organized by J. R. Jones within the Soil and Water Department of the Ministry of Agriculture.[19] He reviewed the position in his *Ground-water maps of Libya* (1964), and the observations wells organized by him permitted studies to be carried out for the 1960–68 period, which proved the serious declines in underground water in coastal western Libya.[20]

The water resources of southern Libya became better known as the result of petroleum exploration, and an attempt was made in 1968 to survey the south-eastern part of the country. A survey was carried out by Wright in the south of the province of Ajdabiyah,[21] showing that enough water existed to support limited and probably economically viable agriculture, provided suitably motivated labour could be organized. An agricultural venture was already at an experimental stage farther south at Kufra.

Since the revolution in September 1969 no significant academic research has been carried out on agricultural topics, but it would seem that ministry sponsored research is going ahead as before.

REFERENCES

1 Publications relating to the agricultural development of Libya during the Italian colonial period have been housed and recorded centrally in the *Istituto Agronomico per l'Oltremare*, Via Cocchi, 4 Firenze, Italy – some are still able to be purchased from this institute. Some of the organizations which published between 1911 and 1942 were:—
Istituto Agronomico per l'Africa Italiana;
Societa Italiana per lo Studio della Libia e delle altre Colonie;
Istituto Agricolo Coloniale Italiano;
R. Universata degli Studi di Firenze – Centro di Studi Coloniali.

2 Higgins, B. *The Economic and Social Development of Libya*, United Nations Technical Assistance Programme, New York, 1953, 1–78.

3 International Bank for Reconstruction and Development, *The Economic Development of Libya*, Washington, D.C. 1960, 1–471.

4 The major research and development agencies cooperating with the Government of Libya during the 1951–61 period were:—
The Food and Agricultural Organization (FAO – Rome)
Libyan-American Reconstruction Commission (LARC);
Libyan-American Joint Services (LAJS);
Libyan Development Council;
Libyan Public Development & Stabilization Agency (LPDSA);
United States Agency for International Development – Mission to Libya (USAID);
United States Operations Mission to Libya (USOM);
The above agencies were cooperating with the following ministries:—
Ministry of Agriculture – especially the Soil and Water Conservation Department;
Ministry of Communications – Meteorological Department;
Ministry of Planning and Development.

5 Cederstrom, D. J. and Bertaiola, M., *Ground-water resources of the Tripoli area, Libya*, prepared cooperatively by the United States Operations

Mission to Libya (USOM) and the US Geological Survey (USGS) Tripoli, 1960.

6 Stuart, W. T. *Significance of the decline in ground-water levels in Tripolitania, Libya, as determined by pumping tests,* USOM and USGS Open File Report, Tripoli, 1960.

7 Ogilbee, W., Vorhis, R. C. and Tarhuni, H. A., *Ground-water resources of the Az Zawiyah area.* USGS and Ministry of Agriculture, Tripoli, 1962.

8 Doyel, W. W. and Maguire, F. J. *Results of water investigations in the Benghazi area,* USOM and USGS, Tripoli, 1959.

9 Theodorov, N. T., *Report to the Government of Libya on indigenous and Italian farm enterprises in the Zawia area,* FAO Report No. 259, Rome, 1954.

10 Azonni, M. M. and Attiga, A. A., *Analysis of available agricultural data in relation to agricultural production and planning,* Technical sub-committee, Draft Five Year Plan, Tripoli 1962.
Note: Ess. Attiga was Minister of Planning up to September 1969.

11 Fisher, W. B., *Agriculture in Modern Libya,* Geographical Magazine, Vol. XXV, No. 3, July 1952, pp. 184–94.

12 Hill, R. W., *A bibliography of Libya,* Department of Geography, University of Durham, Research Papers Series No. 1, Durham, 1959.

13 Hill, R. W., *Agriculture and irrigation in the Tripolitanian Jefara,* unpublished Ph.D. thesis, University of Durham, 1960.
Brehoney, J. N., *A geographical study of the Jebel Tarhuna, Tripolitania,* Unpublished Ph.D. thesis, University of Durham, 1961.
McLachlan, K. S., *A geographical study of the coastal zone between Homs and Misurata, Tripolitania,* unpublished Ph.D. thesis, University of Durham, 1961.

14 Willimott, S. E. and Clarke, J. I., *Field Studies in Libya,* Department of Geography, University of Durham, Research Papers Series No. 4, 1960.

15 Buru, M. M., *El-Marj Plain: a geographical study,* unpublished Ph.D. thesis, University of Durham, 1965.

16 Harrison, R. S. 'Migrants in the City of Tripoli, Libya', *Geographical Review,* Vol. 57, 1967, pp. 397–423.

17 Brown, R. L. *Interaction of Oases and Petroleum Development,* unpublished Ph.D. thesis, 1968.

18 Libyan University – London University Joint Research Project, *General Report;* London, 1970:
Volume 1: *Agriculture and the Economic Development of Libya.* Edited by Professor Edith Penrose, J. A. Allan and Dr. K. S. McLachlan.
Volume 2: *Maps.* Libya Crop Survey Maps and General Land Use Maps with an Analysis of the Agriculture of Western Libya by Computer Maps.
Volume 3: *Tabulated Data from Questionnaire Surveys of Libya* 1966/67 *and Western Libya* 1967/68.
Volume 4: *A Select Map and Air Photo Bibliography of Libya,* with Special Reference to Coastal Libya. Compiled by J. A. Allan.

19 Jones, J. R., *Ground-water maps of Libya,* US Geological Survey, Open File Report, Tripoli, 1964, p. 1–11 with maps.

20 Allan, J. A., 'Some recent developments in Libyan agriculture', *Middle East Economic Papers,* Beirut, 1969.

21 Wright, E. P. and Edmunds, W. M., *Hydrogeological studies in Central Cyrenaica,* Institute of Geological Sciences, London, 1969.

XI

The Evolution of the Moroccan National Movement since Independence

M. Palazzoli

University of Rabat, Morocco

1. *Some General Considerations*

The apparent simplicity of the play of politics in Morocco depends on the dominant position in it of an actor whose strategy and presence eclipse those of the others, and also on the unanimity of the view of the fundamental objectives to be pursued, at least according to their public declarations. But a closer approach immediately dissipates this double impression, and even though they do not always occupy the centre of the stage, numerous actors are moving about on it with diverging options as to essentials, and in conflict over an unspoken struggle for the retention or conquest of power.

1. *The number and type of opponents* can be quite easily explained if one bears in mind the conditions obtaining on the return to independence, which strengthened one of them at the same time that it prepared the ground for the division of the others.

For in Morocco, as often elsewhere, it was the traditional bourgeois conservative forces which unleashed and led the national liberation struggle. Long kept away from the reins of power by the colonizer, they aspired to remove him, and on his departure seized them for themselves, confiscating for their own benefit the modern sector which he had set up in town and country. But here the process took place in rather special circumstances, which gave rise in part to the present balance of forces in the country.

On the one hand the monarchy came out of it considerably strengthened, whereas it could have collapsed, as in Tunisia, in favour of a more charismatic leader than the sovereign. Many reasons can be adduced for this. Very early on, in 1933 on the occasion of the Feast of the Throne, and the demonstrations in Fes in 1934, the nationalists had discovered the profit to be gained from propaganda based on the person of the Sultan, and on the reverence owed to his prerogatives. Moreover, it could be opportune to obtain support of the supreme authority in the land (however reduced its real powers might be at that time), and thus shelter behind it by covering the claims they put forward with the cloak of legitimacy. Once these tactics had been chosen, at any rate, the nationalists clung obstinately to them. Muḥammad V had the sense to realize on his part that it was up to him to make sure of the future of the dynasty by taking over the leadership of the movement, as witnessed for example by the complications attending his journey to Tangiers in 1947. And, as is well known, in exiling him the French rendered the finest of services to his crown: the resistance had taken as its basis the usurpation of Moroccan sovereignty; henceforth it was given a precise, immediate objective. The return of the sultan became the symbol of victory in the eyes of everyone. A legend grew around his person, all the more easily in that the work carried out in depth over the years by the leaders of the liberation struggle had prepared the population for this, and could at last bear fruit. So that for the masses, deeply grieved by the departure of Muḥammad V, independence would mean the restoration of royal power with the totality of its rights which had been taken over by the occupier.

If the monarch came out of this trial with increased stature, at the same time there existed at his side a strong and lively nationalist party, its influence spread among the workers by a vigorous union, and in the country by a turbulent army of liberation which in certain areas refused to lay down its arms: the oarty of the Istiqlāl which could easily have brought into question the authority of the crown and imposed its will upon the State, had it remained united. Some at least of its leaders wanted this, but their dream was never realized. For the nationalists were to be the victims of their own tactics, and perceived very quickly that even though it had been an investment in the short term to raise the standard of the monarchy, once independence was acquired such a policy was likely to rebound on them.

The ruler, in fact, could not without difficulty endure so powerful a rival for long. Personal differences and rival ambitions had always divided the leaders of the movement; it was tempting to play on them. More especially, as in many other countries of the Third World, amongst those who had worked together for liberation a rupture quickly appeared between the conservative old guard, who would have liked to settle down into independence without modifying the structures of the country, at all events not raising a finger against the advantages of the propertied classes, and more progressive elements, brought into the movement later on, who favoured more thorough-going reforms in order to hasten the evolution of the country on a basis of greater social justice. The most striking illustration of this was the split of 1959 which gave rise to the UNFP; its only result was to help the ruler, whose power was obviously strengthened by the disunity of the nationalist forces.

However, the population, very anxious that the reforms promised for the end of the Protectorate should occur, would not have allowed too open a division between these forces, nor would they have understood an open conflict against the king on the part of some of them, beginning with the Istiqlāl. Appearances had to be maintained, the adversary dealt with tactfully, the outlines of the dispute blurred; numerous ambiguities, at least in the beginning, bear witness to this..

2. *Thus the interplay of politics in Morocco is characterized by a marked ambiguity*, having as its main effect a cleavage between the avowed objectives of the contenders and those which in reality they hope to achieve.

The declared objectives are more or less the same for everyone, though each doubtless is eager to accuse the other of betraying them. But everyone refers to them: the struggle against underdevelopment, agrarian reform and a more equitable division of wealth, industrialization, consolidation of independence and vigilant nationalism, non-alignment, building of the Maghrib . . . And glorious harmony appears to reign on essentials: Islam and traditional values, the monarchical form of the State, democracy – to which everyone proclaims his tireless devotion.

But here more than elsewhere appearances are deceptive. The political forces confronting one another in Morocco are in fact clearly placed in the struggle for power which absorbs them; their interests are divergent, in spite of the myth of national unity to which they pay lip-service; their choices differ, and the conflict between them though it may be muffled or subdued, is none the less a social conflict of considerable intensity.

For the conservative forces, represented fairly adequately by certain parties (such as the Istiqlāl, until further evidence, or the Mouvement Populaire), certain bourgeois circles (whose representatives are numerous in the Sultan's entourage and in the government), certain unions and professional groups (such as the UMA), the objective is to share with the Sultan in the exercise of power without changing it in form or substance, or to bring to bear as much influence as possible on his decisions, in order to preserve the present social balance, a body of purely Moroccan traditions, and above all the interests of the propertied class. But as underdevelopment could not be perpetuated or made worse without risk to the ruling classes, they demand through their spokesmen a minimum number of reforms to allow the economy of the country to 'take off' without damage to their privileges, and if possible to their benefit.

On the other hand, for the revolutionary forces, embodied in certain parties (such as the UNFP and the clandestine Communist party) and certain unions (such as the UMT and the UNEM), the goal is the modification of the form and content of power, either by making the monarchy subject to control, or even (though no one dare say it openly) by abolishing it, if it should appear to be tied too closely to the conservative forces, in order that the ideas of socialism might prevail, and a new organization of state and economy, more in keeping with the interests of the working classes, take the place of the old one. That is to say that the 'Left' demands more radical reforms with more conviction (even though the terminology is sometimes the same).

As for the monarchy, its strategy is both simpler and more complex. For it, the problem is to retain the dominant position it gained, with the departure of the occupying forces, at the head of the affairs of the country, in the face of forces attempting either to share its power, or to take it away altogether. The best way of achieving this, as was understood early on, is to play off one adversary against the other while appearing to act as referee, a catalyst, a centre of gravity holding the nation together. But such a position is not easily maintained, because the king has to govern, that is, to take decisions, make choices, undertake reforms. In doing this he commits himself, and cannot avoid breaking with some forces, binding himself more openly to others, and in this way endangering the throne.

In the event, by removing gradually from power the *élite* of the nationalist movement, the monarchy has cut itself off from the active forces in the country; and though the opposition, powerless, divided, sick, is today in the throes of a very serious crisis, the regime itself appears to have reached an impasse: bogged down in its own contradictions, and seriously shaken by the 'coup' of Skhirat, which almost brought it down, it has difficulty in getting a grip on national realities, and clearly has to make even greater efforts at a time when it appears that since July 1971 it has lost the means of dissuasion, if not repression, which permitted it to survive.

Cast into outer darkness, the nationalist movement has retired to winter quarters, for the time being powerless to influence the orientation of power, worn out, aged, embittered, but still rich in hopes not attained at independence.

2. *The Party of Istiqlāl*

Principal architect and catalyser of the national liberation struggle, the Istiqlāl, more than thirty years after its founding, is still without any doubt the most important of the Moroccan political parties: strong, influential, deeply entrenched. Yet it failed to take advantage of independence. Gradually removed by the monarchy from the leadership it could have claimed, weakened by the split of 1959, thrown in 1963 into a semi-opposition, where it is bogged down and bitter, powerless to have a real influence on the future of the regime, giving the impression of a magnificent but immobile machine, impotent for the present, but available, and a very real presence in the political contest, if only for the numbers it can still mobilize. A prisoner of its beginnings, they are, truth to tell, the wellsprings of its remaining vigour, and of all the defects from which it suffers.

1. *The origins of the party.* The party of the Istiqlāl arose, as is well known, from a desire to use for the benefit of the nationalist cause the favourable circumstances resulting from the war, and the prospect of an allied victory which could be discerned at the end of 1943. At this time, in fact, it took over from the Parti National, which had itself replaced the Comité d'Action Marocaine created in 1934 at the instigation of M. Allal el Fasi, and a few political friends. But this time it is no longer a matter of restricting their claims to a few measures which would liberalize the system. Independence is what is demanded (the manifesto of January 1944, approved by the Sultan, is unmistakable in this respect), and as long as this principle was not accepted by France, they refused to support any project for reform proposed by her.

The new party was based on the alliance of three elements which all belong to the most sophisticated segment of the urban *élite*: the traditional bourgeoisie of the northern towns, particularly Fes, well represented by Allal el Fasi (then in exile in Gabon), hostile to the Protectorate which prevented its taking on the leading role which it would otherwise have assumed, and moved by a desire for a rebirth of the nation founded on the Quran; the modern sector of big business, embodied in men like MM. Omar Abdeljallil and Ahmed Balafrej, receptive to European culture, more dynamic, but angered at being kept apart from the management of the economic renewal to which it aspired; lastly, young left wing intellectuals, of less important bourgeois origin, with westernized education, who were to provide the officers of the union movement and later on of the UNFP: Mehdi ben Barka, Abderrahim Bouabid, Abdallah Ibrahim.

All these men, later to be divided by bitter rivalries, were at the beginning believers in the same faith, the same ideal, and the Istiqlāl, even if it never succeeded in bringing together all the nationalists (M. El Wazzani continued to go his own way at the head of the PDI founded by him, and two different organizations were militant in the Spanish zone; the Parti des Réformes Nationales of M. Abdelhalek

Torrès and the Parti d'Unité Marocaine of M. Mekki Nasiri) rapidly acquired a dominant influence, because its prestige and the deepening atmosphere of repression, together with the high cost of living and the burden of taxation, caused malcontents to gather round it in ever greater numbers. Originally a party of notables, with little formal organization, it realized very quickly (following the hardening of the French attitude after the Sultan's journey to Tangiers, and the arrival of General Juin, which destroyed the hope of impending independence) the necessity it was in to organize itself for a long struggle, to penetrate more deeply into the Moroccan masses and bring them into the organization, also to increase its international audience and canvass for support abroad. But the arrest of its leaders and the banning order following the riots of 1952 dislocated it for a while, and the wave of terrorism which broke over the country, especially after the Sultan was deposed, was not in fact under its control, though encouraged by it, coming instead from below, from elements not always directed by the Istiqlāl, a fact which, however, did not prevent its emerging almost intact from clandestinity at the end of the Protectorate, strengthened by the victory of the cause for which it had fought, but assailed by new problems, more dangerous because less simple than those of the heroic period of the liberation struggle.

2. *The characteristics and problems of the party.* There were two major problems confronting the Istiqlāl immediately after the departure of the French: to compete with the monarchy in running the affairs of the country, whereas the king was determined to do all he could to contain the influence of the party and if possible drive it back into the shadows; to keep its unity, whereas a serious difference of opinion among its ranks divided the middle class supporters of the established order from a left wing impatient to overthrow structures which it judged out of date, and to achieve socialism. And we know that in both cases the party lost, because the Palace, by perseverance and guile, managed to remove it from power, and the split of 1959 consummated the division, long since apparent, of the nationalist movement into two rival factions. The present appearance of the party is in large part a result of these events, and also of its origins discussed above; this appearance can be reduced to three dominant characteristics.

a. The first is due to the internal divisions of the Istiqlāl. Doubtless the divorce of 1959 made it more homogeneous by reducing it to its more moderate elements. But the dissensions survive at that level, merely more subdued, less virulent, than in the past, less dangerous too for the cohesion of the party, because they are no longer the expression of a confrontation of classes and interests, but a conflict of generations which can moreover be found in all political and union organizations in Morocco, and which brings into opposition the old guard steeped in Muslim culture, often xenophobic, clinging for years at the head of the party to positions which are by now completely outdated, and a team of young westernized 'modernists', more receptive to economic and social problems, more conscious of the urgent need for certain reforms, occasionally very critical of the regime, and finally keen to restore to the party, by bringing it up to date, the vitality it has lost. But the old guard stands firm, and its leader (less disputed than others) is still full of vigour and fighting spirit; it is in charge of the party machine; the leadership is in its hands; and the militants, the officers of the Istiqlāl, also chosen for preference from the traditional sector, are its devoted adherents. Therefore the takeover is not easy, but to ensure this is at present the party's greatest problem. As long as it has not taken place, the party cannot be expected to adopt a more dynamic, decisive policy.

b. The Istiqlāl in fact – a second characteristic – is a party which has some difficulty in renewing its programme. Doubtless one would be wrong to think of it as the representative of a narrow, retrograde middle class Muslim conservatism, as some have supposed (beginning with its political opponents). The party has approved certain reforms (the carrying out of development plans, the increase of national prosperity, the creation of heavy industry, freedom from taxes of the great mass of Moroccan small farmers thanks to the abolition of the *tertib* in 1961, etc.); it demands others (some nationalizations, the mobilization of savings, changes in the distribution of money . . .), and starting from the years 1960–3 it has managed to give its official policies a bolder image in economic and social matters, as witnessed in particular by the 'Manifeste de l'égalitarisme pour la libération économique' published in January 1963.

But we should not be deceived by this posture, of whose complete sincerity there is some doubt. The party, weakened by the departure of the UNFP, has been subject since 1959 to serious challenges on the left, and the leadership had to work tremendously hard to fight them off. To demand an agrarian reform, for example, is no doubt a realistic and generous attitude, but it can also be profitable when one has adherents to retain (especially when a party created by the Palace in its turn starts trying to attract them away from you) or to regain in the countryside. The Manifesto of 1963 was made public four months before the elections; this is not pure chance. And if the party asks, more urgently than ever since it has been trapped in opposition, for the establishment of a representative government guaranteed by the unhindered exercise of democratic liberties, it is not only to express the political ideal to which a part of the bourgeoisie is naturally attached, but also because it is of the opinion that the interplay of free and regular elections, and the mechanism of a parliamentary regime, could permit it, thanks to the following it still has in the country, to regain at government level positions which it has lost, and thus bring the monarch to come to terms with it.

In actual fact, the middle way ('neither capitalism nor communism') which the party has succeeded in defining in the last few years, is singularly prudent and conservative. In order to avoid an explosion, it is willing to promote a sounder economy, improve the lot of the working classes, distribute a few pieces of land; but without overthrowing established structures or questioning the interests of the propertied classes. If radical reforms are preached, the first aim is to embarrass the powers that be. And the basis of the Istiqlāl's doctrine (since the team of leaders has not been changed) is still passionate ultra-nationalism (seen clearly in the unshakeable determination it manifests in so far as Mauritania, the frontiers, the Spanish possessions in Morocco are concerned, and also its campaigns against French technical assistance and its intransigent advocacy of rapid Arabization of teaching at all levels), coupled with an attachment to the heritage of Islam which is very quick to take offence, and the need to find a religious justification for the choices it makes.

c. But, however serious the crisis of adjustment through which it is passing at present, the Istiqlāl still retains some importance in the Moroccan political spectrum, owing doubtless to the prestige of the memories associated with it, but also especially to its remarkable organization, and the strength of its following in various parts of the country.

The party machine is still in good shape, functioning well; its structure is that of a mass party, well entrenched at the lower levels, strongly built at the top, with numerous militants in all sections, flanked by parallel organizations – such as the UDTM, the UGEM, or the various cultural, sports, and scout organizations brought together in the Jeunesse istiqlalienne – which effectively support its activities. Vertical links predominate. Decisions are taken at the centre, and the regularity of party congresses since 1960, the frequency with which its leading components meet, bear witness to a vitality of which it is the only example among the Moroccan parties. Finally, its press, and especially the daily press, which has appeared for many years without too many vicissitudes (at least compared to that of the other parties), provides useful propaganda for it, even though its circulation is fairly limited, and confiscations are frequent. The real problems, therefore, lie elsewhere: in the progressive diminution of its resources, especially since it has been in opposition, and its former financial backers (people like M. Laghzawi) have abandoned it; and in the level of the oligarchy which governs it, impossible to remove in spite of pressure from the young.

Its empire, moreover, has twice been progressively reduced: after the split of 1959, and at least temporarily after the creation of the FDIC. But the elections of 1963,[1] though they showed this up (the Istiqlāl was outclassed in the mountains by the Front gouvernmental and in the industrial towns of the Atlantic coast by the UNFP), also confirmed, despite numerous pressures and acts of violence in the course of the campaign, the ascendancy still maintained by the Istiqlāl at that time, and which it has certainly retained in the towns of the interior, notably at Fes (where the traditional bourgeoisie, the traders, artisans, and lower professional classes voted overwhelmingly for it), in the rich countryside of the Gharb and the Tadla, in the districts of Safi and Essawira, and at Tetuan, for example.

The future is by no means closed for this party, therefore, especially as the new generation succeeds in gaining control of it. And, moreover, the monarchy treats it with caution, and has never really attacked it head on,[2] no doubt because of what it represents, and because the fund of goodwill which it still enjoys here and there makes it a partner worthy of respect, which in certain circumstances could once more be transformed into a valuable ally; also because it is well aware that the party would like to collaborate, and in any case is not fundamentally hostile to the monarchy as some others are; lastly because it is an essential, irreplaceable element in the delicate balance of political and social forces upon which the regime at present rests.

3 *L'Union Nationale des Forces Populaires*

The UNFP is only ten years old. But its history is enthralling: it is that of the failure of a left wing formation, powerful at the beginning, which failed to exploit the possibilities of revolutionary action which were open to it, and which is today going through a profound crisis, surviving with difficulty, waiting for better days. It is sufficient to say that studying this party is to go right to the heart of the political struggles played out recently in Morocco; and to lay one's finger on the predicament of the Left in this country, where it is at present powerless to offer a viable alternative to the regime.

The circumstances of the birth of the UNFP are common knowledge, and it is known that well before 1959 the heterogeneity of the various sections of the Istiqlāl already contained the seeds of a split which the test of power, the manoeuvres of the Palace, and the progressive clarification of their political positions finally made inevitable.

This secession, which was intended and prepared, as the municipal elections approached, by forward-looking young intellectuals of modest urban background won over to the ideals of socialism, took on the appearance in the early stages of its growth of a democratic movement, apparently arising from the grass roots, directed against the conservative leadership of the Istiqlāl whose removal was desired by the Left, in the absence of a national Congress at which that leadership could be contested. Therefore at the beginning it was not a question, at least officially, of seceding, but of isolating M. Allal el Fasi and his friends by stirring up within the party a movement which would win over the mass of militants. Thus as a first stage provincial congresses were called: they led to the setting up of autonomous federations crowned in March 1959 by the Confédération Nationale du Parti de l'Istiqlal, the first step to the Union founded some months later in September.

But in fact the whole operation was set in motion and led deliberately to its completion, in conditions which appeared to ensure its complete success, since of the three men who planned it, the first, Mohammed Basri, brought to the enterprise the unruly support of the Resistance movement; the second, Mahjoub ben Seddik, the support of the union he controlled; and the third, Mehdi ben Barka, his abilities as an organizer and the party machine of the Istiqlāl, which he believed to be under his control; at the same time the presence of political friends of the secessionists in Ibrahim's cabinet guaranteed them, besides the active support of the government, the rallying (however equivocal and precarious) of all those dazzled by the possibilities of power.

However, the hopes which had presided over the birth of the UNFP were, in spite of so many advantages, rapidly disappointed. It is worthwhile to try to discover exactly why, pointing out the problems the party had to face up to, and following its development with some care.

1. *Problems and choices of the party*. Very early the UNFP had formidable problems to overcome; it is not too harsh to say that it did not manage to resolve any of them properly.

a. *The first* was to draw up a policy. The party attempted to do so. But it never succeeded in opting for a clear, firm strategy, and the line it followed was always wavy, uncertain and ambiguous.

There is no doubt that its programme and the various positions it took up made it irrefutably a party of the Left: in foreign affairs displaying solidarity with the revolutionary movements of the Third World, and convinced that the unity of the Arab world can only come about on a basis of socialism; nationalistic, fighting for the total economic and political liberation of Morocco both in the eyes of the outside world and in connection with the archaic social structures which in its opinion must be destroyed so that greater justice might prevail for the benefit of the working classes; fundamentally hostile to the regime embodied in the monarchy, in so far as it appears essentially to be closely linked with the interests of the ruling classes to be overthrown, with corruption, with the obstructionist and arbitrary nature of the administration; lastly, in favour of representative democracy (even though there is little chance of its working properly in a country which is not ready to receive it) both for tactical reasons (for it could be a means whereby the opposition, even if it did not come to power immediately, might at least stir up many difficulties for the government in power by making use of its mechanisms and profiting from the relative anarchy which it might bring with it), and more sincerely because it is better, according to the UNFP leaders, than the methods prevailing at present, and may lead to a beginning of the indispensable education of the masses by mobilizing them politically.

The UNFP is a party of the Left by its major alignments and also by its social basis, reflected in its electorate, on which the elections of 1960 and 1963 give valuable information: in general an electorate which is more homogeneous than that of other parties, and almost entirely concentrated – except for the district of the Souss and the mining area of Khourigba, where the party is also well entrenched – in the big modern cities of the Atlantic coastline from Agadir to Tangiers (and in the neighbouring countryside), particularly at Casablanca, Rabat and Kénitra, where the union has apparently attracted chiefly the advanced working class of the new medinas (the vote of the bidonvilles and the old medinas is in general more conservative), and a fraction of the intellectual and mercantile bourgeoisie of the better-class areas.

But the label 'party of the Left' is inadequate. It is too inexact, covering a fairly wide spread of possible actions. And like all progressive movements, the UNFP in fact from its beginnings had a choice between two possible attitudes: revolutionary intransigence or reformist prudence; to fight the regime openly, or to accept it while hoping to transform it slowly by its participation; a clandestine struggle if need be, and violence, or legal moderate activity and compromise. The dilemma is not new, nor is it peculiarly Moroccan; but the way in which it is faced and overcome by the Moroccan Left in relation to the realities of the moment should in any case be important for many years for the future of the country. Truth forces us to say that the leaders of the UNFP seem never to have pondered these matters, and in contrast with the Communists, for example, have never made a clear decision between these two possible policies. 'String of contradictory tactics' and 'a mixture of radical socialist knavery and Blanquiste boastfulness', to repeat two biting phrases of a former president of the UNEM in exile,[3] even at the time when the party was sailing before the wind about 1960, the strategy of the UNFP has displayed a fundamental indecision which has been attributed by certain observers to the opposing pulls of a leadership which is mainly 'petty bourgeois' and its more 'proletarian' following, but should probably be seen rather as the result of differences of temperament amongst the leaders, of the presence in their ranks of some opportunists and doubtful elements attracted at the beginning by the prospects of power open to the Union, and above all of a general lack of revolutionary experience among the officers of the party (often more attracted by demagogic solutions than aware of the objective realities which should guide them), and also the result of Moroccan attitudes, which lead politicians to prefer speech to action. Only Mehdi ben Barka, perhaps, understood more acutely than others the problem which confronted the Union – though this does not at all mean that he always acted wittingly. But at least he had the ability to realize that in order to join battle in any real sense, the party had to be properly organized and firmly based.[4]

b. It must be admitted that, although it is of primary importance, the UNFP has not been able to resolve the problem of its organization: it is of primary importance in that a revolutionary party, likely to be the object of government repression, only has a chance of survival if it has firm foundations and a sound structure to help it to stand up in difficult conditions and, if need be, survive in clandestinity. There is no doubt that on reading the statutes of the Union, one gains the impression of a party with a strong structure and an established hierarchy, on a model similar to that of the Communist parties. But the reality is different. With the modest financial resources at its disposal, continually hindered by numerous administrative difficulties, it has in fact so far failed in the successive efforts it has made to improve its organization.

One might explain why this was so by saying that at the outset its leaders were pulled in two contradictory directions, each as dangerous as the other: faith in the spontaneous adherence of the masses,[5] born out of the wave of popularity enjoyed by the party for a while following its participation in government – an adherence which however is almost worthless if it is not based on a firm foundation of direction and order; the other, the reflex of intellectuals who have no faith in those who are not of their number, and think that the troops they lead are only capable of following blindly the line drawn for them in the more rarefied atmosphere higher up – a reflex whose main effect was to cut off very quickly the leaders of the party from its base, and in particular from the workers. Therefore the real organization of the UNFP pays in fact very little regard to democracy – no different in this from other political parties in Morocco – and is above all very artificial, dominated by a small number of primary assumptions which bear little relation to the political struggle in the Moroccan situation, and, to quote once more the same source as above, 'confined within the limits of the electoralist model', which is by no means the one best adapted to the situation in which the Union has to fight. A 'political bureau' of three members was constituted in August 1967 to restructure the Union and prepare its third Congress; but it would be rash to say that new policies have been elaborated since then, and the Congress in fact has still not taken place.

c. Lastly, and a final black mark, relations between the UNFP and the other Moroccan organizations of the Left have always been difficult, and occasionally very strained. This is not surprising in so far as the Communist party is concerned, since it constitutes a formidable rival, drawing its adherents from the same social background, and able to outbid it for support. On the other hand the serious quarrel which for a long time separated the UNFP from the UMT is more surprising, since the most elementary demands of the struggle ought to have obliged union and party to stand together instead of tearing each other apart, and to collaborate closely to ensure the triumph of their objectives; in retrospect this appears to be one of the most significant aspects of the crisis affecting the Left in this country.

Its origins are little known, and must no doubt be sought in the conjuncture presiding at the foundation of the party in 1959, and in the attitude of the 'Centrale' (National Federation of Unions) at that time. Firmly entrenched at the time when the UNFP was created, largely under its patronage and in any case with its help and blessing, and anxious to keep its autonomy and independence from any political group, the UMT, therefore, kept its distance from the beginning; and in so far as the party refused to be entirely controlled by it, it stood somewhat apart, and pursued its own particular interests, in a way which is only too natural, but which degenerated in the following year, firstly into subdued hostility and then into open warfare. The Congress of 1962[6] which was called to smooth over these early divergencies, among other tasks, could only restore a surface unity resulting from hasty concessions on either side; and the rift rapidly widened. Differing positions taken up in regard to the main political problems of the day, frequent confrontations over essential matters (like that of the organization of agricultural unions in 1962), the boycott of the committees of the party by the unionists, and the distribution by party activists of pamphlets attacking the leader of the union:[7] these added up in effect to a real war of attrition, until the time when in August 1967 a solemn reconciliation was announced (perhaps owing to the arrest of M. Ben Seddik, which united the adversaries in their common misfortune).

The reasons for such a conflict are not easily unravelled, because the debates to which it gave rise took place in secret, at the level of the leadership, and the leaders were always at least tacitly agreed on one point: to say nothing to the masses of the real causes of the quarrel, which are therefore conjectural. The clash of personalities and temperaments doubtless played some part in it (the hostility of some people towards the Secretary General of the UMT was passionate and even visceral); but so also did the efforts of men like Mehdi ben Barka to make the union subordinate to the party, and differing appreciations of the political situation and the measures required to combat it; it was this appreciation which made the officers of the Centrale condemn the, in their opinion, over-adventurous line taken by some leaders of the party, and try to limit the predictable damage by holding the union, whose first task was to defend the immediate vital interests of its members, to more cautious 'a-political' positions. The repressive measures directed against the UNFP would in any case appear to justify, *a posteriori*, the prudence of Mahjoub ben Seddik and his team; but it is understandable that such tactics should be labelled opportunist by their adversaries within the party, and some are of the opinion that they could have confronted the future 'adventurist' danger in ways other than the withdrawal of the Centrale, which broke up the unity of the Left Front.

The tragedy of the UNFP, in fact, is that these dissensions arose, without its being able to surmount them, at the very time when the government in power decided to have done with the party. We must now dwell on this by sketching in a rapid account of the relations between the party and the central power since 1959; for though the Union was unable to resolve satisfactorily any of the problems confronting it, it appears to be in part because the regime did all it could to prevent it by making life difficult for it.

2. *The evolution of the party*. Since its creation the UNFP has passed through two phases, the one ascending, the other descending.

a. The first phase, which ended at the beginning of 1963, was a splendid period in the history of the party, during which its influence increased and its position was gradually consolidated at least in certain parts of the country. This period can itself be divided into two distinct stages. Until May 1960 the party had to attract people, to take root, to assert itself: the party participated in government, and maintained quite good relations with the Palace; it accepted the regime and counted upon the broadening of democracy and on compromises with the conservative elements to organize the necessary transitions and undertake the most urgent reforms. But the first persecutions to which it was subjected, and its dismissal from the Ibrahim cabinet, gave its militants a rude awakening. Thrown suddenly into opposition, the UNFP learned that it could expect nothing from collaboration with the traditional ruling class, at a time when the increase in its public audience, and its relative success at the municipal elections,[8] gave it the feeling that its power was sufficiently proved to enable it to take up a more obviously revolutionary stance, and come into direct conflict with the regime; the tone then hardened considerably, provocations increased, and the Congress of 1962 produced a veritable indictment of the monarchy and those elements of the bourgeoisie which supported it.

b. But the party made the mistake of over-rating its own strength and underestimating the capacity of the central power to resist, worried by these violent declarations and the success of the Union which was confirmed by the elections of May 1963.[9] So the party was made the object of repressive measures; torn apart, diminished, deprived of its means of expression, since then it has been licking its wounds. The crisis is very serious: entangled at the outset by its participation in the government and thereby compromised, then over-insistent in circumstances which were not ripe for a takeover, the party could not gain the position of strength it needed, and its enemies defeated it without difficulty. Powerless, trying to avoid both rebellion and servility, either of which would destroy it, paralysed by the inactivity which corrodes and slowly engulfs it, its problem is to survive in obscurity, and its hope is to remain a force to be reckoned with in spite of everything (with since July 1970 the aid of the Istiqlāl if necessary), and to try to turn to its own profit the increasing social unrest in order to take over when the time comes. But could it ever succeed in this? Failure and some mistakes in politics are not easily forgiven. The only way out for the party in the immediate future is to go through a period of sincere self-criticism, without equivocation, with free debate (a thing which has never happened) about the experience of these ten years. Some of the militants appear to have grasped this, especially amongst the young; but much remains to be done before the party can find its way out of the impasse.

Successive positions taken up by the party are a reflection of this evolution.

The declarations from the early period of its foundation are animated by great enthusiasm, weighed down scarcely at all by the polemic with the old guard of the Istiqlāl. The party was convinced that time was on its side: certain of its leaders were in power, and attempting to bring about reforms with the intention of preparing the ground for the socialization of the country; and the clouds which began to gather over its relations with the Palace were not yet dark enough to cast a gloom over the honeymoon period, studded with flattering judgements as regards the sovereign and reiterations of the attachment of the Union to the Throne.

However, from May 1960 the tone changes. According to them the regime had cast aside its mask: it was 'reactionary', 'fascist', 'feudal', and the only remedy was to destroy it. Violent from the outset, these declarations became increasingly loaded with virulence and revolutionary zeal, as the party became aware of what it took to be its strength. Every royal initiative was henceforth contested vigorously, and every turn in the political struggle gave the Union the opportunity for renewed assaults upon the central power, whose imminent fall it predicted. Subsequent to the repression of 1963, Ben Barka's appeal, and certain of his writings, perpetuated to some extent the tone of this second period into the third, where it is otherwise unknown.

Cast down and wounded, in these latter years the UNFP has perforce had to unlearn the vehemence of the heroic period. No doubt the refusal of the system remains, and criticism is often accurate and severe, showing in this way that the party has not turned its back on its first choice, but the tone has changed, becoming cautious and moderate, at times almost plaintive. They dare no longer attack the monarch head on, and even let it be understood that under certain conditions they might be ready to collaborate. And they limit themselves to asking for a minimum of reforms to regain for the party the rights it lost as a result of its imprudence. Fundamentally the objectives have not changed: but since they annoy the central power, whose anger is to be feared, they are formulated in a sufficiently low key not to worry it, so that at least it allows the party to survive.

4 *Front National*

We lack the distance necessary to put into perspective the full significance of the operation which in July 1970 led the Istiqlāl and the UNFP to call a halt to their dispute, and come together in a National Front, whose creation they surrounded with all the pomp of a great historic reconciliation. But it is permissible to formulate already with some degree of assurance a few remarks at least on the significance of the event.

1. There is no need to stress the 'apparent' speed of the process of reconciliation: this impressed all observers, since it took in all no more than four days for the two parties to progress from the simple simultaneous publication of communiqués in which they declared

their common hostility to the king's projected Constitution (18 July), to the drawing up (22 July) of the Charter of Salé, whose promulgation served to mark the official birth of the Front. The referendum, therefore, acted as a catalysing agent, or the pretext for a reconciliation, which however cannot be entirely explained in terms of this one thing. In fact in September 1969 the municipal elections had already been the occasion of the drawing up of a common communiqué by the two parties, who were in agreement over the boycotting of the elections. Since then contacts had increased at all levels, and if the brothers who had been enemies had finally decided to come together again, it was because they were already being pushed in that direction by many forces, not only by the purely conjunctural desire to take up the challenge they were offered.

Within their ranks there were many who were nostalgic for the time when they were united; and the memory, still alive among the older militants, of the struggle once waged together against the occupying power, helped, as the outlines of their mutual grievances became blurred with time, to arouse in them the feeling (expressed occasionally in moments of confidence) that they belonged, after all, to the same family. Since moreover it had at length become obvious to all that the disunity of the nationalist movement benefited no one but their enemies, the idea gradually spread among its divided members that instead of spending their time in mutual recrimination, they might yet heal the breach in order by their united efforts to gain the heights once more.

But in fact it is obvious that it was the changes taking place in both of them that most helped bring about the reconciliation. The principal aspects of this have been discussed. After, at the risk of its own destruction, undergoing a 'crisis of leftism, or adventurism', the UNFP, after the plot of 1963, moved steadily to wiser, more reformist positions, and is now led by the most moderate of its former leaders. On its side the Istiqlāl, originally compromised by its participation in the government, has to some extent regained its reputation, since its long stay in opposition has cut it off from power, and it is subject to pressures from younger, more dynamic elements which are pushing it into more and more radical attitudes.

The objective conditions for the convergence of the two parties were thus realized, and serious reasons of a tactical nature helped to force them to come to an agreement in practice: because the alliance with the UNFP gave considerable support on the left to the Istiqlāl, whose sincerity was still doubted by many; whereas the more vigorous party machine and more articulate press of the Istiqlāl gave to the dismembered, oppressed UNFP a prop by which to climb out of its difficulties.

2. How strong is the edifice which has just arisen in this way? In the immediate future one may be sceptical, even though it has successfully overcome the hazards of the month following the referendum.

No doubt the Front is desirous of being open to all 'nationalist formations' which might wish to adhere to it; and it received immediately the support of most of the opposition unions and, through the good offices of Ali Yata, of the clandestine PLS. It is also true that its sudden appearance produced a shock, which was felt all the more in that it served to wake up with a bang those circles which had been overtaken with heavy somnolence. Lastly it is true too that the unexpected reconciliation of the two parties came as a surprise to the king himself, and contributed towards the rapid failure of the plans of the Palace, deepening still further the gulf which divides the nationalist movement and the Throne.

But, however significant this development might be at the outset, it must not be forgotten that the Front only represents an alliance, in which each party maintains its autonomy; and it is difficult to say whether the sort of confederation envisaged at the moment can prepare the reunion which many appear to desire, or whether it is merely a loose coalition, ready to melt away like snow after a brief appearance. A 'cartel du non' (coalition of those who say no), it was fundamentally a defensive reflex of accumulated bitterness which led to its creation; going beyond the conjuncture which gave it birth, and clarifying the vague terms of the Charter it gave itself, will it be able to propose more positive measures and above all to throw its weight decisively behind them to ensure their success? In any case has it not come too late? Does it change in any way the balance of forces in the country? And do the Istiqlāl and UNFP together still have enough of an audience and enough vitality to obtain together what each has failed to gain apart? Lastly, are they sure of their own men? As far as one can see, on both sides the creation of the Front has been accompanied by some reserves on the part of some of the militants: in particular in the UNFP, where it seems that several of them, especially amongst the young, agreed with some reluctance to collaborate with people yesterday stigmatized by them as 'reactionary' – the reserve with which the UNEM moreover greeted the Front National is very characteristic in this respect.

These reserves mortgage the experiment. It is clear that they could only be overcome – and the Front survive to justify the hopes placed in it at its creation – in so far as it succeeded in gaining immediate successes, defining unequivocally a concerted policy for action, and reconstituting the amity of the movement which had been so divided. It is permissible to doubt their success. And the events of

July 1971 did not create a fundamentally new situation in this respect; though they made the search for an 'opening' by the Palace easier, it is hard to see from the point of view of the nationalist movement how this 'opening', supposing it actually comes into effect, could lead to any other result than the revival of the dissensions dormant in the movement, while definitely compromising it in a new ambiguous experiment in collaboration with the regime which is being progressively worn down, apparently unable to regain the heights.

NOTES

1 The Istiqlāl gained 41 seats (out of 144) with a little more than a million votes (i.e. about 30% of votes cast, and 21% of the electorate; in the municipal elections of May 1960 it had gained 40% of the seats.

2 The severe remarks which the king nevertheless made about it August 1971 perhaps marked a turning point in the relations between the party and the Palace, the beginning of a more open split.

3 Article published under the pseudonym of Hamid Yarmouk by Hamid Berrada in No. 2 of the review *Front* in October 1969.

4 See in particular his book, *Option révolutionnaire au Maroc*, 59 ff.

5 By a sort of residual magnetism the party continued for example to attract large numbers to its meetings, over several months, even when its popularity was waning.

6 At that time the UMT held half the seats on the national committee of the party, and still more on the administrative commission.

7 Which at the end of 1963 seems to have had the idea of encouraging the formation of a 'labour party' with the help of MM. Abdallah Ibrahim and Maati Bouabid.

8 23% of all seats and an absolute majority in the municipal councils of Rabat, Casablanca, Kénitra, Tangiers, Safi, and various centres in the Souss.

9 At these elections the UNFP obtained 28 seats (out of 144) with a little more than 750,000 votes, i.e. about 23% of the votes cast (and 16% of registered voters).

Summary of the Discussion

The discussion of Islamization to which the morning session was devoted, resolved itself by suggestion and counter-suggestion into a discussion of opposites, or at least alternatives – a Ṣūfī Islam against a Wahhābī Islam, Islam as a superior civilization, a way of life, against an Islam associated rather with superior skills and power, the stateless society against the politically centralized society as less likely to be receptive to a new religion, the town against the country as more likely to be genuinely Muslim, the peasant against the nomad. A central thought seemed to be the feeling of a contrast between Africa north and Africa south of the Sahara, expressed in the suggestion that to the south Islam found itself in an environment different from that of its original homeland, in which its spread was correspondingly retarded. The suggestion was pointed by Professor Hunwick's call for a comparative study of syncretism in North and in West Africa. One important difference that might emerge from such a study was touched upon by Dr. Fisher, referring to the paper on the spread of Islam in Egypt and North Africa, that whether or not the content of the faith was relevant to a consideration of Islamization north of the desert, it surely was to the south in the period of reformist Islam. This was because of the exclusive character of the new Islam of the jihād by comparison with the eclecticism of the earlier stage of 'mixed' Islam, in which there was no overriding loyalty to the faith and its precepts. The difference from Egypt and North Africa would then be that Islam of a very 'mixed' variety was there compatible with a most exclusive allegiance; it was a cardinal fallacy on the part of nineteenth-century missionaries in the Maghrib to suppose that because the religion of the rural Berber population was shot through with paganism, their Islam was superficial in the sense that it would yield without difficulty to Christianity. The point in West Africa is made more clear in Dr Fisher's paper, when he discusses the competition of Christian churches for Muslim recruits in Yorubaland. It may of course be that, taking into account Professor Anderson's reservations about the entirely Islamic character of the law in Northern Nigeria, the question of 'mixed' versus 'pure' Islam should be seen in strictly relative terms; nevertheless the suggestion remains of an important cultural difference, however it is to be evaluated. As Dr. Hiskett remarked at the end, what *is* a Muslim?

The discussion in the afternoon session of the papers dealing with modernization, nationalism and independence was more fragmentary, given the wide variety of the subject matter. Papers were taken separately rather than together, and questions were devoted more to elucidation. Dr Allan's paper was obviously relevant to the whole question of the application of capital to the water resources of the Sahara, of which the Aswan High Dam is an extreme if very particular example. Original fears of excessive evaporation from the surface of the lake, or of a major effect upon the water table of the desert, may have been exaggerated, but not only is there the eventual silting up of the lake to be reckoned with, but also more immediate side effects, such as the dwindling of the sardine catch off the coast as the outflow of the river is reduced, a reported rise for the same reason of the salinity of underground water in the Fayyum, and an increase in bilharzia as the irrigation canals remain full of water all the year round. Professor Sanderson's paper was of interest in connection with the discontent of the Southern Sudan with rule from the north. M. Palazzoli's paper, coming after the abortive coup in Morocco in July 1971, provoked considerable speculation about the future role of the army in the situation he described. The feeling was that the coup had been arranged by high-ranking officers wishing to save the monarchy from its mistakes; with their execution, the way was open for more drastic action by more radical juniors.

The following comments and queries were subsequently submitted in writing:

1. *Healing and conversion to Islam*

My worry about Dr Fisher's paper is that he seems to be describing as 'Islamic medicine' a form of magical therapy which was widely practised in pre-Islamic Arabia. The Quran would be particularly potent magic because reading and writing were regarded as focal to the power of the Arabs; water from Mecca because of its exotic character. Both may have contributed indirectly to the spread of an Islamic mythology, but in the first place they were being interpreted in traditional African terms. There is ample evidence of similar treatment of Christian-western material. Speke's watch, Mackay's burning-glass, were called 'spirits' by the Ganda; and Mackay was so concerned that he destroyed his lens in the fire. Missionaries actively encouraged the Ganda view that the Bible was the source of British technological power and could give the same to the Ganda. One of the fascinating aspects of the Christian impact on Africa – not yet sufficiently studied – is the extent to which their teaching (and still more their implicit message) was interpreted in traditional terms and therefore 'misunderstood'. No doubt the same is true of Islam.

When Dr Fisher draws attention to the fact that Muslim doctors offered treatment to all, while Christian doctors (though this is a dangerous generalization even about evangelicals) tended to insist on conversion, I suspect that he is on to something extremely important. There are two, parallel, traditions of therapy in black Africa – one by magic, the other by initiation into a cult. It looks as if the Muslims followed the former, the Christians (though they did not know it) the latter; and the Aladura churches have now taken the missionary model to its logical conclusion.

The Rev. F. B. Welbourn,
Department of Theology,
University of Bristol.

2. *Islamization and the 'stateless' society*

Dr J. A. Ballard asked whether it might not be possible to work out a typology of the mechanics of the penetration of Islam into non-Islamic societies. Instances cited in the papers presented to the Symposium suggested possible similarities to the methods of European penetration and the establishment of colonial rule. Despite obvious differences in their aims, both forms of penetration involved alien agents who had to deal with varying types of African societies and who had used military conquest, trade and explicitly missionary efforts in different situations. Both had, perhaps, found it easier to come to terms with African states than with 'stateless' societies.

In reply to a question from Dr Hiskett concerning the application of the latter point in Northern Nigeria, Dr Ballard referred to M. G. Smith's study of Zazzau, where both the Fulani jihād and Lugard's Residents had made use of pre-existing centralized political and social structures. By contrast David Dorward's recent study in *African Affairs* showed how the decentralization of Tiv society made both colonial administration and missionary penetration a difficult, piecemeal process.

Institute of Commonwealth Studies
University of London.

3. *The army in Morocco*

Question directed to M. Palazzoli:

Your discussion of the political position and programmes of the diverse factions within the Moroccan nationalist movement does not enable us to identify their potential attitudes towards the professional and political interests in the military. To what degree, in your opinion, can we say that:

a. these factions were as surprised as the monarchy by the events of July 1971, and

b. there will be a necessary revision in the basic position of the 'nationalist opposition' as a result of the attempted military coup?

Byron Cannon,
Department of History,
University of Wisconsin.

Conclusion: Islam and the Study of the Region

It is appropriate in conclusion to recall David Dalby's advocacy in his opening remarks of regional studies which should bring together representatives of many separate disciplines in an examination of the problems of an area as a whole. The necessary condition of any such examination, if it is not to be a mere aggregate of specialities, might be thought the discovery of a paradigm in terms of which it can be systematic. Physical geography in itself may conceivably suffice, giving rise to an historical society in which changes in the part affect the whole. The broader the area, on the other hand, the less obvious the community, and the greater the need to establish, not only what is and what is not common throughout, but what is peculiar, and in what sense. In the present case the paradigm proposed for the sake of argument was of a very large area, designated Islamic northern Africa, created by the historical spread of Islam. It is a paradigm which it is doubtless easy to attack and to undermine. Even on its own terms, for example, the suggestion which emerged from the discussion of a major discontinuity between the area to the north and that to the south of the Sahara, might be compared with the common practice of dealing with Egypt as a part of the Middle East rather than Africa, to establish a scheme of at least three different areas for which a common religion forms a very tenuous link. At the same time it is worth summarizing the ways in which the paradigm may be justified.

In the first place, taking account of the possibility that the resemblance is superficial, should Islam in this northern Africa region be considered as an isolated phenomenon whose expansion and distribution should be studied in its own right as an autonomous process, thereby limiting the paradigm for this purpose to an inconsequential description? Or should Islam be seen as resulting in certain common values, doubtless shared with regions as far away as Central Asia and Indonesia, which nevertheless represent in the African context a community of culture between disparate societies with peculiar effect upon behaviour both locally and *vis-à-vis* the region as a whole? Or thirdly, is the spread of Islam to be taken as an indicator of other developments of a more secular nature which may not at first sight be so apparent, arising for example out of the physical geography of the Sahara and the Sudan, which make it possible to speak of a global society or a global economy in the area?

'Historism', more commonly, 'historicism', the theory that something is to be explained solely in terms of its history, is no longer fashionable. Below the surface of events, historians have preferred to quantify rather than qualify in their search for more regular explanations at the level of society, economy, and ecology. At the level of events, on the other hand, it is undeniable that there is a sense, represented by the choice of narrative as a means of exposition, in which the historical sequence is unique, a concatenation whose links may not be rearranged. Much of the time of a professional historian is spent in trying to establish this concatenation, even if the result may depend upon his reconstruction of links which are missing, and its presentation upon his emphasis. It is this concatenation, moreover, which goes to supply the historian with the material basis for his claim to disciplinary existence, and less grandly with the ammunition with which to defend his position by objection to the generalizations of others, be they within the discipline or without. There is a sense, therefore, in which it is essential to study the process of Islamization in Africa as a thing in itself, without going beyond what is necessary to establish the course of events.

This sense is unavoidable in the present context, in which the paradigm of an area created by the spread of Islam is in effect faced by two others, the paradigm of the nation state, and beyond that the paradigm of the Third World. The fact is that put in this way there is no compatibility. Under the heading of 'modernization', both the nation state and the Third World are general propositions against which individual examples may be compared. Islam is not a proposition of this kind. Although it contains within itself a discrepancy between the ideal and the actual, it is not religion, despite its own claims, but a specific example, historically as well as theologically defined. It is impossible to consider it as religion, however this is to be understood,[1] without reference to something other than itself, without speculation, overt or covert, about what it might or should have been. This would be unprofitable; it is better to reduce the other propositions to the same historical, not to say historicist, terms, explaining nationalism, for example, by what it has been rather than what it might become. For any historian, this means dealing in the first place with what people wanted, and secondly with the decisions by which those desires were realized or frustrated. It is at this level of explanation that Islam can be considered as a norm, principles, values and customs which affect the choice of individuals and communities.

Such consideration, on the other hand, raises difficulties of appreciation. It is not merely a question of evidence which makes the spread of Islam in Africa so problematic, in the twentieth century no less than in the tenth. It is precisely this question of a norm, posed generally in the question of what is Islam, what is a Muslim? It arises even for historicism the moment the question of explanation is turned around, and posed from the point of view of the participant, in terms of the future rather than the past. With Hegel, recourse may be had to Spirit – a strategy to which the history of religion is evidently prone –, but this, the extreme solution, is currently a confession of failure. Its merit, of course, is that it is the Muslim solution, and hence, ironically, an excellent starting-point for an inquiry which must discount it as a possibility on technical grounds, as lying beyond the scope of the discipline concerned. Any description of Islam in Africa must certainly allow for the discrepancy between the ideal and the actual, and for the tensions which result. What allowance should be made is another matter. It is certain that Islam, even, indeed especially, Islam at its most scholastic, is on its own terms imperfect *vis-a-vis* both heaven and earth, looking to an unattainable ideal while compromising heavily with custom and with power. It is a moot point how far it is possible to take this Islam as a standard by which to grade particular practices. That in any given situation there might be an awareness of a discrepancy is undeniable; that it needs to be more than a matter of opinion on the part of the actors, is more doubtful. In the case of the nineteenth-century jihāds, for example, the tension between standard and practice was evidently an essential feature of the crises; but was this the result of an eventual realization by certain participants of the objective truth about Islam, or was it merely the adoption of one out of many equally legitimate postures? It is not at all clear that the Islam of ᶜUuthmān dan Fodio was necessarily superior to that of the clerics from whom he broke away, who were accused of compromising with secular authority, merely that a different interpretation had been chosen, or an emphasis placed. Jihād may be a topic of Islamic law, but for that reason may be all the more open to construction. The example of Protestantism and Catholicism invites caution; so, more specifically, does that of the two sons of Ismāʻīl al Walt. (2)

Even if the notion of a 'Spirit of Islam' be converted into that of an innate logic of the faith, therefore, it must be treated with care.

It might very well be true to say that the formal logic of the religion, in which I would include the 'ways' of the Sūfīs as well as the 'schools' of law, precludes such an innate logic as an objective proposition, leaving it only as a subjective 'Here I stand'. Absolute as this may be for the individual or for the community, conservative or revolutionary in its operation, it is then open to evaluation in its social context, as one among other factors which combine to influence each other. The identification, selection and combination of these factors may vary; the accumulation of argument over the Fulani jihād is a case in point.[3] The effect is nevertheless to put the religious norm into perspective, to see it as a reflex. From there it is a short step to considering it as a symptom. This is an especial temptation, because it proceeds now quite naturally from the historical discipline itself. It is the religion which has generated a great deal of the historian's evidence, or has provided it with a great deal of its subject matter; the range of comment in what Lewicki has called *The Arabic External Sources for the History of Africa to the South of (the) Sahara*[4] is itself an indication of the scope of the activities and the knowledge of Muslims on the continent, while much is probably to be inferred indirectly from the main bulk of Arabic literature. There is a sense, therefore, in which Islam in the history of Africa has acted as a 'trace element'; the history of its spread, taken as a phenomenon, is indicative of a whole range of contacts and developments for which more direct evidence may be lacking.

Here, I think, is one of the fundamental problems of African history. The evolutionary model of human history may be approved or decried; it may encounter major objections, it may be severely qualified. The decline and fall of the Roman empire, the emotively named Middle Ages, concepts which were a source of satisfaction down to the eighteenth century, have notoriously survived as a serious problem into the thinking of the nineteenth and twentieth centuries. Conceived as an integral part of this problem, the history of Islam itself has been taken as a major example of retrogression. We find it involving Africa in the attention paid to the cyclical theory of civilization propounded by ibn Khaldūn, now applied as a general proposition to the continent south of the Sahara by Y. Lacoste.[5] Nevertheless, the evolutionary model has become central to the study of history in the so-called 'modern' world, and this is true of Africa, despite attempts made in the name of cultural independence to discover an alternative,[6] all the more because the subject matter, going back as far as the Olduvai Gorge, turns more continuously than anywhere else in the world from the primary model of physical evolution to that of the evolution of culture in a scheme of 'prehistory' running in many ways down to the present day. In this scheme the history of Islam on the continent stands for a major and continuing intrusion, cultural, social and economic, not to say political. To what extent does that intrusion constitute in its turn a process of 'development' in the modern, economic, sense, a process leading to a radical, historical change in the internal structures and external relationships of the societies concerned?

If, for example, we look at Saharan trade, the routes and the commodities, gold and slaves, for which it is now famous, should probably be seen, not on the analogy of transatlantic ventures, but as the outcome, and as the agents, of a complicated pattern in which local exchanges were tied into a network of exchanges from locality to locality covering a very wide area indeed of North Africa and Egypt, the Sahara and the Sudan.[7] Such a network clearly altered with time; it is possible that it should be seen as a question of 'growth', in which such exchanges as they developed served progressively to alter the composition of society both locally and regionally in terms of occupation, specialization and class, with results which might be seen in a statistical age in terms of productivity and demography. Research continues to try to fill in the historical details, witness P. Kalck's recent paper on the Gaoga of Leo Africanus,[8] while a conclusion of this kind is strongly suggested by the data on slavery provided by A. G. B. and H. J. Fisher,[9] and is put forward by L. Brenner in a contribution to the latest regional survey of the subject, *Aspects of West African Islam*, dealing with the North African trading community in the nineteenth-century Central Sudan.[10] It carries the implication that Muslim Africa to the south as well as to the north of the desert is to be included, *mutatis mutandis*, in the same process of historical change which is principally familiar for the history of Europe.

On the other hand, the use of Islam and its history in Africa as a measure of such a process tends to break down on closer examination. This is immediately apparent in the matter of the spread of Islam, when it is necessary to account for the choice of individuals and of societies. Certainly no single explanation will do; it is largely a question of circumstances and conditions. The fact of Islam may be noted; it might be considered almost as a matter of education, of familiarity with things Islamic in the world about. It might be seen more specifically in terms of the employment of such things for particular purposes. Although the functional aspect may be observed, however, the precise and necessary, as distinct from the accidental, 'historical' relationship of the religion to the social structure and to the course of events is much harder to envisage, harder still to document. This is even more the case when the norm is refined and defined, and the attempt is made to establish certain types of Islam in relation to certain types of society. I have argued elsewhere that 'denominations do not necessarily correspond to types, nor types to societies; they may be . . . confused by many variables, not least by the historical dimension . .';[11] in other words, that 'cultural history' of this kind, verging upon a cultural anthropology, tends to founder precisely upon the element of history involved. It seems that the argument must return to the initial point, that Islam in this context cannot be treated as religion in general. However suggestive it may be, it cannot be taken as evidence of anything other than itself.

This is a radical assertion. Produced by a consideration of valid procedure, it casts doubt on the very existence of an intrinsic connection between culture, in the traditional European sense, and the overall state of society. From the historical point of view it threatens what Christopher Hill has called 'total history' with 'partial history', the preserve of the 'partial historian', the specialist, for example, in economic history, or in this case in the history of culture reduced, in effect, to the history of 'ideas'.[12] There is no need to be a Marxist to consider this an artificial dissection of experience. The problem is certainly in the first place one of documentation. Compared with the historian of Europe, the historian of Africa is underfed. To leave it there, however, would be to mistake the issue. Fundamentally it is a question of what in fact would constitute a sufficient documentation. The problem has been faced by sociology, torn between the search for deep structures which may exist only in the mind of the observer and the need to consider the possibly superficial opinions of the people concerned, by the possible discrepancy between real and apparent intention. Confining itself to the actor, history has phrased the question in theological terms, of determinism versus free will. It has the advantage of seeking specific causes for specific events, for which purpose E. H. Carr's resolution of the problem by a distinction between the reasonable and the coincidental is useful.[13] For this purpose, however, it might be thought to beg the question of what is reasonable. In the relationship of culture to society, there is a dislocation between the forms of the one and the structures of the other in the matter of proof. If we could be certain of the advancement of knowledge, it might be anticipated that the proof would stem from an adequate theory of the human mind. Meanwhile it is speculation on the basis of hypothesis.

The result can be seen embodied in *Le Maghreb entre deux guerres*.[14] Berque is well aware of the need to reconcile the structures of economy and society in the period between the two wars with the perception of life for those who lived at the time, the quantity with the quality, in order to calculate the responses which led from the apogee of the colonial system to the brink of its downfall. He does so as an historian, by a concentration on the event as the reality, the point of an analytical 'cone' which broadens downwards into abstraction and generalization. To construct this 'cone', however, he falls back upon linguistic theory; the event becomes a cultural act. It becomes an expression and a sign, a semaphore whose significance, varying widely from observer to observer, is nevertheless not lost. Like a pawn in a game, it elicits a response until finally, as the moves accumulate, the situation is changed and perceptions begin to alter. Islam for example shifts from an 'Islam refuge' to an 'Islam jacobin', from a cultural defence to a cultural attack. What is interesting about this exercise is not so much the satisfaction it affords: if Berque satisfies, it is because of his 'linguistic' intuition, because of his skill at 'reading between the lines'; if he fails, he has failed on his own admission, in spite of his great erudition, for lack of the material. It is the fact that in the end we have a history, the outline of a sequence of events, the 'profil de la durée maghrébine', in which, in the sentence 'la révolution était en avance sur les consciences', the discrepancy between society and culture remains posed as a lack of simultaneity, a lack of coincidence at any given time.

The linguistic model, reminiscent of the historical linguistics of Guillaume, for whom speech preceded language, may or may not be a valuable tool. A different version was used before Berque in North Africa by Fanon, for whom language preceded speech to give a direct and immediate translation of reality into cultural attitudes;[15] the model has since been used academically by Y. Turin in a book whose title is self-explanatory, *Affrontements culturels dans l'Algérie coloniale, écoles, médecines, religion, 1830–1880.*[16] Berque's conclusion, however, acknowledges the fundamental condition. It relates, of course, not only to Islam. This is only one element in the cultural repertoire of his North African 'garden', where business and politics, for example, also have their *moeurs*. At this level it is possible to write a self-contained study of cultural relationships, a 'history of ideas', of which Hourani's *Arabic Thought in the Liberal Age* is an excellent example in this context. To do more, to attempt to overcome the 'epistemological divide', the historian might be advised to turn first to the history of institutions. If man does not live by bread alone, neither is religion simply a matter of theology, politics a matter of opinion, or economics a matter of objectives. We should not need proverbial wisdom, Robert Burns, or Vance Packard to remind us not only of the existence of 'organization man', but of the fact that the outcome of his activities may be unforeseen. Institutions have a life of their own. From the historian's point of view, their basic function may be to generate material. From this point of view, they are prime objects of study, in themselves and in relation to their public. The metamophosis of the Coptic church in Egypt from the church of the majority to the church of a minority, the evolution of the Ṣūfī orders both generally and locally, can be examined in their own right over longer and shorter periods of time for the same kind, if not as a rule the same amount of information as can be obtained from the ecclesiastical history of the European Middle Ages and beyond. At the same time the voluminous sixteenth-century Maghribī collection of legal opinions, fatāwā, the *Mieyar al muerib* of al Wansharīshī, the product of several centuries of active jurisprudence, not only illustrates the workings of an alternative, or at least complementary system of government to that of the sulṭān, by private composition on the basis of the Islamic law, but in so doing reveals, with considerable qualification, much about the problems with which it dealt.[17] When we find these problems taken over by the legislation and the courts of French Algeria, the records of litigation, systematically examined by J.-P. Charney, come perhaps as close as it is possible to get to documenting the way in which Algerian Muslims of the early twentieth century were prompted to act by their problems and their opportunities.[18]

On the whole, documentation on this scale is either rare or unexplored. Nevertheless the study of the institution, whether it be Islamic, a political party, a trade union, a ministry or a business, with an eye to the question of what it was doing together with what it more narrowly did, may prove the most historical method of underpinning the history of 'culture' in such a way as to establish the correlation with the 'base'. Here at least the three paradigms proposed may meet on common ground. Faced by new competition, many Islamic institutions have weakened or lost ground, sometimes to the point of eradication. Some have prospered, economically, socially and politically. There have been new arrivals, like the Aḥmadīya, and new forms. Whatever else it may be, Cairo radio has become a Muslim institution in its own right. The pilgrimage to Mecca has flourished. What matters is the activity, in which Islam combines with other perceptions to give a specific result, an history. The ḥājj is a good example, recalling as it may Weber's view that the pilgrimage to Rome could not be regarded as an economic activity, although it had undoubted economic importance. Opinions on this point may vary, but at least the phenomenon exists as a subject for fairly narrow historical scrutiny.[19] The Murīdīya of Senegal is comparable as a particular history in which politics, religion and economics go hand in hand.[20] A biographical unity is restored, if not to the individual, at least to the office, and to the collectivity which it represents.

Histories of this kind show up most clearly in cases of obvious conflict. European history has come to offer 'diplomatic history' as a specialized subject in which countries and their governments are seen to have technical values for international purposes, whose evolution may be traced. The extension of this highly sophisticated European behaviour to include Africa in the nineteenth and twentieth centuries has meant that the continent has come naturally within the purview of the European subject as normally conceived and practised: the responsibility for the 'Scramble' is very much a live issue, and one with its own peculiar fascination, as, for example, when we find a book entitled *British Diplomacy and Tunis, 1875–1902*, turn for the purpose of Africanists into a description of the way in which the Italian descent on Libya was prepared.[21] At the same time it has meant that the process of colonization has come to be conceived, not so much in terms of a general conflict of cultures, a general imposition of one civilization upon another, but more specifically as an extension of this behaviour to include the African peoples themselves, so that the history of the colonial period in Africa can be seen in terms of an evolving conflict between allies and enemies. The extension was conscious on the part of the Europeans; African peoples were each provided with a reputation which, notwithstanding the general stereotypes of Arab and Black, placed them in the same categories as Europeans. It has, however, been left to present historians to establish the diplomatic character of the European penetration, dealing with Africans as friends and enemies in much the same way as the powers conducted themselves 'at home'. Still more has it been left to them to draw the conclusion that this diplomatic state of affairs runs in various ways right through the colonial period to independence and beyond. Most obviously it has become the thesis of Davidson[22] and Ranger[23] that there was a continuity between initial resistance to the imposition of European rule and the subsequent movements for independence. It is the fate of such theses to undergo endless qualification. The hypothesis, however, remains an obvious one for the discussion of Nigeria, for example, while the appearance of independent African states has meant the reappearance of diplomatic history properly speaking.

Whether such schemes are regarded as intrinsic or conceptual, it is clearly possible to assign the appropriate values to Muslim peoples as to any other, and to watch them change. Equally it is possible to abandon the question of conflict between neighbours, if only because loyalties intersect, and may very rarely override. Even if it be thought that a major consequence of European rule has been a pattern of conflicts, that pattern is itself not simple, with ethnic and political boundaries at variance, quite apart from economic and social divisions. There is, moreover, a sense in which it is irrelevant, or marginal, either because the scale is too great, or else too small, something to avoid rather than to join. In such cases, adaptation may be a more appropriate, if no less rationalist, hypothesis. Certainly it might be more in keeping with 'institutional history'. Just as Charnay can show from his Algerian material the workings of conflict at the level of individuals and little groups, so here again is the opportunity to write an '*histoire des petits*'. If however we ignore the 19 brotherhoods represented by 500 zāwiyas with their 300,000 *khouans* (ikhwān), the 178 zāwiyas of maraboutic origin with their 40,000 descendants or disciples of the founders, and the 622 domed tombs locally venerated, taken by Julien to illustrate the presence of Islam in the Tunisian countryside,[24] and look at the more imposing spectacle of the Moroccan monarchy, beside the well-known collaboration with and opposition to the French, we can note for example the Western education, and the fact that by 1950 the Sultan had become 'the richest landowner in the empire'.[25] Such history is at least as relevant to the present situation as the course of political events.[26]

For the purpose of cultural history, however, the common denominator to be found in such individual cases is perhaps the notion of technique. Returning to Islam, it has developed as a principle of organization. The organization of thought is most apparent in the case of the law, but has extended to bring a vast range of historical, literary and artistic reference into the mental equipment of Muslim peoples. A cardinal feature is what might be termed the 'rabbinical succession' to point the contrast with the Apostolic Succession of the Christian church, the transmission of learning from master to pupil which guarantees the authenticity of the faith, and which becomes a matter of social organization in the corporations of the *eulamā*' and the brotherhoods of the Ṣūfīs. It might be expected that the element of formal logic, applied to any given situation, would help to govern the direction and the outcome; to quote the proverbial maxim, li kull khilāf ḥall fī 'l Shar'.* On the other hand it is possible to see it adopted and adapted, in the first place as a slogan. I have argued elsewhere that in the precolonial Maghrib Islam should be regarded historically as a language of politics, vindicated by, not in, the event.[27] In the same way qawmīya, 'Arab nationalism', and waṭanīya, 'the nationalism of the homeland' might be regarded as declarations, confirmed along with religion with portraits, national days, fasts, pilgrimages and the prayers. In the second place, the corporations have had their uses. While Professor Sanderson observes the power of the Sayyids in the Sudan, work undertaken in Tunisia by M. Rouissi would account for the rapid spread of the Neo-Destour in the

* 'For every dispute there is a solution in the Law'.

south of the country in the 1930s by the disposition of the brotherhoods reckoned up by Julien.

The principle and its embodiment, the logic and its uses, find an echo in the ambiguity of a word such as Islamization in English, transitive and intransitive, active and passive, indicative of a continuous as well as a completed action. Starting from a definition of Islamization as islām, 'submission', when speaking of the spread of Islam in Egypt and North Africa, I developed it in the sense of shahāda, 'witness', credo, creed, to understand it in the sense of a distinction from the non-Muslim world at home and abroad, with certain consequences for social and political relationships, not least in the nineteenth century.[28] These can clearly be seen in the Ottoman empire, where the legal effects of religion, in the shape of the separation of communities, had been recognized by the administration in the *millet* system.[29] So far as Europe was concerned, it was notoriously embodied in the Capitulations, the agreements under which Europeans resident in the empire were governed under their own laws.[30] The mediaeval antecedents went back to the formulation of Islamic law itself; they may be judged by the various agreements between Venice and Florence and Egypt and Morocco in the fifteenth and sixteenth centuries published by J. Wansbrough.[31] The documents are couched in terms of mutual respect, and proceed in detail. The initial reference to the titles of the signatories, Muslim and Christian, establishes reserved positions from which a bargain can be concluded. They exemplify the development in the second half of the Middle Ages of what has been described as 'a new and practical code governing international relations'.[32] In the nineteenth century, on the other hand, the Capitulations as the expression of this code became the lever, first for the early attempts at modernization on the part of the Muslim governments themselves, subsequently for an increase of European influence and control over those governments, so that, for example, the 'protectorate' in Tunisia and later in Morocco can be seen to grow in many ways from the 'protection' of European nationals under the system of consular jurisdiction.[33] Algeria was anomalous only by virtue of conquest, which afforded the opportunity to convert the effects of religion into a principle of state no less than in the Ottoman empire. Defined *as a Muslim* by the Senatus Consulte of 1865, on that account the indigène was condemned to be a second-class subject, deprived of citizenship, afflicted with the Code de l'indigénat.[34]

A similar history, with a different conclusion, might be written in respect of relations with the Coptic communities of Egypt and the Sudan, where the Dār al Islam overlapped the Karāzat al Marqusīya, the Apostolic province of St. Mark, and where the political and administrative relationships were accompanied by a progressive use of Arabic and Islamic language, literary and legal forms on the part of Muslims and Christians alike, until it may be that, like the Capitulations, they created a situation which could be exploited to end the independence of the Nubian kingdom early in the fourteenth century. Meanwhile it would seem possible to extend what amounts to an archaeologist's definition of culture, with forms and concepts in the place of material artefacts as the tools and the products of society, to serve as something of a base for the history of Islam in the continent as a whole.

NOTES

1 Cf. e.g. Geertz, 1968, 1–4; Leach, 1969, 86.
2 See above, 20.
3 Cf. e.g. M. G. Smith, 'The Jihād of Shehu dan Fodio: some problems', in Lewis, ed., 1966, 408–24.
4 Lewicki, 1969.
5 Lacoste, 1966, 42–3.
6 Cf. e.g. Ranger, ed., 1968, x.
7 Cf. e.g. Brett, 1969, 358, 362–3.
8 Kalck, 1972.
9 A. G. B. and H. J. Fisher, 1970.
10 McCall and Bennett, eds., 1971, 137–50.
11 Brett, 1972, 494.
12 *Times Literary Supplement*, 24.11.72, 1431–2.
13 Carr, 1964, 87–108.
14 Berque, 1970.
15 Fanon, 1970.
16 Turin, 1971.
17 Al Wansharishī, 1314–15H.
18 Charnay, 1965.
19 Cf. el Nager, 1969.
20 Cf. O'Brien, 1971.
21 Marsden, 1971.
22 Ranger, ed., 1968, 177–88.
23 Ranger, 1967.
24 Julien, 1972, 63.
25 Ibid., 48.
26 Cf. e.g. J. Waterbury, 'The coup manqué', in Gellner and Micaud, ed., 1973, 397–424.
27 Brett, 1972.
28 See above, 9.
29 Cf. e.g. Hitti, 1960, 727.
30 Cf. e.g. Holt, 1966, 197–8.
31 J. Wansbrough, i.e. 1962, 1963, 1965^1, 1965^2
32 Wansbrough, 1971, 34.
33 Cf. e.g. Coulson, 1964, 150–1; Marsden, 1971, 24–87; see above, 9–10.
34 Cf. Ageron, 1968.

REFERENCES

Ch. -R. Ageron, *Les Algeriens musulmans et la France, 1871–1919*, Paris, 1968.

J. Berque, *Le Maghreb entre deux guerras*, 2nd ed., Paris, 1970.

M. Brett, 'Ifrīqiya as a Market for Saharan Trade', *Journal of African History*, X, 3 (1969), 347–64; 'Problems in the Interpretation of the History of the Maghrib in the light of some recent publications', *ibid.*, XIII, 3 (1972), 489–506.

E. H. Carr, *What is History?*, Penguin Books, London, 1964.

J. -P. Charnay, *La Vie musulmane en Algérie*, Paris, 1965.

N. J. Coulson, *A History of Islamic Law*, Edinburgh, 1964.

F. Fanon, *A Dying Colonialism*, London, 1970.

A. G. B. and H. J. Fisher, *Slavery and Muslim Society in Africa*, London, 1970.

C. Geertz, *Islam Observed*, New Haven and London, 1968.

E. Gellner and C. Micaub, eds., *Arabs and Berbers*, London, 1973.

P. K. Hitti, *History of the Arabs*, 7th ed., London, 1960.

P. M. Holt, *Egypt and the Fertile Crescent, 1516–1922*, London, 1966.

Ch. -A. Julien, *L'Afrique du Nord en marche*, 3rd ed., Paris, 1972.

P. Kalck, 'Pour une localisation du royaume de Gaoga', *Journal of African History*, XIII, 4 (1972), 529–48.

Y. Lacoste, *Ibn Khaldoun: naissance de l'histoire passée du tiers monde*, Paris, 1966.

E. Leach, *Genesis as Myth and other essays*, London, 1969.

T. Lewicki, *Arabic External Sources for the History of Africa to the South o, Sahara*, Wroclaw – Warszawa – Krakow, 1969.

I. M. Lewis, ed., *Islam in Tropical Africa*, Oxford, 1966.

A. Marsden, *British Diplomacy and Tunis, 1875–1902*, Edinburgh and London, 1971.

D. F. McCall and N. R. Bennett, eds., *Aspects of West African Islam*, Boston University Papers on Africa, Vol. V, African Studies Centre, Boston University, 1971.

O. el Nager, *West Africa and the Muslim pilgrimage*, Ph.D. Thesis, London, 1969.

D. C. O'Brien, *The Mourides of Senegal*, Oxford, 1971.

T. O. Ranger, ed., *Emerging Themes of African History*, Nairobi and London, 1968.

T. O. Ranger, *Revolt in Southern Rhodesia, 1896–7*, London, 1967.

Y. Turin, *Affrontements culturels dans l'Algérie coloniale, écoles, médecines, religion, 1830–1880*, Paris, 1971.

J. Wansbrough, 'A Moroccan amīr's commercial treaty with Venice of the year 913–1508', *Bulletin of the School of Oriental and African Studies*, XXV, 3 (1962), 449–71; 'A Mamlūk Ambassador to Venice in 913–1507', *ibid.*, XXVI, 3 (1963), 503–30; 'Venice and Florence in the Mamlūk commercial privileges', *ibid.*, XXVIII, 3 (1965), 483–523; 'A Mamlūk commercial treaty concluded with the Republic of Florence', in S. M. Stern, ed., *Documents from Islamic Chanceries*, Oxford, 1965; 'The safe-conduct in Muslim chancery practice', *BSOAS*, XXXIV, 1 (1971), 20–35.

Al Wansharīshī, *Mi'yār al mu'rib*, 12 vols., lith. Fes, 1314–15H.

INDEX

INDEX

Entries are listed according to the spelling in the text, with cross-references in the case of alternative spellings employed by different contributors, e.g. al Tūnisī, el-Tounsy. No attempt has been made to provide a systematic transliteration of all names or words of Arabic origin, which would render familiar names such as Bourguiba unrecognizable.

jihād, xxiv, 38, 57, 61–2, 63, 81, 143, 145, 149